The Social Production
of Indifference

The Social Production of Indifference

Exploring the Symbolic Roots
of Western Bureaucracy

By Michael Herzfeld

The University of Chicago Press
Chicago and London

Published by arrangement with Berg Publishers, Inc.

This study was originally published in the series *Global Issues*, edited by Bruce Kapferer and John Gledhill, and published by Berg Publishers, Inc.

The University of Chicago Press, Chicago 60637
The University of Chicago Press, Ltd., London

ISBN 0-226-32908-9 (pbk.)

Library of Congress Cataloging-in-Publication Data

Herzfeld, Michael, 1947–
    The social production of indifference : exploring the symbolic roots of Western bureaucracy / by Michael Herzfeld.
        p.   cm.
    Includes bibliographical references and index.
    1. Elite (Social sciences)   2. Bureaucracy.   3. Social conflict.
    4. Social control.   5. Abuse of administrative power.   I. Title.
    [HM141.H47   1993]
    302.3′5—dc20   93-1674
                                                          CIP

for
Peter S. Allen
in friendship

Contents

Acknowledgments

Parts of this book have been presented in oral form. I would particularly like to acknowledge the Department of Anthropology at the University of California, Berkeley, for providing me with the original opportunity of doing so, as well as for the stimulating discussions that followed at the informal conference, held at Berkeley and organized by Paul Rabinow, on "Anthropology and Modernity," in April 1989. An extended seminar discussion of key issues at University College, London, provided focus and food for rethinking. Considerable further development of the theme was inspired by the workshop on "Anthropology of the Center and Periphery," organized a year later in New York by Marc Abélès (Collège de France) and Susan Carol Rogers (New York University) with funding from the Council for European Studies. Final refinements were made possible through a generous two-month fellowship awarded by the Ministère de la Technologie et de la Recherche, Paris, and held in the Laboratoire d'Ethnologie et de Sociologie Comparative at the Université de Parix-X (Nanterre) in May and June 1991. I would particularly like to express my deep appreciation to Marie-Dominique Mouton, the librarian of the Laboratoire, for her generous and practical help, and to Maria Couroucli, Eric de Dampierre, Altan Gokalp, and Roberte Hamayon for their warm encouragement during my stay in Paris.

A large part of Chapter Five is a substantially revised version of an article originally published in the *American Ethnologist* (9[1982]: 644–663), and partially reproduced here by permission, under the title "The Etymology of Excuses: Aspects of Rhetorical Performance in Greece" (Copyright © 1982 American Ethnological Society).

I am indebted to Carol Delaney, Raymond J. DeMallie, Don

Handelman, P. Nick Kardulias, and Gail Kligman, for permission to cite their unpublished manuscripts.

I wish to thank Bruce Kapferer for originally inviting me to join the "Global Issues" series and for discussing the materials and ideas with me with sharp insight and warm friendship; and Marion Berghahn, anthropologist and publisher, for her splendid advice and patience. Katherine J. Hagedorn and Ellen Maly guided the final stages of the manuscript preparation with tact and skill.

A very large number of friends and colleagues responded graciously and constructively, and at very short notice, to my request for criticism of an earlier draft: Marc Abélès, Arjun Appadurai, Talal Asad, Don Brenneis, Jane K. Cowan, Loring M. Danforth, Alfred Diamant, Mary Douglas, Carol J. Greenhouse, David I. Kertzer, Uli Linke, Peter Loizos, Pamela K. Quaggiotto, Deborah Reed-Danahay, and Nancy Scheper-Hughes. They provided friendship as well as intellectual provocation, but they are most certainly not to blame for weaknesses that have survived their scrutiny. I am enormously grateful to them all.

This book is dedicated with special affection to Peter S. Allen, who, over two decades ago, amiably nudged me on my way to becoming an anthropologist. I am profoundly grateful for his gentle but effective prodding at that time as well as for his generosity and collegial support ever since, and hope that the present effort gives him no cause for regret.

The Social Production of Indifference

The Self and the State

Why do some people apparently become humorless automatons as soon as they are placed behind a desk? Why do kindly friends and amiable neighbors become racists and bigots when they discover, or (more accurately) decide, that others do not "belong"? How does it come about that in societies justly famed for their hospitality and warmth we often encounter the pettiest forms of bureaucratic indifference to human needs and sufferings, or that in democratic polities designed to benefit all citizens whole groups of people suffer from callous neglect?

These are the questions that cluster around the theme of this book. They may be summarized more generally: how and why can political entities that celebrate the rights of individuals and small groups so often seem cruelly selective in applying those rights? Indifference to the plight of individuals and groups often coexists with democratic and egalitarian ideals.

Indifference is the rejection of common humanity. It is the denial of identity, of selfhood. We may thus suspect that its appearance in state structures arises from competing claims over the right to construct the cultural and social self. Who "makes" the self – the citizen or the state? Can we even speak of "the state," or is that entity in turn a construct deployed by certain manipulative individuals to legitimize their authority?

In this book, I propose to focus on representations of the instruments of state control, and more particularly on the kinds of offices and agencies that are lumped together under the generic heading of "national bureaucracy." Most studies of bureaucracy look at how they function. In so doing, they address the success or failure of particular bureaucracies in the terms of bureaucracy itself: service of citizens' needs, immunity to patronage, efficiency. Moreover, it is clear that in some states bureaucrats have a relatively high degree of input into policy-making (Aberbach, Putnam, and Rockman 1981; Diamant 1989). It is no part of my purpose to dispute the value of these goals. On the contrary, I proceed from a fundamental puzzlement: how does it come about that repression at every level from that of the totalitarian state to the petty tyrant behind a desk can call upon the same idiom of representation, the same broad definition of the person, the same evocative symbols, as those enshrined in the most indisputably democratic practices? To speak of anomie or dysfunction is a description, not an explanation.

The term "Western" in the subtitle is intentionally ironic. It enshrines a stereotype. The various countries lumped together under the rubric of "the West" conventionally celebrate certain features that separate them from the rest of the world: democracy, rational government, scientific and technological inventiveness, individualism, certain ethical and cultural commitments. One does not have to take all these claims at face value in order to appreciate how important they have been in shaping a sense of common culture for centuries. "The West" is a symbol of shared identity.

Behind the mask of commonality, however, appear enormously different legal regimes. Anglo-Saxon liberalism and German neo-Kantian authoritarianism, for example, may have radically opposed consequences, even though both lay claim to reason grounded in nature (Pollis 1987:587–588; Bottomley and Lechte 1990:60). "The West" acquires a variety of meanings in the hands of different actors and in response to varied international models. But that is just the irony of its predicament, and it gives us the opening that our exploration requires. The idea of a coherent, unified rationality is neither coherent nor unified in itself. I do not intend to show here what is "Western" and what is not. That is the language of absolute identities – the conceptual idiom that I have set out to criticize. Instead, I shall attempt to show when, why, and how social and political actors manage to invest such suppositious entities as "the West" with compelling significance in everyday life.[1]

Calling oneself "Western" is a question of identity, and the bureaucratic management of identity – personal, social, and national – is what this book is about. Nationalist ideologies usually lay claim to some kind of constructed "national character." Their bureaucracies have the task of calibrating personal and local identity to this construct. Identity is at the heart of all anthropological inquiry, and an anthropological approach to national identity is well equipped to explore the relationship between national identity and more localized models of social and cultural being.

Bureaucracy is one of those phenomena people only notice when it appears to violate its own alleged ideals, usually those concerning a person's place in the social scheme of things. Consequently, in most industrial democracies – where the state is supposed to be a respecter of persons – people rail in quite predictable ways against the evils of bureaucracy. It does not matter that their outrage is often unjustified; what counts is their ability to draw on a predictable image of malfunction. If one could not grumble about "bureaucracy," bureaucracy itself could not easily exist: both bureaucracy and the stereotypical complaints about it are parts of a larger universe that we might call, quite simply, the ideology and practice of accountability.

The conventions that govern talk about bureaucracy are very much like the equally conventional habit of groaning at puns. In both cases, there is a play on the discrepancy between formal or anticipated properties (precisely defined rights in the case of bureaucracy, an exact correspondence between words and meaning in the case of puns) and actual experience (the violation of personal autonomy in bureaucracy, the disruption of everyday semantics in puns). In actual practice, the charges against bureaucracy may be quite unfair, and listeners may find puns revealing and funny. But comic dismay is expected in both cases, and in both it must be freely given. The response has nothing to do with personal belief. It has everything to do with convention.

1. I should also make clear that it is not my intention to discuss the formal properties of bureaucratic organizations, a task arguably best left to political scientists. There is an increasing interest in the ethnography of administration among social scientists. See, for example, Britan 1981; Richman 1983. These works take inquiry to a much more intimate level than, for example, the macro-analyses and cultural generalizations of Crozier (1964, 1971).

This is crucial to understanding bureaucracy as a social phenomenon. The fact that people have stereotypical expectations of bureaucratic unfairness offsets their sense of personal failure: there is safety in numbers, in being reassured that everyone knows all about bureaucrats. Rejecting the hateful formalism of bureaucracy is itself a conventional, formal act, and identifies areas of tension between official norms and more localized social values. Representations of bureaucratic evil are comforting precisely because, like the symbols studied by the ethnographers of small-scale societies, they are collective.

Not all bureaucratic encounters are dismal; for some lucky individuals, the system works every time. But their good fortune then raises a problem for the practice of social relations. In cultures that value individualism and entrepreneurship, failures to get what one wants suggest moral deficiency and demand self-justification. In the industrialized societies of Western Europe and North America, no less than in remote villages in Greece or Italy, people find it necessary to explain away their inability to deal effectively with the bureaucracy.[2] Everyone, it seems, has a bureaucratic horror story to tell, and few will challenge the conventions such stories demand. Hearers know that they will soon want to use the same stereotypical images in turn.

Clients are not the only people who tell such stories. Bureaucrats, too, often seek means of exonerating themselves from blame. "Buck-passing," which clients recognize as a symptom of some alleged bureaucratic mentality, is in fact part of the same discourse

2. This applies equally to industrialized cultures and to those, notably in the Mediterranean area (Peristiany 1965), that have been characterized as agonistic. The distance between "rugged individualism" and "agonistic self-interest" arguably has more to do with whether one is attributing the quality in question to a collective self or an exotic other than with any fundamental difference in moral orientation. Pollis (1987: 590), however, has argued that "[t]he concept of individualism so central to the Anglo-Saxon notion of rights was nonexistent in traditional Greek culture." She goes on to suggest that it was not "individualism" but one's position in a kin-based network that "defined the self." This statement, while accurate, should not be allowed to obscure the lack of fit between formal concepts of individualism and informal social values within "Anglo-Saxon" societies. In order to avoid reifying "the West," a problem to which Pollis rightly draws our attention elsewhere in her article, it is crucial to bear in mind "Western" intellectuals' tendency to contrast their own idealized political *models* with the "corrupt" *practices* of other cultures – a theme that will emerge frequently below. On the conceptual links between nationalism and various kinds of so-called individualism, see especially Bottomley and Lechte 1990: 60; Handler 1985: 210, 1988; Herzfeld 1982a: 57–60.

of accountability, personhood, and superior force. While disgruntled clients blame bureaucrats, the latter blame "the system,"
excessively complicated laws, their immediate or more distant
superiors, "the government." While people often act as though
clients and bureaucrats were two separate classes of human beings,
separated by some Manichean division of good from evil, they are
demonstrably participants in a common symbolic struggle, using
the same weapons, guided by the same conventions. Bureaucrats
are citizens too; and, as one ethnographer of public policy
management has observed, "the most basic goal of any bureaucrat
or bureaucracy is not rational efficiency, but individual and
organizational survival" (Britan 1981: 11).[3] While some social
scientists (such as Goffman 1959; Handelman 1976; Schwartzman
1989) have focused on the practical devices with which clients and
bureaucrats negotiate with each other, there has been little discussion of the role in such interactions of the conventions of explanation, and especially of attacks on "the system."[4] This is the
theme of secular theodicy.

Explaining the Evils of Bureaucracy

The concept of theodicy as I use it here is derived from Weber.[5]
Weber was interested in the various ways in which religious systems
sought to explain the persistence of evil in a divinely ordered
world. We need not take time here to consider his comparison
of several major religious traditions, but it is worth noting that

3. This statement, despite its tone of sympathetic practicality, still perpetuates
the censorious implications of opposing rationality to self-interest that we shall
observe in other writers (such as Banfield 1958). It also emphasizes personal tactics
and interests without explaining how these both reproduce and influence cultural
values. Britan's approach, however, is preferable to the Eurocentric cultural determinism that I am criticizing here, unless his statement is read as an equally deterministic endorsement of entrepreneurial individualism.

4. Perhaps because a high proportion of bureaucracy studies have dealt with the
West (but see Riggs 1962 for an early exception), they have not seemed to be symbolic
at all.

5. Tambiah (1990: 153) briefly suggests a parallel with religious theodicy.
Obeyesekere's (1968) analysis of theodicy shows that it exists in popular as well as in
canonical religion, a possibility that Weber did not pursue. In applying the model of
bureaucracy and its critique, we can see the operation of theodicy in official explanations, which tend to suppress protest, and in popular reactions to bureaucratic
inefficiency and venality.

he linked the urgent need for theodicy to the idea of transcendence – the idea that a moral principle, or a deity, could transcend
the specifics of time and place. In some religious systems, notably
Christianity, this might take the form of salvation. The secular
equivalent of salvation is the idea of a patriotic and democratic
community, one that tolerates neither graft nor oppression.

European nationalism resembles religion in that both claim
transcendent status. This might seem not to apply to nationalism,
whose frame of reference is a specific geographical and historical
space. Nationalisms all claim transcendence, however, in two
important senses. First, internally, they claim to transcend individual and local differences, uniting all citizens in a single, unitary
identity. Second, the forms of most European (and many other)
nationalisms transcend even their own national concerns, in that
the principle of national identity is considered to underlie and
infuse the particulars of nation and country. Gellner's (1986: 124)
claim that there is nothing particularly interesting or different
about specific nationalisms is less an analytic observation than a
somewhat backhanded voicing of the ideology itself.

Religious theodicy asks how, if there is a truly universal deity,
evil can exist in so many nooks and crannies of daily experience?
Weber (1963: 138–139) links the answer to this question directly
to that of transcendence: "the more the development [of religion]
tends toward the conception of a transcendental unitary god who
is universal, the more there arises the problem of how the extraordinary power of such a god may be reconciled with the imper-
fection of the world that he has created and rules over."

It is not too fanciful, I suggest, to compare this problem with
that faced by the members of many modern nation-states. In the
most promising beginnings of independence may lie the seeds of
a horrendous tyranny; in laws promulgated by the most benign
democracies lurks the possibility of bureaucratic repression. Not
all *risorgimenti* turned into Fascism, not all Enlightenment philoso-
phies led to concentration camp administrations; but in even the
most liberal national democracies the bureaucratic capacity for
petty tyranny remains a scandal of perception if not of fact.

The explanation, I shall argue, lies in the confusion of expressive form with practical meaning: symbols of hope may always
become instruments of despair. Weber, who clearly recognized
this problem, was intensely ambivalent toward bureaucracy: a
necessity for the securing of various practical freedoms, it also

threatened to become a rigid "iron cage" (see Mouzelis 1968: 20–21).

For ordinary people, then, including bureaucrats bewildered by the apparent ineluctability of forces that compel them to deny their own moral judgment, some sort of explanation is needed. Such explanations are not necessarily believed by those to whom they are offered. But it is not at all clear that belief is the issue.[6]

Where Weber posits theodicy as a way of propping up belief against the evidence of a flawed world, I suggest instead that secular theodicy, at least, serves a more pragmatic goal. It provides people with social means of coping with disappointment. The fact that others do not always challenge even the most absurd attempts at explaining failure does not prove them gullible. It may instead be the evidence of a very practical orientation, one that refuses to undermine the conventions of self-justification because virtually everyone, as I noted above, may need to draw on them in the course of a lifetime.

This helps us to dispose of the contrast that is often posited between the passive "fatalism" of oriental peoples and the action orientation of the West – a first step toward conceptually unravelling "the West" itself. Weber (1976) suggests that Calvinism, with its doctrine of predestination, was the crucial stepping-stone in the evolution from a fatalistic to an activist orientation: effort in the material world to confirm one's status as a member of the elect replaced the more contemplative acceptance of fate that allegedly characterized oriental and primitive religions. Weber's discussion of the role of this doctrine in the West thus did not prevent him from treating the East as excluded from the march toward rational government. He made it clear, moreover, that nationalistic self-satisfaction had its roots in the idea that the elect might know themselves to be predestined for greatness (Weber 1976: 166).[7]

This mode of explanation is still very popular in attempts to compare the industrialized West with other parts of the world. It informs, for example, a recent account of the persistence of patronage and resignation to official dictates among Middle Eastern

6. See Needham 1972 on the serious objections to applying "belief" as an analytical category to the study of collective action.

7. In Weber's own terms, "it is important for the general inner attitude of the Puritans . . . that the belief that they were God's chosen people saw in them a great renaissance. Even the kindly Baxter thanked God that he was born in England, and thus in the true Church, and nowhere else."

populations (Presthus 1973). We shall discover, however, that resignation is a poor gloss on actual social practice: the invocation of fate can serve highly calculating ends. The citizen of an industrialized state who complains of bad luck in drawing an intolerant judge or tax official is not responding at all differently from the Turk or Greek who, having tried every possible avenue, must now face derision at home, at work, or in the neighborhood, and seeks to minimize this social damage.[8] In Weber's analysis, the use of predestination is effectively retrospective: once people had demonstrably succeeded in their industry (in both senses of that word), their heavenly destination would be plain for all to see. Their character was a part of their fate, to be revealed in the course of events throughout which they had continually to keep up the struggle for success. As we shall see, such eminently practical concerns are not in any sense the exclusive prerogative of northern European Protestants.

Thus, what marks off the condition of modernity is not doctrinal impulse, but increasing centralization and scale. The symbolic values that are activated, however, are sometimes remarkably consistent from one level of social integration to the next. The symbolic roots of Western bureaucracy are not to be sought, in the first instance, in the official forms of bureaucracy itself, although significant traces may be discovered there. They subsist above all in popular reactions to bureaucracy – in the ways in which ordinary people actually manage and conceptualize bureaucratic relations.

There are clearly differences in the efficiency and level of integration of bureaucracy among different countries. But to attribute these differences to variations in national character, or still more generically to a contrast between oriental and occidental personality types, is simply a vicarious fatalism in its own right – an assertion, never demonstrated but often taken on trust, that "they" cannot escape the constraints of culture and society to the extent that "individualists" are supposedly able to do in the West. Presthus (1973: 54) portrays the Middle East in these terms:

8. As F.M. Marx (1962: 170) observes in a comment that recognizes the stereotypical character of arguments such as that of Presthus, "much of what seems to defy the institutional 'engineering' under auspices of Western technical assistance to less developed countries is itself present in the Western bureaucratic pattern, too." Diamant (1962: 86), who cites Presthus's Turkish work with approval, nonetheless remarks that a productive reading of Weber would dispense with "polarization of political authority (or political culture) types along a Western-non-Western continuum."

"'Inshalla,' the belief that God's will determines the course of human events, fosters a somewhat negative attitude to self-aid and innovation." Culture, no less than biology (and perhaps implicitly because of it), is seen as destiny.

And yet that mark of differentiation is itself part of the same logic and symbolism as that of (for example) the supposedly backward peasants of the non-industrialized Mediterranean lands. The latter may in fact also treat their successes as a consequence of character, saying in effect that one is predestined to be a certain type of person. In this sense, their position is remarkably close to that of Weber's Calvinists. They, too, are entrepreneurs. The one clear contrast lies in the far more massive scale at which collective action is possible in industrialized countries. The idea that fate subsumes character is elevated, in the modern nation-state, to a much more broadly inclusive level, giving rise to the grim predestinations of national character and destiny.

To the extent that a Middle Eastern cultural attitude of the kind Presthus describes really exists, it is no more usefully treated as a resignation to the inevitable than Calvinist notions of predestination. Like these, it is a theodicy, useful for explaining away one's own misfortunes or the successes of one's competitors.[9] If Middle Eastern attitudes do exhibit generic divergences from the values of post-Reformation northern Europe, these must be seen as a consequence rather than a cause of international inequalities. Such cultural contrasts, so judgmental in their implications and so easily evoked at the level of national entities, also subsist at more local levels, particularly between a capital city and its provinces. They spring from real experience, and from the resulting conviction that since those in authority cannot be trusted, one must seek more intimate bases of reliance. If the state has proved unable to fashion a perfect national universe, people have grounds for seeking self-exonerating explanations of their own failures to deal with bureaucratic mismanagement.

The concept of a secular theodicy is part of a larger argument

9. Entrepreneurship, a virtue in the Protestant West, becomes mere grasping or deviousness when perceived in exotic others. Since it often operates on a smaller social scale than Western industrialism, moreover, it lends itself to Western prejudices about the selfish behavior of "natives." Clearly, the scale of operations is a condition of what we recognize as modernity: hence Anderson's (1983) vision of an extension from face-to-face relations by means of "imagining" a larger community. But the practical logic of Calvinist-capitalist and village versions of destiny is the same.

in which I propose to treat nation-state bureaucracy as directly analogous to the ritual system of a religion. Both are founded on the principle of identity: the elect as an exclusive community, whose members' individual sins cannot undermine the ultimate perfection of the ideal they all share. Both posit a direct identification between the community of believers and the unity of that ideal. This is what Weber (1963: 50) meant when he claimed that "[i]t was Moses' great achievement to find a compromise solution of . . . class conflicts . . . and to organize the Israelite confederacy by means of an integral national god." We may view the continual reaffirmation of transcendent identity as an effect of some bureaucratic labor. The labor itself is highly ritualistic: forms, symbols, texts, sanctions, obeisance. If some bureaucrats fail to do their jobs wisely or fairly, it does not invalidate the meanings of these formal accoutrements, although it may undercut the authority of particular officials – and it certainly calls for a comprehensive theodicy. Just as anticlericalism often coexists with deep religiosity (Herzfeld 1985: 242–247), those Greeks (for example) whose experience of bureaucracy leads them to exclaim, "We have no state (*dhen ekhoume kratos*)!" are thereby affirming their desire for precisely such a source of justice in their lives.[10]

Symbolism and the State

Much has been written by anthropologists about the symbolic aspects of the modern nation-state (for example, Binns 1979–1980; Cohen 1974; Gajek 1990; Handler 1985; Kligman 1981; Linke 1985, 1986; Löfgren 1989), and I make no claim to novelty in emphasizing the symbolic aspects of government power. Such writings have been valuable in showing that symbols can be emotionally manipulated for political purposes. The danger with this approach, which derives from Durkheim's separation of the sacred from the profane, is that it often treats that distinction in highly literal, one might say ecclesiastical, terms. As Douglas (1986: 97) notes, that is an unhelpful development, for it disregards the ways in which highly charged symbols pervade areas of everyday

---

10. Elsewhere, I discuss this usage in the context of historic conservation and its bureaucratic management in a Cretan town (Herzfeld 1991).

experience that are not obviously political – sacralized intrusions into profane social space.

Unobtrusive symbols, however, are often the most potent of all. Their connections with received ideas about self and body, family and foes, give them unusual potential for manipulation. They seem natural and obvious. When drawn from physical nature, they exemplify what Douglas (1970), emphasizing their surreptitious force, has called "natural symbols." These include race, blood, and kinship. For better or for worse, such ideas have served state ideologies well. Weber (1963: 90) pointed out that bureaucracies have tolerated and even exploited popular religion to induce cohesion and obedience. The social symbolism of family and local groups, and especially the highly sacralized rhetoric of blood, has a similar utility.

In the earlier chapters, I shall provide more details about the specific forms of the symbols that nationalism shares with local-level societies. The most widespread of these forms is the imagery of blood as the common substance, or essence, conferring common identity. Like all symbols, this complex can take on a wide variety of meanings, some of which may diverge radically. Indeed, symbolic ambiguity is central to my argument. Because some symbols have proved extremely durable, it is often assumed that their meanings are constant. Nothing could be further from the truth. While blood may become the basis of differentiation in general, for example, the question of whom it includes and excludes is the most important issue here. It obviously makes a great deal of difference whether one remarks of an in-law that the latter is "not a blood relative," of an enemy state that "we shall shed their blood in revenge for ours," or of an ethnic minority that "we should not mix their blood with ours." These are widely separated levels. Even at the same level, however, the symbol of blood can be used both to include and to exclude. It is a device of extraordinary affect and power.

Blood is the key metaphor in representations of kinship in Europe and elsewhere. Adam Kuper (1988) has recently given us an astute account of the rise, in the nineteenth century, of an "illusory" distinction between primitive societies based on blood and kinship and modern ones based on the contract. This idea persists in the enduring distinction between tribal anarchy and bureaucratic rationality. What is so extraordinary here is that the metaphor of blood-kinship clearly suffuses the rhetoric of the state even as the latter denies its relevance. While modernity is largely defined by a commitment to rational management and immunity to family interest, the rhetoric of state is redolent with kinship metaphors. Those who serve familial interests at the expense of larger, communal ones are treated as though they were guilty of the political equivalent of incest.

There are, of course, very sound practical reasons for the desire to eradicate favoritism of any sort. My intention here is not to decry the intentions or the reasoning that underlie such impulses. The danger to democratic institutions does not, I suggest, lie in critiques of political or civic processes, which it is after all the stated aim of such institutions to protect. That same aim, however, may be seriously subverted if we lose sight of the metaphorical basis of much bureaucratic rationality. The familial and bodily symbols of nationalism are not simply metaphors. They are powerful emotive magnets, and they can be, and are, deployed by capricious officials and citizens. In the hands of totalitarian regimes, they can become an instrument of mass suasion. For all the enormous intellectual labor that has gone into the creation of a primitive "other," the collective bureaucratic self is cast in the very language and imagery that is conventionally attributed to that other. A sense of paradox arises from pious objections to the alleged "amoral familism" of Mediterranean or Latin American peasants, objections often raised by their own governments, when official rhetoric still makes the family the moral core of the citizen's affective bond with the state.

This is not to say that such rhetoric indicates bad faith. To the contrary, it is presumably based on the assumption that the family provides an easily understood model for the loyalty and collective responsibility that citizens must feel toward the state. Just as internal strife can disrupt a family to the point of dissolution, so civil war can arise from various forms of political factionalism and subvert the most generous intentions of officials at every level. But the rhetoric of kinship, which may provide a strong basis for day-to-day solidarity when applied by disinterested officials, can also serve more sinister aims – sinister, because they consist of the special interests that they purport to deny. The rhetoric of "the common good" does not always serve the common good.

It is one of the goals of this book to show how and why this can happen. It is not my intention to brand officialdom in general, or to investigate the psychological motives of those in whom we recognize the worst of bureaucratic repression. Instead, I intend to ask how it is possible for these people to wreak such widespread damage. I shall argue that they draw on resources that are common to the symbolism of the Western nation-states and to that of long-established forms of social, cultural, and racial exclusion in everyday life. Any symbolic form, removed from its original context and given new meanings by official fiat, may easily relapse into something akin to its previous significance. It also provides members of the public with a means of conceptualizing their own disappointments and humiliations, and with an argument that, under some circumstances, may lead them to acquiesce in the humiliation of others – the social production of indifference.

In the opening chapter, I offer an argument for treating the world of the bureaucratic West within the same framework as the smaller-scale societies traditionally studied by anthropologists. Mary Douglas, to whose comprehensive work on classification and symbolism this book owes a great deal, has made a cogent case against overestimating the importance of scale and sociocultural complexity in determining the relations between institutions and the way people think (Douglas 1986: 21–30). Her argument attacks the false dichotomy between primitive and modern modes of social organization,[11] and points out that most anthropologists today would reject the stereotype of a tribal society forever mired in unchangeable tradition.

To her argument, however, I would add a further dimension: that of the historical relationship between modern industrial societies and the local societies that they had to unite within themselves in order to constitute themselves as nation-states. In that long process of transformation, certain symbolic forms were carried forward. While their meanings often changed, they have in many cases remained extremely volatile, liable to manipulation and misprision in equal measure. Douglas treats the social basis of identity, a theme to which we shall return in Chapter Three under the heading of "iconicity," without attending to the semantic slippage that has enabled seeming continuities of symbolic form to conceal potentially disruptive ideological changes. Earlier and modern societies, or national states and local communities, may

---

11. Indeed, Douglas later (1986: 99) proceeds to discard Durkheim's distinction between mechanical and organic solidarity as immaterial to what she sees as Durkheim's major contribution to the analysis of the social bases of cognition.

share specific symbols, but their significance is obscured if we do not consider their contexts of use or the historical processes of transformation that conjoin them.

In Chapter Two, I attempt a more comprehensive delineation of indifference and its relationship to systems of classification. In pursuit of this goal, I examine three studies that all focus on change. One, an ethnographic account of a Portuguese fishing village, offers the sort of evolutionary view of encroaching modernity that Douglas so rightly rejects, although its author builds on her work to show connections between the symbolism of a pre-bureaucratic social order and the new way of doing things. A similar contradiction appears in the second study, an ethnographic account of peasant workers in northern Italy, since the author of that study follows Weber's pessimistic account of the "disenchantment" of the modern world – a common sociological conceit in the early years of the twentieth century (see Nisbet 1973). In the Italian study, however, nuanced historical analysis allows us to see the source of the continuities: they are not just formal, nor are they indicative of growing conceptual complexity, but they spring from changes in the distribution of local power and the effects of outside forces. Finally, I turn to a very recent, comparative account of nationalism and exclusion in Sri Lanka and Australia. This work, also a study of transformations, serves to focus attention on the fact that any ideology, no matter how consistent its formal expression, may produce radically divergent applications and interpretations.

This is crucially important, and is addressed more fully in Chapters Three and Four. Chapter Three examines the formal properties of stereotypes, both those commonly entertained about bureaucrats (the conventions of disdain) and those that appear to guide bureaucrats' own actions. In both cases, we find ourselves examining the use of conventional images for what often turn out to be far from disinterested goals. Chapters Three and Four examine the role of individuals and groups in taking seemingly transparent symbols and investing them with different meanings, some of which are derived from older or more local contexts than those ostensibly in force. In Chapter Three the focus is explicitly on stereotypes, in Chapter Four on the forms of language in general.

These chapters provoke questions about accountability. If people can shift the meanings of institutionalized forms, who is to hold them responsible? Alternatively, what devices can officials use to escape the constraints of accountability? And how do their clients cope with a world in which officials can duck their responsibilities so easily? These sets of strategies are mutually complementary, and belong to a shared symbolic order. We are back to the issue of theodicy here. Moreover, we will find that officials' dependence on a symbolism derived from local-level interests allows or compels them – according to circumstances – to depart from received interpretations of the law. It is not only the state that determines the bounds of the acceptable.

Chapter Five is an ethnographic demonstration of these points, particularly of the role of secular theodicy. Theoretical arguments about the way national bureaucracies work have not paid sufficient attention to the common ground on which bureaucratic practices and popular attitudes rest. Yet it is clear that, in the absence of such common ground, bureaucrats would feel no need to excuse their actions, nor would citizens have any hope of reversing them. In looking closely at one particular set of popular attitudes, then, I hope to say something of a more general nature about the relationship between secular theodicy and official ideology. While there are special reasons for examining the case of modern Greece in particular, the data presented in Chapter Five suggest the possibility of comparable data elsewhere – data that would help us to explore further the mutual dependence that we discover in institutional structures and individual strategies. Finally, in the closing chapter, I offer some suggestions about where such a comparative exercise might lead.

I do not claim that anthropology can or should supplant the insights of other disciplines into bureaucratic practice, nor would I expect, from the vantage point that I have sketched here, to provide a comprehensive account of bureaucratic process. I suggest, however, that anthropological sensitivity to immediate context – ethnography – helps shift the focus away from perspectives that are already, to some extent, determined by the institutional structures they were set up to examine.[12] I have chosen to call my subject "Western" bureaucracy in part from a playful sense of

12. Bruce Kapferer has suggested to me that most analyses of bureaucracy have so far been caught up in Western assumptions about the separation of person from action, a posture that he suggests can usefully be contrasted with Indian concepts. This reinforces my earlier point about the role of rationalist views in determining the existing perception of bureaucracy and the prevailing focus on bureaucratic organization at the expense of symbolic frame.

irony: it is not at all clear what "the West" is, even though its existence and its association with bureaucratic rationality are often assumed. By making central such a problematical identity, I seek the sort of productive discomfort that characterizes anthropology through continual realignments of cultural and social comparison. This is an approach that offers a perspective on how people contend with the forces that try to control who they are.

One World or Two?

Bureaucracy: The Symbolism of Rational Government

One of the most commonly held assumptions of modernity is that the bureaucratically regulated state societies of "the West" are more rational – or less "symbolic" – than those of the rest of the world. This division is based on a circular argument, which provides the definitions of rationality and then finds it at home. It treats rationality as distinct from belief, yet demands an unquestioning faith not radically different from that exacted by some religions. Even critics of the state bureaucracy implicitly accept its idealized self-presentation. The nation-state represents perfect order; only the human actors are flawed. This has all the marks of a religious doctrine.

Yet our methods do not reflect the resemblance. It is as though we confronted two different worlds: symbolic analysis is appropriate for the soft definitions of religion and ritual, but the real world of government organization calls for sterner approaches. The implications are sometimes bluntly ethnocentric: "traditional or primitive societies" have "ritual" where the industrialized West enjoys the benefits of "rationalism" (Riggs 1962: 20, 30).[1] Even in indisputably "modern" societies, however, the separation of reason from

---

1. Riggs (1962: 35) insists that his model does not describe particular societies, and that it could be used to isolate comparable features in American bureaucracy. His examples, however, are clearly ranked on a scale of modernity, and, while he does explicitly recognize that the features he attributes to "developing" societies reflect social inequalities, he apparently sees the resulting pattern as occurring in spite rather than because of the global domination of Western "rationalism."

ritual must obscure the practicalities of interaction between official rationality and daily experience. Nor will it do to dismiss as irrelevant the cosmological cast of commonly held ideas about bureaucracy, with their evocation of fate and chance, of innate personal as well as national character, and of blame and accountability. Formal regulations and day-to-day bureaucratic practices alike are fully embedded in everyday values; the idea of organizational reason is itself a symbolic construct with powerful ideological appeal.

Consider again the conventional attitude to bureaucracy, and juxtapose it with this definition of ritual (Tambiah 1979: 119): "Ritual . . . is constituted of patterned and ordered sequences of words and acts . . . whose content and arrangement are characterized in varying degree by formality (conventionality), stereotypy (rigidity), condensation (fusion), and redundancy (repetition)." Almost without modification, this definition would also fit the popular view of bureaucracy because it describes some familiar aspects of bureaucratic practice: stereotype and practice meet on the common ground of convention.

One therefore cannot make sense of modernity without paying equal attention to the symbolic roots that it so determinedly rejects. Riggs (1962: 20) claimed that Western bureaucracies were less responsive to the constraints of culture than were the "folk" systems of the Third World, the latter perhaps being a more suitable object of study for anthropologists. Intermediate ("developing") administrative systems displayed a combination of pure bureaucratic reason and culturally determined interest. This is at best a circular argument. Moreover, it predisposes analysis against any recognition of the cultural construction or symbolic import of Western bureaucratic practice. As a political scientist has wisely noted, however, "[p]ublic bureaucracies are sometimes portrayed as running roughshod over their societies, but they are bound by many thin but strong bonds to their societies and their values" (Peters 1989: 40). My goal is to explore some of those connections in the specific domain, so central to both administration and ideology, of the management of cultural and social identity – in other words, precisely where values play a defining role.

Max Weber articulated the ideal type of modern bureaucracy as a rational edifice built upon the secure foundations of a statistically regulated system of economics. He saw, however, that the stereotype of the unhelpful, interest-directed, buck-passing bureaucrat ran directly counter to the ideal type of the responsible government rationalist. This does not prevent bureaucrats from appealing rhetorically to the ideal type in order to represent – or, rather, recast – their self-interested acts as public service. Despite many subsequent attempts to draft Weberian ideas into the service of Western administrative rationalism, Weber himself was well aware that the progressivist goal of a purely legal-rational bureaucracy was hardly feasible in practice (Diamant 1962: 70).

A bureaucrat's ability to conjure up the image of rational devotion to public service may mask calculation of a more self-interested kind.[2] The rhetoric of predictable formalism is the key here; the routinization of expressive form plays a vital role in the consolidation of power (Bauman 1983: 150–151).[3] Indeed, as Marx noted, the self-perpetuating formalism of bureaucracy is what makes its power seem so unshakable (Lefort 1971: 290).

This formalism draws on Judeo-Christian and Indo-European concepts of the superiority of mind over matter, of thinkers over actors. It places rationality above and beyond mere experience, transcending the particularities of historical time and cultural place, and treats it as the outcome of an evolution leading from acceptance of the natural order to active volition, or, in Henry Maine's terms (see Kuper 1988: 27), from status to contract.[4] Weber's insistence that Calvinism induced a productive work ethic in Europeans is an elaboration of this same thesis of a typically European, historically developed free will.[5]

This thesis treats European culture as the culmination of historical consciousness. The resulting model of "transcendence" – the separation of eternal truth from the mere contingencies of society and culture – crowns an intellectual genealogy usually traced back to fifth-century B.C. Athens (see Humphreys 1978). Its history

2. Shore (1989), for example, has recently given us a compelling account of the ways in which Italian university bureaucrats exploit the rhetoric of public service for highly self-interested ends.

3. It is surely an exaggeration to say of bureaucracy that "language can be said to 'have' people rather than people 'having' language" (Ferguson 1984: 60); this may indeed be more usefully seen as an elegant rendering of political theodicy, as discussed here, whereby actors evade responsibility for their deeds. Skilled officials can always seek refuge in the authority of established rhetorical forms.

4. This distinction has an enormous tenacity in social science. Riggs (1962: 29–30), for example, contrasts the ritualistic concerns of officials in "developing" countries with the Western model of contractual obligations to which they are nominally expected to adhere.

5. The idea that non-Europeans are inferior because they are intellectually passive dies hard. See Herzfeld 1987: 84–87.

is manifest destiny, the European spirit marching to the ultimate emancipation of intelligence from gross flesh.[6] Its particular realizations include the idea of perfectly context-free, abstract language and, in the field of bureaucratic administration, a rational Western model untrammeled by "ecology" – in other words, by whatever is specific to a particular culture (for example, Riggs 1962: 19).[7]

There is a tremendous irony in all this, however, because the very idea of transcendence is itself highly contingent. It is also truculently political. "A system of thought presenting itself in terms of universal liberation through rationality is hard to refute" – and those who do not seem to understand it "become the modern barbarians living in the dark" (Tsoucalas 1991). Its cultural specificity becomes apparent from the degree to which it becomes transformed into quite different ways of doing things in these politically marginal places. While it has allowed local establishments to don the aura of the European Enlightenment, it has also served as a yardstick by which older and more powerful nations could disdain those clumsy imitators on the edges of Europe.

The idea of transcendence is of obvious utility to European nation-statism and its functionaries.[8] As a filtering out of eternal verity from the circumstantial or contingent, it is the basis of authority in virtually all ideologies of state: it represents state power as naturally or divinely ordained, depending on the available

6. Onians (1951: 464–465) has charted the complex intellectual prehistory of such ideas in early European thought, showing that the idea of a transcendent intelligence arose gradually from a complex and widespread symbolic system. Vico (1744) was an early critic of Cartesian mind-body dualism on the grounds that any concept of pure abstraction necessarily overlooked the embodied and physical basis of all thought. Established ideas about mind and body are tenacious, however, even when scientific authority challenges them and scientific thought appears to race ahead of them (Béteille 1990: 500).

7. This does not necessarily follow from the thinking of Weber, who seems never to have doubted that "the kind of administrative staff one might expect to find in a given political system would vary with the form of legitimate authority claimed and accepted in that society" (Diamant 1962: 82; the comment is specifically addressed to the work of such authors as Presthus on Turkey). But while Diamant (1962: 82) notes that "[t]here is today general agreement that little can be gained by treating departures from the legal-rational bureaucratic model as 'irrational'," this perception has not proved sufficiently influential to undercut either the stereotype of Western rationality or its use as a rhetorical weapon both within and against the bureaucracies of supposedly non-Western countries.

8. I have avoided the simpler term "statism" throughout this book, as it is used by political scientists in the very precise meaning of social policies calling for strong bureaucratic intervention.

theology. This is the rhetorical foundation for Marx's view of bureaucracy, summarized by Mouzelis (1968: 9–10) as follows: "Its
main task is to maintain the *status quo* and the privileges of its
masters" through "the bureaucrat's creation of special myths and
symbols which sanctify and mystify further his position."

The state, as a rhetorical construct, is logically opposed to individual agency.[9] In Kapferer's (1988) felicitous terms, the legends
of people undermine the myths of state. Whatever the prevailing
system of government may be, the possibility of reinterpreting
official pronouncements in terms of immediate social experience
must always threaten it. This is reproduced on a more cosmic
scale, when, in Darwin's work (see Greenwood 1984), the idea of
an immutable natural world order that was liable to only one kind
of classification gave way for the first time to a theory according
to which physical characteristics were contingent, accidental, and
infinitely and interactively mutable. This new view of the world
contradicts all notions of national "purity" – a foggy confusion of
race and culture that continues to affect the bureaucratic handling of identity. It is hardly surprising that bureaucrats, especially
minor officials, would succumb to this way of thinking, especially
since social scientists were no less prone to it. As late as 1904, Max
Weber (1976: 30) himself still suspected that the supposedly fundamental cleft dividing Western rationality from Oriental thought
was at least partly hereditary in origin.[10] Even so understated a
form of biological determinism, which is itself fatalistic, should
properly make us wary of any hard-and-fast distinction between
the Calvinist view of predestination and the alleged fatalism of
Middle Eastern peoples. We shall return to this point later.

9. European nation-statism does endorse "individualism," but this is a reductionist doctrine that formalizes agency. On the state as rhetorical construct, Delaney (n.d.), in an argument close to mine, shows how changes in the rhetorical
management of kinship metaphors substantially contribute to the establishment
of nationalist ideology.

10. The potential embarrassment of such genetic determinism in Weber's thought
perhaps also gives an alternative cast to Diamant's (1962: 86) benign assessment
that "Weber was convinced of the fundamental variability of social institutions and
did not consider Western institutions as 'natural' models for all other societies."
Much turns on what Weber would have meant by "fundamental," and his modest
uncertainty about the actual role of heredity in determining cultural difference
makes it virtually impossible to arrive at any clear conclusion. Diamant (1962: 71)
wisely avoids speculation over what Weber's reaction to Nazism would have been.

Arguments of Blood

Biology certainly offered a persuasive model of destiny to nine-teenth-century scientific rationalism. The ancient humoral classification of human races persisted, not only in scientific theory, but also, and especially, in the sphere of ethnic politics and prejudice. These two strands fuse dramatically in the writings of the eugenicist Francis Galton, a major influence on the immigration policies of Anglo-Saxon countries (see Lewontin, Rose, and Kamin 1984: 27, 88). Greenwood (1984: 84) ironically summarizes Galton's view of an essentially unchanging racial organization of humankind: "It appears that races are as they are because they were as they were." A classification founded in unchanging nature, which Greenwood (1984: 67–68), following Ernst Mayr (1982), calls "essentialist," also implicitly or explicitly provides the rationale for the essentialist claims of nationalism (see Geertz 1973: 240–241), and a model for the tautologous reasoning that underlies the bureaucratic handling of identity.

Weber's view that cultural difference might be hereditary is an excellent illustration of how easy it has often been to conflate two kinds of essentialism, biological and cultural. An essentialism that turns blood into destiny – what Caro Baroja (1970) calls "the myth of national character" – is itself a doctrine of predestination, and depends as much on after-the-fact readings of events as fully as the rhetoric of fate in Greek villages and among Weber's Calvinists. To paraphrase Greenwood's Galton: a nation is what it is because it was fated to become what it was fated to become. Possibly the most dangerous word in all the vocabulary of racism, nationalism, and nation-statism is "is." We hardly notice its corrosion of historical contingency.

The humoral system of classification, in which blood served as the point of departure for a moral code ranking whole peoples in order of their physical strength, mental agility, and moral courage, explained away all forms of cross-categorical switching as temporary aberrations from an inevitable state of categorical grace. It organized, in Douglas's (1966) fullest sense, an ideology of purity. Physical miscegenation meant moral pollution – precisely the pollution that the eugenicists and their successors aspired to eradicate. It provided the organizing metaphor for the conflation of identity with morality, and especially of national with bourgeois values. "Nationalism and respectability assigned everyone his place

in life, man and woman, normal and abnormal, native and foreigner; any confusion between these categories threatened chaos
and loss of control" (Mosse 1985: 16). As Greenwood (1984: 40)
rightly notes, this thinking has constituted the basis of ethnic
stereotypes to our own day. With the invention of blood-typing,
a four-fold system bearing a convenient formal resemblance to the
humoral model, some eugenicists actually proposed using it as the
basis for permitting and rejecting new immigrants (W. Schneider
1990: 93–94).

Such ideas still persist in the conflation of Enlightenment values with the symbolism of blood. For some French Rightists, "only
allegiance to universal values of peoplehood, democracy and the
French Revolution can define French nationality. Those who ad-
vocate living together despite differences are, therefore, challenging the principles of unitary community politics on which the
French system has been constructed. *Ius solis* [right based on
residence] is thus regarded as less authentic than *ius sanguinis*
[right based on blood]" (Bottomley and Lechte 1990: 54). Law,
science, and popular discourse could all invoke the ubiquitous
symbol of common blood, transubstantiating it into national
character and what French-speaking Canadians call *patrimoine*
(Handler 1988) – or, in terms of Kapferer's illuminating distinction again, converting popular legend into a myth for the nation-
state.

The solidarity of blood is, as David Schneider (1984: 174) has
observed, "an integral part of the ideology of European culture."
So fundamental was it, in fact, that Europeans, faced with various
forms of fictive kinship in other societies, found it difficult not
to infuse the latter with their own blood imagery. Of several celebrated accounts of "blood brotherhood" among North American
Indians, for example, none is unequivocally indigenous (Tegnaeus
1952: 42), while among certain Plains groups "[i]t is likely that
the conscious recognition of blood as a symbol of kinship is a relatively recent development, justified by a folk etymology," which
may well have in turn arisen from the influence of Euro-American
ideas (DeMallie n.d.: 12).

In Europe itself, blood had by the early nineteenth century
become the elixir that would convert local social relationships
into national culture. Arthur de Gobineau, viewed by many as
the intellectual precursor of Nazi "race science" and certainly an
early proponent of the thesis that the "Aryan race" had brought

civilization into being, thought that the inventiveness of the superior European nations came from the presence in their veins of "Teutonic blood," without which "our civilization cannot flourish" (1984[1856]: 280) – a view strikingly similar in its phrasing to the more extreme expressions of Aryanism from Fichte to Hitler (Poliakov 1981: 77). This quest for a Germanic heritage of blood, strongly formulated in Spain by the Castilian monarchy and directly linked to its active policy of discrimination against "New Christians" (converts of Jewish and Muslim origin), was also elaborated by the French nobility from the time of Louis XIV as a means of asserting its own claims to power against the increasingly powerful Bourbon Kings (Poliakov 1968: 144–145; Poliakov 1987[1971]: 24–27; Poliakov, Delacampagne, and Girard 1976: 69–70). Gobineau's thesis must be read in this wider context. It was the view of a French aristocrat: he was deeply suspicious of the thesis, represented by his contemporary François Guizot, according to which the most important part of the French heritage was Latin ("Gallic"). Guizot, as we shall shortly see, favored the admixture of "races," whereas Gobineau was strongly opposed to it even while realizing that it was inevitable and already far advanced. There is thus a strong correlation in nineteenth-century France between racial ideology and social position, and we should be careful to read Gobineau's thesis as a late elaboration of aristocratic and patrilineal notions of considerable antiquity. Indeed, as Guillaumin (1981: 57–58) has noted, "race" itself appears in French as a designation for aristocratic or otherwise prominent families – which, given the use of family surnames transmitted through males, practically meant "patrilines." In one of the best known of Gobineau's fictional writings, set on the Greek island of Naxos, we find "race" used in precisely this sense of a patriline whose nobility rests in part on its French ancestry (Gobineau 1872: 63), and whose idealized female representative must be close to the ancient virtues and splendidly unaware of the passage of corrupting time (see André 1987: 301–302; Gobineau 1936: 117–118).

The rise of Western civilization came, Gobineau argued, from the admixture of the practical or "utilitarian" disposition that this blood added to the "speculative" psychology of the "southern" and "oriental" races who made up the bulk of the world's populations. This bracketing of "blood" with moral and psychological dispositions, which was also fundamental to the humoral argument, places human nature in the framework of eternity. It also makes time irrelevant, and this makes it enormously useful to nationalist historiographies. Gobineau was explicitly horrified by the movement of time, which progressively undermined his Eden of racial purity (A. Smith 1984: 211–212). The desire to obliterate the taint of pollution brought by historical contingency rests on a consistent symbolism of pure blood.

For Gobineau, these ideas about blood were replicated in natural laws – in particular, in a "law of repulsion" that ensured that people of different "blood" or "race" would not normally desire to intermarry: repulsion of the physical essence reproduces moral aversion (A. Smith 1984: 179–180). Some "races" were forced to mingle their blood with that of others because of propinquity or slavery, and in this Gobineau saw the roots of disaster. It is instructive, if we are inclined to dismiss such ideas as mere metaphor, to consider the highly literal way they resurfaced in racist science after the discovery of blood types – to the point where one French eugenicist could write: "if two drops of blood from people of different races are placed on a glass slide and they are brought into contact, one notices that the two drops cannot mix, and there is a clumping" (Chateau 1938, cited in W. Schneider 1983: 561). This is surely a symbolic elaboration of Gobineau's "law of repulsion," but – like so many such echoes – it substitutes an irreversible condition of nature for Gobineau's horrified vision of racial decline. For Gobineau, the law of repulsion was doomed to give way to an equally compelling "law of attraction" through which the Aryan race would absorb "inferior" elements (Poliakov 1987[1971]: 266). Such prognostications of decline were unacceptable to later racist ideologues, so many of whom nonetheless persisted in claiming Gobineau as their source of inspiration.

Blood, in Gobineau's (1984[1856]: 272–274) view, is the source of a nation's moral character. This association is grounded in imagery found at the local level throughout Europe, especially in the constellation of ideas commonly glossed as "honor." Blok (1981) has argued that in the industrialized nations of northern Europe the state has monopolized this morality.[11] Honor became the hallmark of both nationalism and European identity: the deliberate Westernization policy that the Kemalists brought to Turkey

11. It is not necessary to accept the gloss of "honor" for a pan-Mediterranean code, as Blok suggests we do, in order to appreciate the utility of his identification of the array of concepts so translated in a variety of nation-state ideologies. The transformation of honor from a familial into a state-level value reflects the more

in the 1920s, for example, included substituting formulaic nationalistic oaths such as "I swear by my honor as a Turk" for religious
ones (Spencer 1958: 645).

Such concepts are fundamental to the definition, in many European cultures, of the person. They became generalized as "national character" in the ideologies of nineteenth-century romantic
nationalism (Caro Baroja 1970). Similar processes have ramified
throughout political life. In the massive rethinking among Italian
communists that followed the demise of East European state
communism in 1989–90, those who wished to drop the old ham-
mer and sickle and the party label of "communist" encountered
a widespread belief that the "name" of the party went together
with an unmistakable physiognomy (Kertzer 1991); this clearly
springs from a popular form of innatism, based on the twin concepts
of blood and name as the primary constituents of family identity
(Di Bella 1980, 1991), according to which the basis of all character
is genetic. While some of these usages do not always make the symbol of blood explicit – here, for example, it is instead ideas of
name and physical appearance that play the central role – they
do appear to fit a larger social ideology expressed, as we shall see,
in images of the sharing and exchange of blood and found throughout much of Europe and beyond.

Persistent Symbols, Meanings in Flux

It would be much too simplistic to dismiss the rhetoric of blood
as uniform in its political significance just because it shares a
common idiom that we also recognize as that of modern racism. On the contrary, it is vital to the argument that I am making
to note that the symbolism of blood is in part an empty semantic vessel, capable of being filled with a variety of ideological
messages.[12] It is precisely because ideas about blood are so common and so loosely defined, and because the radical distinction

---

general appropriation and formalization of kinship idioms, twin processes that I
discuss at various points throughout the present work. These processes are perhaps most obviously applicable to the symbolism of blood in the effects they had
on the rights of taking vengeance and bestowing pardon for homicide; see Dupont-Bouchat and Rousseaux 1988: 55–57.

12. Kuper (1988: 9) notes that the idea of primitive society, based on blood
and soil, underlay not only imperialism and nationalism, but also much of Marxism.

between biological and cultural inheritance on which anthropologists insist is very definitely not a part of that received wisdom, that the symbols can service such divergent ideologies.

The historical record makes this semantic instability clear. Greenwood (1984: 109–126), for example, has observed that the uses of humoral imagery in medieval and Renaissance Spain could produce, in the very different situations of Castille and the Basque country, vividly contrasted social ideologies: in Castille a hierarchy of nobility that could be extended to all other regions of Spain by royal fiat, among the Basques a severe and exclusive egalitarianism that treated all Basques as essentially noble and everyone else as of common birth. This combination of uniqueness and superiority in the Basque blood reappears in scientific guise in modern Basque nationalism under the claim, echoing others we have just heard, that the heavy preponderance of Rh negative sets the Basque population apart from all its neighbors (Connor 1991: 10).

Blood symbolism is exclusive; only its specific referents vary according to each ideologue's situation. Thus, Gobineau thought that the effect of Teutonic blood was to induce a powerful sense of political differentiation among the superior European nations, with the result that they would not easily lapse into indolent self-satisfaction; his rival, the conservative Guizot (1856: 32–37), argued instead that political differentiation was dangerous but that the class differences and cultural variety of the Europeans would preserve them from decline through intermarriage and the consequent mixing of blood. Guizot saw in the racial mixing of conquered and conqueror, which Gobineau (in Tocqueville 1989: 256–257) regarded as the greatest danger confronting any expansionist imperial power, the source of strength that had made France superior to all its neighbors (Poliakov, Delacampagne, and Girard 1976: 70). Whichever position one took, the conceptual framework was invariably, it seems, one that social anthropologists immediately recognize as that of endogamy and exogamy: internal admixture was acceptable, miscegenation – however defined – unambiguously wrong.

The argument between Gobineau and Guizot, like the contrast between Basque and Castilian uses of humoral classification, shows that the exclusions supported by blood symbolism may vary enormously. As Kapferer (1988) has argued, both hierarchical and egalitarian ideologies can easily become instruments of extreme intolerance. Where hierarchy may engender suspicion among classes or castes, or may (as in Sri Lanka) reject the presumed threat to order brought by outsiders, an egalitarianism of insiders easily legitimizes solidaristic forms of racism within the dominant ethnic or cultural group. In both, morality becomes the means and the reason of exclusion and violence. It was, similarly, not a long path from Gobineau's aristocratic despair to the Nazis' determined brutality. The issue is not whether these theories were in some sense the same, but how mutable was the meaning of their shared symbols.

The practical ambiguity of political symbolism has two major consequences. First, it means that formally consistent symbolism can be used to justify a variety of positions: this is the importance of formalism to the exercise of power. Second, it can provide an entire armory of self-justifying rhetoric for wildly inconsistent bureaucratic decisions: today's insider may, according to convenience, become tomorrow's foe. As long as the rhetorical form remains constant, the application may be quite capricious. Its constancy is indeed the enabling condition for interpretative license. As Handelman (1983: 5) points out, the mask of finite possibilities permits the tacit acceptance of a considerable range of actual interpretations. Like national history, which it reproduces in countless petty enactments, bureaucratic procedure cannot afford to change its forms if its practitioners want to change its meanings.

Blood and Self-Evidence

The association of blood, war, and intellect constitutes the conceptual foundation for the ideas of identity that we find ensconced in much European classification of persons. Distilled and intensified through the selective filter of a national educational system, as Loizos (1988: 648) has shown for the intercommunal killings between Greeks and Turks on Cyprus, it rationalizes feral actions. In Loizos's terms, it gives meaning to behavior that "normally" – that is, when the victims are seen as insiders rather than outsiders – would be outrageous and even psychopathic. It invests violent deeds with logic, as Simic (1982: 215), following Djilas (1958), appears to suggest for the apparently "dispassionate" mutual killings of Christians and Muslims in Yugoslavia (see also Boehm

1984: 60–62). It accounts for the ease with which Nazi leaders could harmonize mass murder with a view of themselves as decent family men (Mosse 1978: 226) – an emphasis that once again highlights the importance of familial metaphors for systematic indifference to those who are different.

Blood, the metaphor of biological kinship, is especially associated with masculine pursuits of violence. In highland Crete, where approval greets killings in which an avenger has "taken the blood back" (Herzfeld 1985: 157; see also du Boulay 1982: 550–553; Loizos 1988: 648), the tough mountain shepherds say that drinking red wine perpetuates the blood and ensures a desirable proliferation of male offspring. Perhaps this view distills an ancient symbolism of sacrifice, in which wine served as a substitute for blood, semen, and the person-forming fluids of the head (see Onians 1951: 218). In today's ethnographic record, these finer distinctions all seem to have become subsumed by the central figure of blood. Writing of several Mediterranean cultures, for example, Wilson (1988: 529, n. 222) has suggested a connection between the blood shed in feuds and the blood of procreation and virginity that a bride yields to her husband (and by extension to his agnates also) at marriage; the parallels between internecine feud and incest (literally "mixing of the blood" in Greek and other languages) offer a striking converse illustration.

Blood is the basis of the Greek *ratsa*, or patriline, an obvious cognate of "race" that also glosses the Spanish *raza* (a vaguely agnatic notion of collective identity right up to the concept of all Hispanic peoples) and the Italian *razza*. Blood is the medium of cultural exchange and recapture. Its importance appears to derive in part from an early Indo-European ideology. In that symbolic system, the distinction between the blood "inside" the body and the blood "outside" the body served as symbolic discrimination between patrikin and affines (Linke 1985: 357–361) – in other words, between the members of a male-centered descent group and those who married into it. This preference for the predictability of unilineal descent over the unpredictability of matrimonial alliance seems necessary to the emergence of centralized state systems; thus, as Hamayon (1990: 739–774; n.d.) has observed, religious systems like shamanism, by favoring alliance over lineal descent and ambiguity over certainty, do not encourage the centralization of power. Patrilineal descent, on the other hand, readily serves as a metaphorical vehicle for the transformation of social groups into national entities. The elaboration of blood as the medium of this conversion may take vivid form. In the nineteenth and early twentieth centuries, for example, Hungarian artists often depicted scenes of the legendary blood contract through which local chieftains voluntarily submitted their authority and special interests to a single national leader (Sinkó 1989: 76–77): the physical mingling of the blood of descent in the melting pot of national unity dramatically illustrates the process whereby the state takes over the language and substance of kinship for its own purposes.

In the nineteenth century, too, the fundamental distinction between patrikin and affines sometimes appeared as a genealogy of nations in which some "races" allegedly possessed male, active qualities whereas others possessed female, passive ones. These ideas fully reproduce the logic of patrilineal kinship: the male principle encompasses and absorbs the female (see Biddiss 1970: 110; Horsman 1981: 76). In Gobineau's thinking, conversely, true race is always both aristocratic and male; the necessity of its dependence on female procreation is the source of its inevitable corruption by "female" races (André 1987: 32). Although sometimes used to justify miscegenation as a means of conquest, a program fundamentally at odds with Gobineau's gloomy fears of corruption and utterly rejected in practice by such doctrines as Nazism and apartheid, the symbol of a male bloodline has thus served as a conduit through which ancient, local concepts of social superiority could progressively become transformed, in these later developments, into the idiom of brutal repression.

This semantic lability inevitably has ironic consequences. For example, it is easy to forget today that Gobineau entertained an admittedly complex and nuanced admiration for the Jews, whom he regarded as a relatively unmixed population whose competitive and self-isolating spirit would spur European culture to still greater heights, while he despised the population of modern Germany – the one country where his ideas were to achieve the status of political dogma – as racially mixed (Biddiss 1970: 254–259; Poliakov, Delacampagne, and Girard 1976: 76). The outward symbolism of blood and patriline was constant, but, for that very reason, it could sustain wildly divergent meanings and applications, serving as a common ground for the Enlightenment, Romantic nationalism, and Fascism. Similarly, at a more domestic level, we find in the ambiguity of this idiom some suggestive answers to our initial puzzlement about the coexistence in a single culture of generous hospitality and bureaucratic pettiness. Shared symbolism may disguise the most shocking transformations of intention, both over time and within cultural space.

Thus, the Nazis made free use of blood symbolism, at once familial and familiar, to invest their most feral practices with the force of common sense. One of its forms was already available in the notorious "blood libel" against the Jews, used by the Nazis – as it had been for centuries before them – to furnish the pretext for collective vengeance (see Mosse 1978).[13] Other uses of the same symbolism, although perhaps more trivial in appearance, were not in practice inconsequential. Like the composer Richard Wagner, whom he greatly admired, Hitler was a vegetarian who accused the Jews of corrupting the world through their consumption of meat (Poliakov 1968: 458–459), so that in a sense exterminating them could be seen as the revenge of nature at large. Again, semantic lability emerges as the enabling condition for what appears to be utter inconsistency, that of the vegetarian who is prepared to commit genocide: here, the symbolism of familial revenge is deployed on a universal scale. More generally, the Nazis' use of blood symbolism follows anthropologically well-known patterns of exclusion, and especially the association of difference with impurity (Douglas 1966). Thus, they defended the shedding of Jewish blood on the grounds that it was tainted by such categorical anomalies as venereal disease and incest (see Linke 1985;1986: 246–256).[14]

Such metaphors unite whole societies in the pursuit of violence. The logic of nationalism treats the nation as a family. New states are especially liable to develop such devices through their

13. This once common idea, according to which the alleged Jewish use of the blood of Christian children in rituals was used as justification for killing of Jews, displays the structure and imagery of blood exchange in a particularly stark form. On Nazi symbolism of the blood, see also Linke 1986; on the roots and practice of Nazi exploitations of folklore, see Gajek 1990; Kamenetsky 1977, 1984; Linke 1990.

14. "Incest" is "blood-mixing" in several languages, including Greek. On the attempt to justify genocide as a punishment for the "non-Aryan" practice of meat-eating, the basic historical assumption is presumably derived from early Sanskritic scholarship. Today, even among those Europeans who do eat meat – surely the great majority – we find the same distaste for the notion of consuming once living creatures, although the relevant symbols are differently deployed: powerful categorical barriers separate "meat" from "animal," and "killing" from "slaughtering," and these symbolic disjunctures are reproduced in the physical separation of slaughterhouses from the urban centers they serve (Vialles 1987: 23–25, 137–139).

educational systems, and may displace or coopt family affect for
the purposes of national solidarity (see Handelman and Shamgar-
Handelman 1990, on Israel). Conversely, political alliances are
portrayed in the language of kinship and affinity, and are often
created through the "merging of blood" in dynastic alliances.

Kinship and its extensions furnish a rhetoric of political pollution. Thus, the foes of a certain Greek Cypriot politician represented him as the "brother-in-law" (wife's sister's husband) of the
leader of the Turkish Cypriot community (in other words, the
enemy) because his wife was Indian and therefore foreign. This
"syllogistic reasoning" (Loizos 1975: 284), which at times of great
political tension takes on a thoroughly literal "feel," turns on the
language of blood, a language so uncompròmising in its categorical distinctions that it cannot accommodate the possibility of intermarriage between Christians and Muslims.

It is an irony of history that a similar logic, echoing Nazi "race
theory" and, beyond that, the ideas of Gobineau, once marked
the perception of political alliances in Sri Lanka: the myth of Aryanism died hard in South Asia, especially as it was one of the few
mythological devices for achieving self-respect that the British
occupiers, with their Sanskritic scholarship, were willing to offer
their more educated local subjects (see Kapferer 1988: 91–92).
Perhaps to be viewed in the same framework is the recent report
from a Soviet journal that Saddam Hussein was the son of Josef
Stalin![15]

Accusations of illegitimate political filiation or affinity invoke
the essentialist taxonomy of blood (see D. Schneider 1968, 1974).
Other metaphors may lack the specific symbolism of blood, but
are always predicated on ideas about the embodied person and
its relationship to wider cosmological questions of accountability,
intention, and innate character. These include the countless places
of social life where indifference reigns, where the pettiest of tyrants – protected from inspection by the very banality and triviality
of their power – are capable of inflicting a range of suffering no
less significant simply because it is less dramatically visible. Here,
too, in the citadel of reason that constitutes the ideal type of
bureaucracy, suffering can spring from a bookish devotion to the
written word. If the schoolroom is where children first learn to
extend familial affect and rage to national loyalty, it is often through

15. Reported in *Newsweek*, 21 January 1991, p. 6.

attention to fine print that an unscrupulous or racist bureaucrat can make "the state" appear to be an ineluctably indifferent or callous instrument.

Our task is to explore this often inadvertent sanctioning of indifference: the indifference that permits and even tacitly encourages genocide and intracommunal killings, to be sure, but that also perpetuates the pettier and less sensational versions of the same logic. Compactly expressed, as I have already hinted above, indifference is a rejection of those who are different, made tolerable to insiders because it is presented in terms that are at once familiar and familial. Indifference is arbitrarily selective. Like "benign neglect," which is one of its varieties, it provides a moral alibi for inaction. Someone must always be willing to activate that excuse, and one of my goals here is to show why it is so easy for individuals and organizations to do so.

Anthropologists' political commitments have often led them to the critical study of violence and prejudice. They have also been perennially interested in questions of category violation – the ways in which people's ideas about order are threatened or undermined. It is much rarer to find anthropologists concerned with the translation of the one into the other, although the recent study of intercommunal killings on Cyprus by Peter Loizos, briefly mentioned above, has taken an important step forward by showing that individuals may translate the more virulent forms of nationalist rhetoric into extreme violence against the categorical outsiders. Leach (1965) long ago pointed out that the act of killing was a form of classification in itself, since it indicated the boundary between friends and enemies. Violence, like all taxonomy (Douglas 1975), can become self-evident, and thus appear to be a necessity. By the same token, destructive, routinized inaction can become an apparently inevitable dimension of everyday social experience.

Gellner (1988: 234), in an apparent evocation of Weber's (1968: 16) definition of discipline as habituation to authority, notes with apparent surprise that modern liberal democracies have proved much more pervasive of their citizens' lives than have the most tenacious tyrannies of the past. In part, this is a matter of technology. One can imagine the intellectual exhaustion that would ensue from any attempt to challenge even an infinitesimal part of the arbitrary directives that come to us at every moment of (at least) our waking lives. Modern mass media have powerfully intensified this capacity for the inculcation of habit (see Bourdieu 1977). Handelman (1990: 269) has suggested that these directives function under conditions of domestic intimacy that inhibit action: they are "affective rather than effective." But this does not mean that they are unimportant. On the contrary, they are ideal instruments for transforming models of action into passive consumption. The mass production of official forms works in much the same way, and the conventions of complaining about the bureaucracy only serve to reinforce the effect of a pervasive familiarity.[16]

Teleology/Tautology

In conventional anthropological thought, symbolism implies religion. Nationalism certainly exhibits an enormous capacity to worship itself in the form of a code: language, manners, dress, art, morals. Festivals of national folklore often have this self-promoting religiosity, although, as Kligman (1981: 139–151) has argued for the state-organized Caluş festival under the Ceauşescu regime in Romania, they may also incorporate the persistence of more localized loyalties at the same time.

Durkheim's famous argument (1915) that religion is society worshipping itself thus seems appropriate to nationalism as well, as Gellner (1986: 56–57) has noted – and as Durkheim (1899: 20) himself seems to have recognized. Indeed, it probably works rather better for nationalism than it does for religion. Applied to ordinary religion, Durkheim's thesis is flawed from a number of points of view, not least of which is the way in which it reifies society. That very limitation, however, is what makes Durkheim's thesis so applicable to nation-statism. His view of the moral order even provided one self-consciously Westernizing country, Turkey, with the actual arguments for sacralizing national society as a homogenous entity (Spencer 1958: 653).[17] In modern nation-states, it is

16. Weber (1946), who thought that the persistence of symbolic affect was strengthened rather than undermined by the process of routinization, described bureaucracy as "among those social structures which are hardest to destroy." The routinization of symbolism, like the habituation to discipline that Weber saw as characteristic of bureaucratic workers, makes it seem ordinary in much the same way as certain everyday metaphors ("table *leg*," for example) have come to seem literal. On the death and revival of metaphors, see Ardener 1971: 224–225; Bolinger 1975: 423–424.

17. Spencer differentiates the Turkish case from more totalitarian forms of na-

relatively easy to trace the historical development of the state's self-reverence and the special interests that infuse it.

A Durkheimian view of nation-statism permits us to treat the rationality of bureaucratic identity management as a refraction of the sacralized national order.[18] Once created, national identity is both a moral fact and a collective representation in the clearest Durkheimian sense. It also subordinates smaller identities – kin group, village, region – to the encompassing collective good. In displacing them, however, it must draw upon them for symbolic nourishment, for they provide the language that the people best understand – much as the early Christian Church, in an earlier spate of universalizing, had coopted many pagan rituals and sacred spaces (see also Kertzer 1988: 45).

Social scientists have often overlooked the implications of this historical relationship between the national and the local, and the organic part played by symbols in creating the new order out of the old.[19] They have treated parochial or kin-based forms of interest

---

tionalism. Even the most careful architects of ideology, however, can never be entirely sure what new meanings will be read into their formal doctrines. The Durkheimian architect of Turkish nationalist ideology, Ziya Gökalp, was a Kurd (Spencer 1958: 648); this minority has since been conceptually assimilated into the nationalist vision as "mountain Turks." Fallers (1974: 71), who acknowledges Gökalp's interest in the ethnic basis of nationalism, nonetheless ignores the specifically Durkheimian inspiration of Gökalp's thinking, and also does not accord him the central role that Spencer attributes to him. In assessing the connection between social theory and biography, we should also note Durkheim's evident concern, as a secular Jew, "to elaborate the legitimating ground of liberal state structures" (Boyarin 1991: 16), as well as the ultimate irony of his admiration for what he considered to be an innate German capacity for collective thought and action (see Mitchell 1931: 98).

18. This is the inverse of the process described by Bauman (1983: 91–92), in which ritual required the foregrounding of metaphorical properties, and proved unpersuasive as a means of making converts or winning admirers when it was instead read as literal. Bauman is concerned, as I am here, with the relevance of the Weberian concept of routinization to an understanding of rhetoric and its effects. See Kertzer's (1988: 65–67) useful discussion of the Durkheimian "civil religion" view of American politics and its extensions to other societies. While Kertzer is right to criticize the inattention to social conflict that such models display, we may again meet this objection with the modification that they do at least describe the intended effects of nationalism: the framers of nation-state constitutions design the rhetoric of unity specifically to do the self-fulfilling work of teleology.

19. See, however, Kertzer 1988: 114–119, for an incisive account of the Italian Communist Party's response to Christian symbolism, and Kertzer 1991 for evidence of pervasive traditional values in people's "reading" of the Party's official insignia.

as "amoral" (Banfield 1958) and symbolism as irrational. If instead, however, we interpret the machinations of Italian villagers as moral defenses of family interests, and the symbolic conjurings of supplicants to saint's shrine and bureaucrat's office as *faute de mieux* manifestations of practical knowledge, we come much closer to the critique of ethnocentric rationalism that is, as Tambiah (1990: 50) has cogently argued, the crux of Durkheim's position. We can then also take up a more critical stance toward the effective cooptation of Durkheimian sociology by nationalism, which models its rationalist argument on the exercise of power in science and religion alike (Tambiah 1990: 31).

As should be clear by now, the study of national bureaucracy is substantially illuminated by Kapferer's case for treating nationalism as a form of religion. He claims that it is not simply a matter of the state's taking on the trappings of religion, although well documented cases of this – as, for example, in the Soviet Union (Binns 1979–80; see Kertzer 1988: 42–46 on other cases) – do clearly exist. For Kapferer, nationalism is itself a religion, because, like any religion, it demands the reification of an immanent and encompassing entity as the sole object of ultimate veneration. But Kapferer does not fall into what some have seen as Durkheim's error of assuming that such systems come into being without help from interested human agents. On the contrary, he demonstrates the unceasing interplay between political motives and cultural reification. It is not necessary to argue that there is an essential, Ruritanian national character to see that Ruritanian bureaucrats would be lost if they could not brandish the idea as a touchstone of personal authenticity. That is what, among many other pieces of paper, passports are for.

Whether or not religion can meaningfully be described as society's self-worship, then, nationalism can certainly be so viewed. Ironically, what makes nationalism different from religion, more "modern," is its far clearer congruence with the Durkheimian model of religion. It is an intentionally created, ostensibly autotelic, and largely self-referential ideology. By recognizing its capacity to revere itself, moreover, we do not necessarily assume that it is successful in controlling the hearts and minds of its citizens, or that it is necessarily an evil monster. It does, however, control public attitudes and enforce a degree of conformity with these in everyday life.[20] Every bureaucratic action affirms the basic teleology of the state.

Just as nationalism can be viewed as religion, bureaucratic actions are its most commonplace rituals. There are other such everyday rituals: Hegel saw the reading of the morning newspaper as a secular replacement of prayer – a point that Anderson (1983: 47–49) has interestingly related to the role of "print capitalism" in generalizing the social model to national culture. Some of the public rituals of nationalism are obvious enough, from coronations (Cannadine and Price 1987) to the ponderous march of warheads through Red Square (see Binns 1979–80). The centrality of public ritual to political legitimation has been extensively discussed (Cohen 1974; Kertzer 1988). But religions are rarely content with public rituals alone, and bureaucracy similarly requires rituals of personal commitment – practices that are sometimes less obviously ritualistic.[21]

Religions demand private or small-group acts of allegiance, such as prayer, confession, and penance. These provide a moral standard to which more powerful actors force those who are less powerful to calibrate their actions. In much the same way, bureaucrats exact their own array of self-exonerating, supplicatory, and punitive practices. These practices, which ostensibly align personal identity with state authority and always affect the play of selves in some way, spill over from the actual confrontations of bureaucrats and their clients into the most intimate moments. Whenever citizens blame the bureaucracy for some embarrassing humiliation, they reaffirm the teleology of the state itself.

The pettier practices of bureaucracy are often as cyclical and even as calendrical as any rite of seasonal passage – doing one's

20. Douglas's (1986: 18–19) defense of Durkheim against the charge that he represented institutions as autonomous, sentient beings follows a similar line of reasoning, although she gives greater emphasis to the role of cognition and seems to find little difficulty in reextending Durkheim's case back to religion.

21. Blau (1963: 166), for example, recognizes the office party as a ritual, seeing it as a rite of solidarity analogous to the dances of Andaman Islanders. Blau (1963: 233) also, following Merton (1957: 199–200; see also Handelman 1978: 8), treats the excessive attention that some bureaucrats pay to formality as "ritualism," creating inefficiency at the practical level. Formulations of this kind, however, overshadow the significance of ritualism as a rhetorical strategy in the hands of skilled actors on both sides of the desk.

tax returns, for example. Concomitantly, they reaffirm one's required allegiance to a clearly defined code of law while also suggesting the need to placate its local enforcers. Those who disobey get "treated like dirt." They are, to invoke a well-known anthropological definition of symbolic pollution (Douglas 1966), "matter out of place."[22] To the self-appointed guardians of conceptual, functional, and moral purity, intruders must be cleansed or eradicated; only one's "own people" are "in place" and beyond corruption. Thus, strident political puritanism can logically inhabit the same rhetorical space as the most flagrant breaches of propriety.

Mention of Douglas's durable argument, itself partially of Durkheimian inspiration, reinforces the case for using methods developed for the study of ritual in small-scale societies to examine the petty regularities of bureaucracy in a modern nation-state. Douglas's thesis is about order, a concept with deep-rooted implications in all the Indo-European languages that surface in modern confrontation with the most advanced high technology (see Zonabend 1989: 189). Even the most centralized bureaucratic nation-state relies on a model of social organization that encapsulates concentric loyalties, and this idea also, along with the blood symbolism discussed earlier, has deep roots in Indo-European conceptual history (see Sahlins 1989: 110). State order, moreover, is perhaps the most massively organized and systematically controlled symbolic system that the world has so far known, and it appears to provide the template for today's emergent idioms of a more transnational order. The English-language use of the term "order" (both a perfect state of obedience and the act of commanding it) suggests the extent to which ideology and practice constantly reproduce and reinforce each other.

In much of the recent and partially justifiable criticism of anthropology as exoticist, there has been a tendency to throw out the baby with the bathwater. We recognize that the discipline, born of colonialism and of European claims to world supremacy, has embarrassingly close historical and conceptual ties to European nationalism. While this may direct some searching criticism at the methods we use to study small-scale societies, it no less con-

---

22. Note again the intimations of "corruption" – the charge levelled at those who manage to break into the system; their own view is much more likely to be that it is "gift-giving" (Greek *dhorodhokia* means "bribery") or "reciprocity."

vincingly strengthens the case for applying them to bureaucratic
nation-states, especially those of Europe. While we continue to entertain the possibility of treating nationalism as a form of religion, we should certainly expect to gain useful insights from an
analytical tradition crafted from some of the same key ideas as
European nationalism.

We can approach this from another, related angle. Much bureaucracy appears to consist of the management of taxonomies
(see especially Douglas 1986; Handelman 1976, 1978, 1981, 1990).
As Handelman (n.d.: 2) remarks: "Bureaucracy is no less the construct of cultural cosmology than are the usual subjects of anthropological work." But it is also important to embed this realization
in a wider concern with the symbolic representation of authority
by those over whom it is exercised. To treat bureaucratic practice
apart from popular reactions to it – the secular theodicy with
which I am concerned here – is implicitly to accept the disembodied rhetoric of officialdom.

Part of the problem certainly seems to lie in the ways in which
anthropologists habitually think about their discipline. Symbolic
classification belongs to the domain of the exotic,[23] bureaucracy
to that of the modern and mundane. This distinction reflects a
certain division of labor in the discipline: while many students of
symbolism (such as Ahern 1979; Strecker 1988; Tambiah 1968)
have addressed the question of efficacy – how does symbolism
actually work? – this interest has for the most part been poorly
reciprocated by those whose job it is to study the "mechanical"
aspects of political life, including bureaucracy. Ironically, the "hard-
soft" binary opposition in our own thinking has reinforced that
division of labor, and has left the symbolic analysis of bureaucracy
relatively marginal within the discipline. The anthropological study
of modern political forms runs the risk of reproducing the ideology of modernity itself, with its hard-soft dichotomies. It is time
to reverse that self-serving argument by attending to the forms and
uses of secular theodicy.

23. While it is true that terms such as "cult" are really colonialist glosses on a
very differently organized local reality (Kaplan 1990), we can benefit most by
turning such formulations upside-down and examining the secular activities of the
nation-state as "cults" and "rituals." Perhaps, in so doing, we violate the "native"
ideas of that "tribe" of politicians (see Abélès 1989) and functionaries; but that
is no worse, and may arguably prove much more revealing, than the similar use
of ethnocentric terms for exotic peoples throughout anthropology's long history.

Bureaucracy Between West and East:
The Greek Case

The ethnography of Greece provides a rich source of material for our investigation. It is a land of spectacular hospitality and intensely personal social interaction, a place where accepting food is an avowal of affect and refusal prompts the complaint, "You don't love us." It is also a country whose own inhabitants complain bitterly about the indifference and hostility of bureaucrats. Two images, apparently at odds with each other: yet both are about social boundaries.

Both images are aspects of national self-stereotypes, the one as flattering as the other is critical. Both, moreover, incorporate national stereotypes, in that the generous host and the unyielding bureaucrat can invoke the authority of national laws and values to "explain" and even extol their respective actions. Most important of all, both are explicitly discussed, by Greeks and others, in terms of the highly charged opposition between "Europe" and "the Orient."

Greece has an extraordinarily ambiguous, complex historical relationship to the idea of Europe itself, and more generally to the stereotyped entity that we call "Western" culture (Herzfeld 1987a). Greece occupies a peculiar position on the conceptual borders, in time and space, between the polar images of "Western democracy" and "Oriental despotism" – a play of antithetical stereotypes that brings into sharp focus the conventional identification of "rationality" with "the West." Most discussions of bureaucracy treat the West and the Third World as contrasted entities, characterized, respectively, by bureaucratic rationality and familial loyalty (Peters 1989: 42).[24] In noting the play of these stereotypes in Greece, I am not trying to argue for or against either characterization: indeed, such a stance would work against the theoretical argument of this book. The stereotypes are consequential in an entirely different way. They are both an

24. Diamant's (1962, 1966) was a lone early voice that wisely cautioned against such a rigid polarization of the world's political cultures. On the whole, the habit of thinking in these terms is too entrenched in European social science as well as in many bureaucratic systems to retreat easily. It has also provoked reactions of a comparable kind. In a world hitherto dominated by Western economic and political interests, stereotypes serve as rhetorical weapons, not only in the race toward "development", but now also, and conversely, as a way of keeping the "Great Satan" and his evil technology at bay.

instrument and an effect of the peculiar circumstances under which Greece became in independent, modern nation-state. Their usefulness to us here lies in the fact that, as cultural representations, they connect local disparities of power with global political events.

Greece has been an ideological battleground for sharply contrasted stereotypes. The country's formal bureaucratic models were imported from Western Europe: the first king, who arrived from Munich in 1833, brought a clutch of Bavarian administrators, all versed in Napoleonic law. These outsiders encountered a powerful tradition, firmly entrenched during the centuries of Ottoman rule, of patronage and favor-peddling. National debates rage over which cultural models to invoke in explaining the country's problems: do we blame the meddling West or the corrupt East, or both? This is the central question regarding the theodicy of Greek political life.

The problem was compounded by the certain knowledge that educated Greeks had in fact played an extremely prominent role in Ottoman administration. While bureaucracy was introduced to the fledgling Greek state on a "Western" model, moreover, it arrived with an already tarnished image. As early as the seventeenth century, certain disgruntled French nobles had actually described the monarchical bureaucracy in their country as "Turkish" despotism (Jacoby 1973: 43)! Almost exactly a century later, Adamantios Koraes, one of the leaders of the Greek movement for independence, witnessed the French Revolution in Paris, and waxed enthusiastic about its message of liberation through the exercise of pure reason. As Tsoucalas (1991) shows, Enlightenment concepts were so transformed in Greece that "[e]ven today, 'corruption' has been found to be not only functional but also socially necessary for 'modernization.'" The lack of fit between idealized Western universality and the special interests to which it was calibrated in Greece underscores the cultural and ideological specificity of such concepts, and eventually leads us to ask what the "West" itself might be.

Greece also, and for related reasons, seems to exemplify in extreme form some of the more common features of nineteenth-century European nationalism. Above all, as Just (1989) has now noted, "blood" is more clearly the guiding metaphor of Greek identity than it is of some other nationalisms: the most pervasive idiom of particularistic relationships appears at its starkest

where the universalizing idealism of the Enlightenment under-
went greater local transformation than elsewhere. Whether or not
the Greeks had few other concepts around which to mobilize their
ethnic identity, as Just (1989: 77) claims, they undoubtedly saw
in the blood metaphor a means of uniting local folk symbolism
with the racial argument of Eurocentrism. In Schneider's (1968)
terms, the Greeks did not distinguish clearly between the respective metaphors of substance ("blood") and code ("kinship"). This
conflation, which may be more general than Schneider originally
recognized (see Béteille 1990), permitted the easy transformation
of familial into national terms: infused with one blood, the nation
is a single enormous kin group (*singenia*) or "patriline" (Modern
Greek *yenos*; Classical Greek *genos*) defined by its common "birth"
(Classical Greek *genesis*; compare the Latin *natio*). In this transformation, blood – which, as the carrier of kinship, is liable to
progressive dilution – is assimilated to the blood of Christ, whose
sanctity is inexhaustible.[25] The martyrdom of national heroes
expresses this religious conflation to the fullest degree.

The patrilineal emphasis, which sounds so exotic in the European context, has in fact enjoyed a considerable lease of life there
even in recent decades, as is indicated by Ceauşescu's Romanian
utopia and its subsequent transformations (Kligman 1991), and
perhaps also by concepts of cultural and even political "patrimony" (Handler 1986; Kertzer 1991). In Turkey, Atatürk adapted
Ottoman symbols to invest with powerful rhetorical force the pair-
ing of a "father state" and "motherland" (Delaney n.d.). In Greece,
the transubstantiation of patrilineal society into national culture,
of heredity into heritage, is conveyed by the dramatizing of the
early intellectual proponents of Greek independence as the
"Teachers of the *Genos*" – the mind directing the blood. These
examples make explicit what is elsewhere often left unsaid: that
the basis of the national culture is a society defined, in many
instances, by its agnatic continuity.

Perhaps the source of the relative visibility of blood symbolism
in Greek nationalist rhetoric is the same as that of the disjunction
between Enlightenment rationalism and day-to-day administrative
and political practice. Greece has not developed a bureaucracy as
free of patronage as some of its richer and more industrialized

25. Iossifides (1991: 144, 151) provides ethnographic support for these symbolic
equations.

neighbors have in Europe. The reasons for this state of affairs are embedded in Greece's continuing econonmic dependence and in the support that outside interests have always provided for privileged elites within.[26] As Peter Sahlins (1989: 291) has pointed out for the contrasting conditions obtaining in French and Spanish Catalonia, localism feeds on neglect or repression by the central authorities. When state efficiency fails to materialize at the local level, or is impaired by powerful mediating interests that protect local solidarities, the emotive symbolism of blood, body, and patriline may get far more play. It conceals in a single rhetoric the very real differences and strains that divide the state from more intimate social entities.[27]

Greece makes an exceptionally good case study by virtue of the enormous body of relevant materials now published. Greek bodily and familial symbolism is portrayed in an extraordinary range of historical and folkloric studies that link it to the country's millennialong tradition of literacy. The religious literature, Christian and pre-Christian, is especially rich. Other writers have already pointed out that religious symbolism pervades even the most aggressively secular domains of Greek life (Hirschon 1989), and that formal doctrine is reciprocally informed by the very "folk religion" that its practitioners so often condemn as superstitious or heretical (Stewart 1991). A rich folklore, much of it recorded to support the nationalists' goal of demonstrating continuity with the ancient past, allows us to identify relationships between the symbolic forms of ritual and religion and some of the practices associated with the modern bureaucracy. Here and elsewhere in the European Mediterranean anthropologists have already noted parallels between patron-client relations and the practice of pleading with saints for their intercession with God (Campbell 1964: 342; Boissevain 1969: 78). The symbolic underpinnings of modern political life are a good deal more ramified than this one parallel might suggest, however, and the pattern of connections between cosmology and social practice is arguably more accessible here than anywhere else in Europe.

26. I do not propose to discuss this at length here, but for a good range of assessments see especially the above-mentioned article by Tsoucalas; Couloumbis, Petropulos, and Psomiades 1976; Mouzelis 1978.

27. It is no coincidence that Greece has attracted such a rich literature on the role of both honor and patronage, beginning with Campbell's (1964) seminal linking of these twin dimensions of social and political life, especially given that blood is the symbolic medium for the rendering of honor.

The Greek focus is thus a choice dictated by specific historical considerations, but I shall also use examples from other European countries. My goals are both more generic and more particular than that of studying a single system in its entirety. They are more generic in that I hold that the symbolic roots of bureaucratic interaction are, with slight modifications, common to most of the European world and through it to most industrialized and industrializing countries. Thus, the Greek data offer us the basis of a model that can then be examined in other contexts. My goals are more particular in that I shall be concentrating on a particular set of metaphors and images that bureaucrats and their clients activate frequently in their dealings with each other: blood and kinship, the writing hand of fate and the division of territory.

The ethnography of Greece here serves as a means to a larger end: the intense focus it offers on the stereotyping of "Western" society that pervades the practice of bureaucracy. If at times the indifference or interestedness of Greek bureaucrats may seem more dramatic than what may occur in other parts of Europe, I suggest that this is not the consequence of some innate Greek character trait, an argument that would simply reproduce the essentialist prejudice that I am trying to dissect. I prefer to see it as the outcome of specific historical circumstances, especially of the political and economic inequality that subsists both within the country and in its relations with the international powers on which its survival as a state has always depended. These circumstances have dramatically highlighted the internal contradictions of European nation-statism in a country considered both the idealized ancestor and a dependent and politically marginal minion of the West. Greece is not the main focus of this book, but the Greek materials may help to lay bare some of the common features of bureaucratic interaction that lie more deeply submerged elsewhere.

Stereotypes and Strategies

In drawing the greater part of the material for this study from the ethnography of modern Greece, I will be dealing with a culture and a society in which the Eurocentric and the "native" have both become local strategies. They are part of all Greek citizens' experiential realities. They are the building blocks for Greek explorations in identity. They also serve to highlight the main features of common discriminations between Europeans and others.

State logic usually seeks to render eternal and inviolable certain principles of national sovereignty that gloss over the ever labile issue of who "we" are. This is what nationalist essentialism is all about. But such essentialism is no less a creation of stereotyping than the nation-state itself. Attacking "the state" and "bureaucracy" (often further reified as "the system") is a tactic of social life, not an analytical strategy. Failure to recognize this is to essentialize essentialism. Ethnographically, it would lead us to ignore the multiplicity of sins covered by the monolithic stereotypes of "the bureaucracy" and "the state."

Categories can be challenged, classifications breached. (In religion, too, schismatic heresies and blasphemous rejections of the divine order are part of human experience.) We may again recall Mary Douglas's dictum that "dirt is matter out of place." Even this happy formulation has been too often and too easily treated as a sort of static axiom, allowing us to forget that the boundaries of place itself are contestable. Those who actually do the job of delineating the contours and extent of place also get to say what is dirty, what is holy, and what is reassuringly and familiarly clean. They, not nature, define the ordinary; and, like all human actors, they may have to defend their choice.

Thus anthropology, with its propensity to focus on the exotic and the remarkable, has largely ignored the practices of bureaucracy (see, however, Britan and Cohen 1980). Yet this silence is, as Handelman has observed, a remarkable omission. It is also suggestive. Skilled actors that they are, bureaucrats put a face of unemotional neutrality on their every action. It is only when one makes a conscious effort to contrast their practices with those of everyday sociality that the systematic oddity of what they do begins to emerge with any clarity.

Handelman has already pointed out that bureaucracy exhibits taxonomic features that makes it amenable to social anthropological analysis. What is more, he has drawn our attention to its close resemblance to ritual and symbolic systems, although he has not pursued the analogy in detail. Both he and Jan Brøgger (1989: 145) have noted the parallels between bureaucratic attempts to define disorder and Douglas's model of symbolic pollution. Zonabend (1989: 159), too, in her remarkable study of a remote Norman community bedevilled by the construction of a nuclear power station, has noted that disorder is no less disruptive to a modern European community than it is to any other. Equally important for our present concern with the persistence of ancient metaphors is her acknowledgment that the concept of order found throughout the Indo-European languages has not withered away under the conditions of modernity. The concern with purity and pollution – which certainly underlies modern American and European racism – may be even more appropriate to modern nationalism than to the exotic symbolisms of cassowaries and pangolins. A Californian without a driving license is categorically as anomalous as a Nuer twin. Because Californians of such anomalous status would otherwise find it virtually impossible to use credit cards or cash a check, the state must issue them nondrivers' driving licenses: an amusing and relatively benign illustration of how culturally streamlined expectations of personhood come to determine official practice.

Like most symbolic systems, bureaucracy does offer some grounds for dispute, especially in matters of interpretation. Disgruntled clients must fight on two fronts at once. First, there is the actual arena of dispute over rules and decisions – the area in which, if the bureaucracy truly serves citizens' interests, there is a fair chance of remedial action. In addition, however, every disgruntled client must deal with the larger social ramifications of failure – an aspect commonly ignored by social scientists. Citizens who fail to get what they want may seriously lose standing in their home communities unless they are able to produce a convincing, or at least socially unimpeachable, defense of their actions.

The stereotype of the government bureaucrat, in most European countries and many other places besides, is thus an important part of the reality of existence within a modern nation-state. This is not the same as saying that the stereotypes are correct. What we do find, however, is that bureaucrats and clients alike invoke simplistic images of an inexorable system and its faceless servants for ends that have to do with self-justification. Citizens whose failure to extract some advantage from officialdom brings the neighbors' ridicule in full flood are the ones who claim that the machinery of state is remorseless and impersonal. They save face by invoking the faceless. Little attention is usually paid to these idioms of self-exoneration. Because they invoke much of the same symbolism as bureaucratic practice, however, and because bureaucrats also use them in order to deal with complaints from clients who may also be friends or kin, they are the key to understanding the social forces that temper both the rationality and the caprice of bureaucrats.

Even the most rationalistic view of bureaucracy must also acknowledge its potential for caprice. No system is proof against self-interested manipulation. This book is situated in the conceptual space between intention and use, that ultimately uncontrollable zone where the very fixity of symbolic form provides a cover for the tactics of power-grabbing, humiliation, and indifference. Attitudes to bureaucracy are, as I noted earlier, a convention that may have little to do with the reality of bureaucratic functioning. But in a world where human beings make history, as Vico and Marx both argued, one need only ask what a disembodied bureaucracy could actually be to make the absurdity of such a notion fully apparent. Bureaucracy, as Weber recognized, is a system demanding accountability, and accountability is a socially produced, culturally saturated amalgam of ideas about person, presence, and polity. Despite its claims to a universal rationality, its meanings are culturally specific, and its operation is constrained by the ways in which its operators and clients interpret its actions. Its management of personal or collective identity cannot break free of social experience.

CHAPTER TWO

The Roots of Indifference

Persistent Themes

The subtitle of this book includes the metaphor of "roots." This suggests a search for origins. Anthropology, however, has moved away from both original forms and questions of pure identity. Even in the study of ancient Greece, as Humphreys (1990: 536) has happily observed in another context, we can now see clearly that "the categories used in nineteenth-century studies of Greek religion – native/foreign, civilised/primitive, rational/irrational – were developed by the Greeks themselves in their reflections on religious belief and practice from the sixth century BC onwards."

Why, then, in a study ostensibly devoted to the social life of modernity, do I suddenly revert to what looks like a search for traces of past cosmologies? What is the purpose of seeking conceptual remnants of which modern social actors are probably unaware, and whose significance seems to have more in common with nineteenth-century nationalism and survivalism? The reason lies in a challenge to the uses that nationalism has made of history.

Nationalism seeks to identify civil institutions with a pure form of some putative national culture. It flattens the erratic temporality of history, turning the unpredictable succession of events into retroactive proof of a glorious predestination (see also Anderson 1983: 19) – Weber's Calvinist project writ very large indeed.[1] In later chapters, we shall consider some of the ways in which both

---

1. In certain respects, this project is complementary to that of Victorian survivalist anthropology, which posited a sort of manifest destiny for Western civilization and used this assumption to justify the colonial adventure.

bureaucrats and their clients represent government as fate: the former to intimidate, the latter to explain away. In rejecting the survivalism of Tylor, as Tambiah (1990: 46) points out, we may still make use of the Victorian anthropologist's recognition that failure to carry out an instrumental act can be explained away by some sort of after-the-fact rationalizations. Once we realize, with Weber, that all rational actions "derive their legitimacy from value decisions whose ground is anterior to instrumental decisions" (Tambiah 1990: 163), we may logically examine the actions of bureaucrats and their detractors within a common framework. Austin's (1971) important insights into excuse construction will prove helpful here.[2] Successful excuse-making entails converting the rationalizing of mistakes into the claim that these mistakes were predestined to happen all along – whether by fate, by the rules of the social game, or by transcendent logic.

The social grounding of bureaucratic practice is crucial here. Official forms claim historical origins; my concern here is to demonstrate instead their social uses.[3] Anderson (1983: 15) is obviously uncomfortable with Gellner's (1986) view that nationalism is "invented" from above, as I am with Hobsbawm and Ranger's (1983) oddly comparable view of "the invention of tradition." Both the approaches criticized here fail to recognize the role of the ordinary person in taking the grand images presented by the leadership and recasting them in the more familiar terms of local experience, and influencing their public evolution in turn. For this reason, describing national identity and heritage as pure fiction is a kind of essentialism in itself.

Thus, in pursuing "symbolic roots," I hope to demonstrate an intimate, two-way relationship between manifestations of state power and the numerous levels at which a sense of local community is realized. Much as has recently been argued for "folk" and "official" religion (Stewart 1991), I contend that, while we can certainly point to official and subversive political attitudes as ideal types, any suggestion that these are separate universes must seriously cloud the issue. The roots of official intolerance and indifference lie in popular attitudes, upon which official discourse builds to make its own case. Genocide would arguably be inconceivable

2. The relevance of Austin's work for understanding excuses in their cultural context is discussed in greater detail in Chapter Five.
3. This again is consistent with an Austinian perspective, or more generally one derived from speech act theory, on the expressive dimension of social life.

were there not already some conceptual models in place, perhaps less violent, but certainly no more tolerant of social or cultural differences. Recognizing this does not constitute the sort of cultural determinism that would cite cultural values in defense of genocide. On the contrary, we should critically examine how those in power use existing symbols and rhetoric to produce such pernicious determinisms.

The task is thus to identify the materials out of which each state constructs its own origins, and to trace the ways in which powerful interests – or pettier actors – have coopted those materials in order to build their own authority. In the same materials, too, citizens find the resources they need to fight back against importunate officials who claim to be doing the bidding of "the state." Just as anticlerical sentiment often uses the rhetoric of religion, so, too, the ideals of the state can be used to denounce the venality of its representatives; in some countries, including Greece, Jesus – victim of the Pharisees – is sometimes represented as the very archetype of resistance to church and state alike. Bureaucratic indifference and the secular theodicy that seeks to explain it away are cut from the same rhetorical cloth.

To begin unpacking these commonplace complexities, and to get some sense of their relationship to historical experience, I shall rely heavily here on three recent ethnographic studies. Two of these works are Europeanist ethnographies, and are offered quite explicitly as attempts to theorize the ethnography of Europe as well as to contribute to that ethnographic literature itself: Douglas Holmes's *Cultural Disenchantments* (1989) and Jan Brøgger's *Pre-bureaucratic Europeans* (n.d.[completed 1989]). Both explore the strains of modernization in a post-Weberian framework of analysis, although their interpretations are significantly divergent. The third work is Bruce Kapferer's *Legends of People, Myths of State* (1988). This is not an ostensibly Europeanist study at all. It is a comparison of Sri Lankan and Australian nationalisms. As such, however, it introduces a challenge to the common assumption that modern nationalism is necessarily and invariably constructed on a fundamentally European model, and shows how even that model may be altered through transportation – whether or not in the very specific historical sense in which Australians understand that term.

Brøgger and Holmes tread the difficult path between the survivalist view of traditional forms that I have discounted here and the analysis of cultural tenacity as resistance and strategy. The results of their efforts, as we shall see, are in marked contrast to each other. Kapferer's book raises important questions about the relationship between egalitarianism and hierarchy that balance the assumptions of the two Europeanist works. Perhaps most revealing of all, it finds in the Australian experience of fighting the Turks at Gallipoli a curious replay of the Renaissance battles between Turk and Christian and a source of reevaluation of the place of Greeks and Turks in the global scheme of things. Kapferer thus reminds us, in timely fashion, that these peoples of the interface between Europe and the Orient are subject to taxonomic imperatives even when these have moved to the opposite end of the earth – that they can be made to serve willy-nilly, as soldiers going to their deaths in battle or as derisive caricatures in the classroom, as pawns in the proxy wars of Western powers, and as bearers and victims of colonialist and racist stereotypes justifying their own humiliation.

It is clear that the most modern nation-states of the "West" share a complex and pervasive symbolism. Old values and symbols persist, not as taints of foreign "backwardness," but as the organizing framework both for an older order and for what seeks to replace it. The new never fully escapes the trammels of the old. The following discussion of the three works, which leads to a broader examination of the persistence of symbolic form through changing social and political conditions, should show that it is more valuable to trace the processes of transformation in an enduring cosmology than to pursue a Manichean confrontation between the pollutants of the old order and the purity of the new.

Enchanted Nazarenes

Jan Brøgger's account of Nazaré, a Portuguese fishing village, shows us a community locked by its highly unusual matrifocal kinship structure into what the author regards as a typically medieval state of culture. Belief in the supernatural, reliance on close kin bonds, a prebourgeois understanding of marital relations, and the open enjoyment and celebration of sexuality mark a cosmos that has withstood successfully, in Brøgger's view, the combined effects of bureaucratic rationalization and its sociocultural counterpart, bourgeois respectability. Brøgger expends a surprising amount of effort persuading us that this Atlantic community is usefully seen in the context of "Mediterranean" values. For this reason, he expresses surprise at finding women openly enjoying sexual jokes, and argues that their lack of prudery represents an arrested earlier phase of what Elias (1978) has called the "civilizing process." It is in fact no longer so clear that all Mediterranean societies exhibit the same sense of sexual embarrassment (see Clark 1982). In Portugal, ethnographic studies – none of them cited by Brøgger – have already noted a high incidence of both bastardy (Brettell 1986; O'Neill 1987) and premarital sex (Cutileiro 1971). But Brøgger's portrait of a Portuguese fishing village displays the discursive conventions of "Mediterraneanism," even though Nazaré is actually not on the Mediterranean littoral, in order to discover there a fixed-state model of social life that he can contrast with full incorporation into the modern nation-state.

Brøgger's analysis speaks directly to a theme I have already enunciated above: the official association of disembodiment with bureaucratic practice. He unequivocally and interestingly argues that the concealment of bodily functions represents an intrusion of categorical restrictions in much the same way as does the imposition of bureaucratic order. This important proposition points to the process of separating the sensory from the sensible – which underlies the formalism of state-sanctioned civility. The difficulty with Brøgger's handling of the question lies in the extremely literal way in which he reads the forms of categorical order as these appear in fully industrialized and bureaucratically organized societies. He assumes that the outward acceptance of bureaucratic and cultural "formalism" represents a radical break with the Gemeinschaft-oriented past.[4]

4. Mouzelis (1978: 134–136) discusses the parallelism between administrative and cultural formalism, arguing that it serves to protect elite interests. Riggs (1962: 21) defines formalism as "the degree . . . of discrepancy between the formally prescribed and the effectively practiced." Tsoucalas (1991) suggests that the label of formalism ill describes cultural situations such as those in Greece, where "objective" public ethics become transformed through the prism of more particularistic social values; his argument is historically more cogent than Brøgger's because, instead of arguing for a unilineal evolution from one type of society to another, he suggests the transformation of one set of values as a result of their refraction through the social experience of a different culture. In general, attributions of formalism or its absence are liable to debate on specific historical grounds. Thus, in the case of Brøgger's analysis, historical evidence suggests that communities like Nazaré were subject to heavy bureaucratic control ever since the age of the earliest Portuguese explorations in the New World (Pina-Cabral 1991) – a circumstance

Brøgger's argument originates in the progressivist implications of Elias's historical sociology of manners, and in a literal reading of Weber and Tönnies: "The establishment of a number of new social categories with the rise of the modern *Gesellschaft* created an equal number of possibilities for trespassing" (n.d.: 145; see Tönnies 1957). Despite Douglas's (1986) sensible reminder that scale is largely irrelevant to the complexity of social phenomena, scale and complexity are all too easily confused.[5] Thus, for Brøgger's "pre-bureaucratic," read "simple." To a thesis already constrained by its Mediterraneanist assumptions, Brøgger here adds a variety of survivalism that recalls Banfield's (1958) model of "amoral familism." The latter attributes a morality based on the rationality of common interest to "modern" society. It necessarily excludes the possibility of alternative loyalties – a possibility to which Weber's classification of ideal types had in fact catered.

In one important respect, however, Brøgger's argument very clearly anticipates my own. The resemblance lies in recognizing bureaucratic responses to disorder as ways of dealing with symbolic pollution. He calls on Douglas's insights into the social basis of classification to suggest that there is, in practice, a continuum between the taboos of a "pre-bureaucratic" society and those of the modern state. The weakness of his particular case stems from his reluctance to abandon the alienating before-and-after dichotomy. As a result, he manages to hint that these people really live in a different world, one in which their perceptions are so radically different from our own that they belong to another era altogether – a classic exoticizing device (see Fabian 1983). Thus, for example, he clearly sees the recognition of luck and sorcery as characteristic of the prebureaucratic way of thinking – a piece of Mediterraneanism in which, admittedly, he may have been inadvertently influenced by Douglas herself (1979: 40). Although he is right to see in Douglas's analyses of symbolic classification a way of bridging the gap between small-scale societies and modern, industrialized ones, and although he certainly recognizes the rhetorical play of talk about luck and ability in the former (n.d.: 124), he

---

that renders the survivalist implications of the "pre-bureaucratic" label especially suspect.

5. We shall return to the problem of scale in Chapter Four when discussing Anderson's model of "imagined communities." See also the brief discussion of scale later in this chapter.

spoils these important insights by opposing bureaucracy to luck, instead of recognizing bureaucracy as the heir to the symbolic mantle – and import – of luck. He does not seem to accept that even in the most "modern" societies, people may not accept the rationality of bureaucratic action because they know that – just as in any small-scale village – its bearers are human beings like themselves, and because they see "the system" as no less capricious than the most demonic fate. He fails, in short, to address the problem of political theodicy.

This observation allows us to pinpoint one of the main problems with the concept of bureaucratic rationality as it is so often misunderstood. Weber apparently recognized that its claims were inevitably tied to particular social formations. In this sense, it is a rhetorical phenomenon: it announces the grounds on which it will be seen to "work" and proceeds in circular fashion to include or exclude all actions on the basis of their alleged conformity to those grounds. Even in its most universalist form, its apparent transcendence of cultural particularities depends on the rules of a logical game that does not lie outside culture.

Brøgger, however, has chosen to read the evolution of modern society in a very literal way. The association of Protestantism with a universalizing view of how cause and effect work, an idea that clearly derives directly from Weberian sociology, also goes hand in hand with the rise of bourgeois ideals of respectability (see Mosse 1985). Like Gellner (1988), who sees in the rise of literacy the rationalization and literalization of thought rather than the primary cause of ever more ramified confusion and misunderstanding, Brøgger accepts the literalism of bureaucracy at face value. For this reason, he must then find a way of explaining the villagers' apparent immunity to the rationality of state bureaucracy. He finds this in a family structure that does not, in his view, encourage extensive cooperation – essentially Banfield's argument, transposed to a somewhat different kinship mode.

Brøgger's Nazarenhos may indeed have resisted the intrusion of the bureaucratic state in many areas of their lives. It does not follow from this, however, that the now irresistible new order will necessarily impose its own interpretation of events upon them, although they will undoubtedly take full advantage of its rhetoric in order to survive. Any state bureaucracy depends on a literal reading of all linguistic forms. This mask of uniformity is precisely what often allows individual citizens to reinterpret. Brøgger's error here is also Gellner's: both give too little attention to the reception, as opposed to the intended interpretation, of what are supposed to be unambiguous messages. This reluctance to acknowledge the reconstitutive role of social actors, moreover, gives rise to a candid but unfortunate social determinism: "In order to change the people of the *praia* [literally "beach"; community of fishermen] into modern rationalists, nothing less than a basic change in the social organization of relationships would be necessary. This is likely to happen only when the traditional *Gemeinschaft* is taken over by the bureaucratic state and the Nazarenos are integrated into an industrial market economy and their dependence on the lineages [*sic*[6]] and personal relations become less important than their dependence on social security, banks, and salaried jobs" (Brøgger n.d.: 126). At that point, presumably, the last vestiges of *Gemeinschaft* thinking will turn into folkloric relics, having nothing to do with the forms of modern bureaucratic interaction – the very project that has led so many European nationalisms to develop a "science" of carefully edited folklore.

This view, moreover, assumes that the disengagement of personal from functional roles has actually taken place: that, in other words, rationality has replaced patronage. Certainly, functional centralization is what the state claims to be doing. Such a rhetoric, however, may mask the intensification, not the disappearance, of political ties that depend upon personal relationships. As a recent writer on Italian university bureaucracy (Shore 1989) has demonstrated (see also Davis 1973: 152), the assumption that bureaucracy is rational and therefore unlikely to be the locus of extensive patronage is a non sequitur: the pursuit of personal advantage may indeed feed off the very institutions of bureaucracy that are supposed to displace it, and is as rational and calculating in the terms of the social level to which it is relevant as is the rationality of bureaucratic action at its own level of organization.

This in fact is what Holmes's post-Weberian ethnography, also set in an Italian context, articulates so well historically (1989: 212–213). The change is located in the rhetoric – the cultural forms that bureaucratic literalism confuses with social organization. Other things change too, of course: the scale of operations, for one. But people develop subtle means of creating new kinds

---

6. "Lineage" is a somewhat misleading term; "clan" might be more appropriate to the shallow genealogical depth intended here.

of affective bonds out of the most unpromising materials. All bureaucrats and their clients alike are potential *bricoleurs*, working both within and upon "the system."

The moral congruence between different levels permits the effective transfer of attitudes from one to another when the scale of social interaction changes, as in the shift from local to national concerns. There is in fact some evidence of this in Brøgger's careful descriptions of tensions and strains within the Nazarenho community. He shows us its most marginal members as true pariahs, excluded from most forms of contact with other villagers, and especially from intermarriage with them. He argues that this comprehensive ostracism occurs "because members of a *Gemeinschaft*. . . cannot risk the odium of contamination which a normal relationship to marginal persons implies" (Brøgger n.d.: 78). The implication of symbolic pollution is clear, and makes excellent sense.

What is much harder to accept, however, is Brøgger's apparent claim that this idiom of symbolic exclusion weakens and dies with the arrival of the *Gesellschaft* – that pollution is any less the concern of rational bureaucracies than it is of the intimate local community. In fact, the reverse is true. Pollution concepts may be refocused or redefined; but they still persist. During my urban field research on Crete, for example, a conservative trade unionist warned me to avoid fraternizing with a well-known local communist, for fear of the effects that such a relationship would have on my dealings with others in the town. The effects of such warnings in an (admittedly small) urban setting were less chilling than they might have been only a little over a decade earlier to be sure, but that is only because the current political disposition in Greece has removed the old label of "anti-Greek" (which in fact is exactly paralleled by the McCarthyite "un-American") from today's communists, a label, moreover, that was devised and applied by national authorities and carried in the national media, from the time of the Civil War (1944–1949) until the fall of the military junta (1974). The attempt to evoke that once ferocious form of ostracism could not work as well as it once did, but this was the result of changes at the national level; it is certainly not a practice that unambiguously marks off national from local politics. On the contrary, it shows the effects of national politics on local perceptions as much as the reverse. This is a symbolism of inclusion and exclusion, purity and pollution – a language that local communists also use. The effectiveness of European bureaucratic taxonomies lies exactly where the "rationalist" position would least expect to find it: in their capacity to conjure up the most traditional categories of blood, family, lineage, and reciprocity – categories that the alleged enemies of the state also share.[7]

Despite the problems that I have outlined here, Brøgger has given us a detailed ethnographic account of a society almost certainly on the verge of radical change. My disagreements with his argument concern not the likelihood or the magnitude of that change, but where it will be located. He predicts that the traditional values and beliefs will soon disappear, having served some useful adaptive purposes during the earliest phases of state-directed bureaucratic and industrial intrusion (Brøgger n.d.: 136). He may well be right about some of the specific forms. But others will probably persist, if not as external symbolic forms, then as structures of thought that will continue to provide an organizing framework for people trying to come to terms with change, and that will permeate the reactions of the bureaucrats themselves. What bureaucracies do is, in this sense, not appreciably different from what all attempts to consolidate power entail. They batten on to an existing cultural vocabulary. People – bureaucrats and clients alike – then make their respective accommodations to this new order. In so doing, they are not necessarily accepting it. They may be doing just the opposite, by playing the letter of national law against its intentions.

Disenchantments of the Bewitched

To explore these issues further, we now turn to a work that invokes Weber in a very different and, to my mind, much more productive fashion. Douglas Holmes explicitly offers his account of the peasant workers of Friuli (northern Italy) as a contribution to the theoretical elaboration of European ethnology. Unlike Brøgger, for whom the "disenchantment of the world" of which Weber wrote

---

7. Kertzer (1991) has described an example of the kind of confusion that can result from rationalist political ideology: doctrinaire Italian communism, which formally abjures emotion in political life, nevertheless appealed to it as perhaps the sole effective means of retaining the Party name and emblems in the face of changes in Eastern Europe in 1989–1990.

is a disruptive process, Holmes documents a gradual cultural process that responds to the infiltration of wage labor among economically depressed peasants. He suggests – in contrast to Brøgger[8] – that the nonrational aspects of that world may never really disappear, although, in the sphere of religion, bureaucratic interference by the ecclesiastical authorities had long ago dispossessed the "unofficial" forms of religion of much of their internal significance and reasoning. In Holmes's account, people fell back on the symbolic resources already at their disposal in order to make sense of new circumstances. Those whose roots were firmly in the local peasant traditions found it hard to organize politically to resist the harsh domination of latifundists and factory owners. At first only the marginal denizens of the towns – apparently unlike the pariahs of Nazaré – could provide an effective conduit for externally inspired change. Bureaucratic regulation, far from replacing older values with an efficient rationality, merely cloaked internal patronage – the sexual exploitation of the more attractive factory women (*favorite*), for example – with its cold and unanswerable authority. This domination, moreover, succeeded in large measure because the Catholic Church had already managed to infiltrate the local value system and to deploy the symbolic forms of that system to its own lasting advantage. Recall here the coexistence of intense patronage and a strong symbolism of national blood-community in Greece. In both cases, a widely accepted symbolism may nourish persistent disjunctures between optimistic religious or political ideologies and the real horrors of social experience – conditions that cry out for theodicy.

Holmes documents several centuries of change in the lives of the Friulani, change that Brøgger assures us must soon come to the Nazarenhos. Perhaps because Holmes's conclusions are largely empirical where Brøgger's are more speculative, they seem less firmly tied to the vicarious fatalism of bureaucracy. His social actors seem to have had a more varied experience of bureaucratic domination, although he does make it very clear that in one respect bureaucracy remained constant: generation after generation of landlords and factory owners used the conceptual precision of accounting methods to exercise an increasing degree of repression and control.

8. But Holmes is apparently in agreement with Weber; see Diamant 1962: 83.

There is one domain, especially, in which Brøgger and Holmes treat related materials in instructively different ways. Brøgger asks how the Nazarenhos interpret ownership of their households under laws according to which possession is stiffly contractual. His view appears to be that there is no connection between the two kinds of ownership: the villagers simply reinterpret contracts in terms of their own models of domestic and spiritual interdependence. The image he evokes requires what, as I have suggested, his approach most sorely misses: the capacity of local people to reinterpret official forms and invest them with meanings radically divergent from those of the law. Holmes, by contrast, suggests that the creeping changes he enables us to follow in the determination of house and land ownership represent a gradual encroachment of the capitalist version of rationality on preexisting concepts of ownership, which in turn suffuses the local perception of what was happening. It is entirely possible, even likely, that the peasant-workers he describes did not fully appreciate what was happening to them, but the long stretch of time over which he examines the documentary evidence does at least allow us to see the process as one of power struggles and engagement carried out in a common rhetorical idiom, rather than the sudden replacement of one discrete system by another.

Like Brøgger, and working in the same Weberian tradition, Holmes makes explicit the connection between religious and social change. He sees in the relegation of local religiosity to the domain of superstition a product of ecclesiastical routinization analogous to, and connected with, the bureaucratic routinization of transactional relationships. He shows that a set of religious images can carry widely divergent sets of meanings, and that such divergences both reproduce and parallel a similar split between the theory and the practice of contractual relations. As I noted in Chapter One, it is more useful in both the administrative and the religious domain to focus on the clash between ideology and practice than to divide the official world from that of the "people." The official world is itself peopled.

Holmes's account suggests that, in Friuli, the structures of "folk belief" – as opposed to its symbolic forms – have been fatally weakened by the intrusions of the state and the church. In other words, we do not see in his description of the present state of affairs any evidence that might suggest that the Friulani confront bureaucracy with a conceptual armor fashioned from older ways of viewing the world. On the contrary, the folk beliefs seem to have become merely a refuge from the oppressive horrors of modernity rather than a structural model for confronting it. Here, however, Holmes is clearly talking about symbolic forms -- the *benandanti* (benevolent witches), for example, whose name still survives in a close etymological cognate (Holmes 1989: 154). Do people only take refuge in these ideas as an escape from the present? Or do they use the conceptual structures that articulate these symbolic forms to deal actively with that same present? Holmes's evidence would suggest that the answer to the second question is negative. As he points out, it was really only the marginal, landless workers who provided the initial base for political mobilization. Nonetheless, it would seem a fair question to ask, now that they have finally begun to interact more aggressively with the state and its agencies, whether the Friulani might not model that interaction on their "enchanted" repertoire of demonic and saintly forces, as Stewart (1991) now suggests the Naxians do in dealing with the evils of modernity.

There is one area in which students of southern Europe have suggested just such a development, as I have already noted, and that is in the modeling of patronal relations on the prototype of saintly intercession. In these analogies of saintly and patronal relations, it is not entirely clear which is modelled on which, and it is probably easier to assume that both represent a particular conception of the person who is caught between, and dependent upon, overwhelmingly dominant powers. Holmes's account of patronage does not attempt to make connections of this sort.

His careful attention to historical process, on the other hand, allows us to trace the rhetorical objectification of "traditional" social ties. This is extremely important, because questions of cultural authenticity, vital to the essentialist claims of virtually every known nationalist ideology, are no less crucial to the daily reproductions of nationalism that we call bureaucratic interaction. This point, which will be brought up repeatedly in later chapters, deserves clarification here.

The social relationships of the *Gemeinschaft* were supposedly based on reciprocity. Inequality does not abolish the rhetoric of reciprocity, but it does undermine its substance. Thus, in many parts of the world, the inequalities of patronage are marked by the paraphernalia of reciprocity, and Friuli used to be no exception.

In feudal Friuli, indeed, gifts (*onoranze*) were offered by tenant to landlord as a ritual affirmation of their mutual, but asymmetrical, bond. The lord, in turn, bestowed a variety of benefits on the tenant. As Holmes (1989: 98) demonstrates, however, the increasing bureaucratization of the landlord-tenant relationship led to the unilateral insistence by the landlord on the maintenance of the *onoranze* alone – a petty assertion of his rights, but one that came as an especially nasty burden for a tenant already in extreme economic straits. Thus, even the institutions of feudal reciprocity, in which the tenant received some degree of security in exchange for his fealty, gave way under the pressures of bureaucratic "rationalization" to an increasing disjuncture between rhetorical symbolic forms and social reality. Note, too, that it is the ritual aspect that stays firmly in place. Contrary to what the model of bureaucracy as a rational system might lead us to expect, it often entails an increased emphasis on ritualistic acts.

Moreover, the rhetoric of reciprocity and of gift-giving remained firmly in place. It would not be fanciful, I suggest, to compare this situation to the acting out of hospitality that is such a feature of modern tourism. Hospitality is part of a reciprocal set, and it marks a contextual definition of relative rank: the host is always superior, at least in a symbolic and contingent sense, to the guest. I have argued elsewhere (Herzfeld 1987b) that the cumulative inferiority of the nonreciprocating guest reaches its extreme in the selfish and insensitive tourist, who finds that "the natives are friendly," but fails to understand that this friendliness masks an enduring contempt. In both the contractual "gifts" of Friuli and the pay-by-ticket generosity of tourist "hosts," we see the same masking of silent attitudes, and the same imposition of a constructed and increasingly ritualized authenticity. It is the claim to authenticity that allows the bureaucrat to justify a stance of intransigence. Conversely, only the evocation of an alternative source of authenticity – either by appealing to a fictive relationship or by invoking some morality even higher than that of the state itself – gives the client any chance of breaking through at all.

In Holmes's account of Friulian contractual history, we are able to follow a gradual detachment of the rhetoric of social relations from the ever grimmer experiences of the principal actors. As this detachment proceeds, authenticity becomes more and more of an explicit and autonomous issue. The meaning of cultural disenchantment lies in this process. Authenticity displaces charisma and social relations as the basis of authority and the goal of representation.

This has some important consequences. Above all, the cultural validation of authority now appears to be more important than the repetitive and ritualistic confirmation of the social bond between landlord and tenant, just as the propitiatory rituals of an earlier age now work to confirm the power of the priesthood rather than the relationship between supplicant and saint alone. The gift becomes not a mark of some actual social relationship but the fetish whereby the landlord reifies – objectifies – the unilateral character of his power over the tenant. This observation anticipates an argument that I shall be pursuing in later chapters: that bureaucratic procedure typically objectifies society as a model made out of language, and then performs certain operations upon that model. Authenticity is a ritualistic system of securing one's place in the cosmos.

This sounds like sorcery. The analogy, I suggest, is not far-fetched. Bureaucrats work on the categories of social existence in much the same way as sorcerers are supposed to work on the hair or nail clippings of their intended victims. Their religion is nationalism, and their actions, like those of most ritual practitioners, pragmatically aim to draw the powers of the reified cosmos into the pursuit of immediate goals. As Tambiah (1990: 24) has remarked of the artificial distinction between magic and religion, "[a] narrow yardstick of 'rationality' misses the rhetorical and illocutionary aspects of ritual performances." Or, to rephrase this telling reflection in terms immediately relevant to our discussion, a narrow distinction between prebureaucratic and disenchanted states of the world overlooks the rhetorical character of the numerous ways in which state functionaries conjure up, and conjure with, the very notion of "rationality." It is thus appropriate, now, to turn to a study in which the conceptual work of sorcery is brought into explicit juxtaposition with the practices of nationalism.

Bureaucratic and Nationalistic Sorceries

Bruce Kapferer's *Legends of People, Myths of State* is an exemplary foray into ethnographic comparison and the study of difference.

Contrasting Sri Lankan and Australian nationalism as respectively hierarchical and egalitarian, Kapferer shows how both ideologies contain within themselves the logical prerequisites for violent intolerance. There is much in his argument that is germane to my present concerns, particularly his ideas about the lability of symbols and even of outward ideology, and about the relationship between nationalism and religion.

Kapferer presents Sri Lankan nationalism within a largely Dumontian framework (see especially Dumont 1966, 1977, 1980), suggesting that for Sri Lankans the state subsumes and encompasses the individual. He draws heavily on mythological texts and ritual practices to show that unity is morally good and should encompass the expression of individual sentiments and identities; these, if allowed free rein, become the source of evil. Thus, for Sinhalese Buddhists at a time of internal stress, the Tamil "others" amongst them, erstwhile friends and neighbors, represent the threat of fragmentation and may legitimately be attacked when this fragmentation starts to become manifest. The state subsumes the person; therefore, in the syllogistic reasoning of nationalism under stress, the differentiation of persons (or ethnic groups) is a moral attack on the state, and invites retaliation.

Kapferer contrasts this hierarchization of unity and plurality with the egalitarian ideology of Anglo-Australians. They, he says, oppose the nation (people) to the state (an instrument of potential repression). Especially in ceremonies such as Anzac Day, celebrating the Australians' contribution to the Allied war effort at Gallipoli, this opposition takes explicit form in confrontations with authority. One might expect an ideology of egalitarianism and disrespect for authority and class to generate only tolerance. As Kapferer shows, however, this is not the case. Rather, Anglo-Australians reject the formation of ethnic enclaves within the nation as a form of unacceptable separatism that justifies reprisals against such groups. I am oversimplifying his subtle argument here, but the fundamental principles, thus starkly outlined, may thus show even more clearly that hierarchy and egalitarianism do share a common core of potential intolerance of difference. They locate difference in divergent aspects of social and cultural relations, but they can call on similar rhetorics (as we shall see) and they turn on the principle of a unity that, as Kapferer recognizes, must acknowledge some kind of internal differentiation. As I noted in Chapter One, a symbolic elaboration of kinship does not necessarily exclude radically divergent meanings. By the same token, hierarchy and egalitarianism can, as Kapferer shows, be equally supportive of intolerance.

The other key aspect of Kapferer's study for my present purposes is its prefigurement, at least in an implicit sense, of the present discussion of the stereotypical management of concepts of European identity. That prefigurement concerns the role that Turks (the enemy at Gallipoli) and Greeks (one of Australia's largest ethnic minorities) play in the debate about Australian identity. Kapferer argues that the fight against the Muslim Turks reproduces the great medieval and Renaissance battles of Christendom, in which the "Turk" was always the stereotypical enemy. Despite the vicious fighting, the Anzacs came to regard their Turkish foes as heroic figures. Conversely, they show great resentment of the Greek minority within Australia, despite – or perhaps at times because of – the fact that Greek-Australians lay privileged claim to European and democratic identity. Outsiders are only acceptable if, to evoke the language of purity and pollution once more, they "know their place."

Kapferer's discussion becomes especially useful to this analysis, however, when he turns to patron-client relations. The major difference between the Sri Lankan case and the normative pattern in Europe is, he claims (Kapferer 1988: 110–112), that the client seeks to become "embodied" and "incorporated" in the patron in Sri Lanka, rather than merely "connected" to the stronger party. Thus, the client will engage in sorcery to break into this larger, more powerful, encompassing entity, identifying personal problems with the collective suffering and identity of the latter: "One sorcery shrine in Colombo makes this explicit in its architecture. Supplicants must enter its premises through the jaws of a lion [which is]. . . the lion of state" (Kapferer 1988: 111).

It is precisely because, as Kapferer insists, the principles of Sri Lankan Buddhism are differently organized from those of European Christianity that we can see some common structural principles at work. In both cases, the state takes on the symbols and rituals of something that lies "beyond" the nation in order to transform the state into that ultimately cosmological verity. Because the western state has made the abandonment of the irrational the basis of its authority, much as politicians make the rejection of rhetoric the basis of their rhetoric, its actions appear to be simply the implementation of logic. This infuses the entire range of patron-client relations with a differential access to reason, not palpably unlike the earlier distinction between those with greater or lesser access to divine intervention. In the presentation of *onoranze*, Holmes's Friulian tenants lost power because a practice that marked local authority was now being transformed into a structure of authenticity. We should not be blinded by this luminous reification of social relations as cultural truths. It is the peculiar alchemy of the Western nation-state, but it is no less cosmological than the Sinhalese order upon which the modern Sri Lankan state rests, and it is no less cosmological than the enchanted world whose symbols it has usurped in order both to deprecate their meanings and to deploy them for new arrangements of power. Moreover, the fact that the modern world appears disenchanted in relation to its seemingly reverent forerunners should not lead us to take its rationalist claims too literally. It, too, rests on utopian and cosmological foundations. As these become discredited in turn, notes Tambiah (1989: 347), and as their rhetoric is stripped bare by the explosion of ethnic hatreds, a new disenchantment has set in, contesting the authority that national governments had sought to enshrine in the symbolism of the state.

Rhetoric, Bureaucracy, and Classification

The rationality of the nation-state emerges in this focus, as it does under the pressure of the new disenchantment, as a rhetorical construction. This does not make it irrelevant, but it does turn it into a very different kind of phenomenon from what it claims to be. Instead of a world order founded upon pure science, we now confront a culturally specific order founded upon its own very recognizable features. There is considerable irony in this situation. Essentialist claims by the state to cultural authenticity only work insofar as they are able to overlook the cultural roots that make those claims rhetorically plausible.

Once in being, a nation-state has to establish a pervasive reinforcement of its culturally constructed logic in every aspect of daily life. The main framework consists of a set of national categories: those that define who belongs and who does not. These categories are relatively simple, few in number, and rigid. They suppress the relativity of all social categories in daily use, so that one may no longer claim different identities in different situations. Identity, once negotiable and subject to considerations of context, now becomes an absolute label. This transformation, an alchemical conversion of popular dross into official gold, is crucial to the invention and survival of bureaucratic national identities of all kinds. The conversion of the *foranus* (Latin), one who is an "outsider" to whatever group happens to be relevant at the time of discussion, into the implacably unambiguous category of "foreigner," is a true conversion of political authority into the authenticity of the nation-state.[9]

This basic discrimination creates a model for all types of state classification, and all of these lay the same claim to absolutely fixed and nonnegotiable meaning. We owe to Don Handelman a series of attempts to show how anthropological analyses of classification could shed light on the significance and operation of bureaucracy. Handelman's interest has focused predominantly on what he calls the "systemic" aspect of bureaucratic classification (especially 1990: 78). This has not prevented him, however, from recognizing the symbolic properties of the phenomenon. In the final section of this chapter, I would like to take up some of his suggestions for the purposes of my own analysis.

Handelman has shown how bureaucratic classification emerged in Western Europe in conjunction with new forms of administrative organization (1981; see also Lincoln 1989: 6–12, 197, n.). In an argument derived largely from his reading of Foucault, Handelman shows that these taxonomies were not necessarily more logical than what had preceded them. They were, however, calibrated to the needs of certain institutional structures, and they became instruments of power and surveillance that could be used quite variably by differently situated actors.

These taxonomies, as I have already noted, also entailed the state's arrogation of violence to its own agents. Whatever one may think of his psychological generalizations on the subject, Edmund Leach (1965) was right to make a connection between small-scale violence, categorical violation, and the larger violence of warfare. While one may not want to agree with his attempt to show that warfare was a form of sexual sublimation and human sacrifice, war as exemplifying the treatment of "matter out of place" simply provides a limiting case of what bureaucracy does all the time. It

9. Note also the progressive semantic and political conversion of *paganus* (Latin), or "country dweller," into a categorical outsider to the religious in-group.

is a resistance to the dangerous powers that arise from categorical ambiguities. This is where we begin to discover the conceptual link between insiders who are not quite "of us," the usual victims of bureaucracy, and outsiders who have to be treated as though they might become "of us" and who must therefore be made victims – if this is not too strong a word – of oppressive hospitality. Pushing acts of hospitality to extremes always carries the risk of hatred and war.

Brøgger, Holmes, and Handelman all evoke, as I have done, the structuralist view of pollution as a means of understanding the peculiar tyranny of bureaucratic classifications. Anomaly, matter out of place, depends on the power of the classifier, not on some intrinsic ("essentialist") property (Lincoln 1989: 165). Handelman's interest is largely in the systemic properties of bureaucracy, although, in a new and so far unpublished paper on Chinese imperial bureaucracy, he especially emphasizes one difference from cosmology of a traditional kind – that "[t]he taxonomic work of bureaucracy is always understood to be under the conscious invention, control, and implementation of human agency" (Handelman n.d.: 2; see also 18). This, once again, is the best argument for applying the Durkheimian view of religion to nationalism: in nation-state societies, we can discern the authorship of official teleologies and place them in historical context.

In assessing the symbolic basis of modern bureaucratic practices, we should set this historical accessibility against Weber's view of the modern world as "disenchanted." To the extent that the bureaucracy is efficient, it is also inhuman (see Jacoby 1973: 148–151). Nonetheless, its basis remains that of belief – belief, now, in rationality and efficiency, rather than in a world managed by identifiable spiritual forces. More than that, it is a mark of identity. Inasmuch as Europe is seen as the home of reason, being bureaucratic in various ways means being European. To Weber, moreover, the rise of the bureaucracy was accompanied by that of the quintessentially European virtue, individualism.

In Mary Douglas's own study of modern bureaucracy, *How Institutions Think* (1986), we encounter a view of institutional action somewhat similar to what I have sketched here. In her view, Durkheim's attention to the process of sacralization, of placing certain aspects of social life beyond criticism or analysis, is precisely what characterizes the operation of institutional structures today. Rejecting the conventional view of Durkheim as a doctrinaire thinker who refused to account for the role of individual agency in social life, she shows clearly how taxonomic systems seem to push further and further away from grounded reality toward an all-consuming abstraction. Wine-growers' vineyard names, for example, give way to formal "type" names shared among large numbers of producers. She pays less attention, however, to the ways in which these systems may continue to be manipulated by canny actors – the uses to which a wide range of seemingly fixed-reference labels may be put. In studying institutions, we study reification, and we try to gain access to the motives and achievements of those who do the reifying. Work on the outer forms of classification should not obscure their lability, but should illustrate this as an aspect of social practice.

Douglas (1986: 21) argues that scale is not particularly relevant to the centrality of symbolic classification, except perhaps in that vastness of scale may obscure the symbolic aspects of social experience – an observation that is very much to the point here. She cogently demonstrates that institutional constraints on cognition do not disappear when the institutions themselves are larger, despite a common tendency to associate large-scale administrative organization with modernity and rationality, and consequently with an absence of symbolism. There is, however, a correlation to be made with size, one that I have already noted briefly in connection with Brøgger's analysis of cultural change. This is the shift from a social to a cultural idiom, and is largely the outcome of the emergence of European nationalism. The larger the entity becomes, the more "stretched" the notion of binding kin ties; indeed, as both Fabian (1983: 75–76) and Kuper (1988) have argued from very different perspectives, the absence of kinship seems to be one of the defining characteristics of the West's view of itself. The familial idioms lose their literal sense and come to seem correspondingly more metaphorical, less "real." Indeed, it was logically necessary for the idea of kinship to recede into the mists of metaphor in order for modern governments to claim reality and reason as the core of the nation-state. This does not make the idiom less compelling – far from it – but it does remove it from critical inspection. Under rationalistic regimes, all symbolism and metaphor becomes "mere."[10]

10. Lloyd (1990: 25–38) argues that the distinction between the literal and the metaphorical was, in ancient Greece, largely a rhetorical and political one, grounded in agonistic social practice: metaphor and myth were what other people did, while

Carol Cohn (1987) has given us a gripping illustration of this process in her description of the rhetoric of defense intellectuals, the people charged with rationalizing the unthinkable (nuclear war) into an acceptable form. Her account illustrates Tambiah's (1990: 24) argument that rationality is better seen as a process, as rationalization. In a world of apparently scientific thought, symbols produce what ought to be nonsensical accounts if judged by the logic of their own users: weapons become humanized while humans are expendable, and the entire horror is achieved by the symbolic conversion of mass death into male-generated "birth" – the metaphors of invention in the nuclear armament industry. In short, alchemy occurs: in the crucible of state science, entities are transformed into their opposites – precisely the capacity of symbolism that furnishes the main argument of this book. Such trans- formations are extraordinarily alluring. Even to a philosophically alert feminist, the androcentric rhetoric turned out to be danger- ously seductive (Cohn 1987: 690, 716–717). Men she actually liked, and was willing to view as decent and interesting human beings, were already inextricably engaged in the same rhetoric. It would be hard to better her account of the personal process through which "mere" symbolism is made to perform the labor of persua- sion for unseen managers of power.

One consequence of the relegation of symbolism to the realm of the "mere" is that the role of actors in actually shaping its meanings becomes highly inaccessible. The symbolism acquires the patina of permanence. Yet in practice symbolism is never inert; its meanings emerge in social interactions, the local refractions of larger processes of change. Rhetoric is not simply the pure art of classification. It is the practice of symbolic action – a process in which fixed form is often not only the mask, but even the enabling condition, for labile meaning. Post-Weberian social science has not dealt adequately with the role of rhetoric in the produc- tion of social experience (see Bauman 1983). This is an especially serious failing when we try to analyze systems whose operators

---

one's own logic was literal and factual. (Compare the strikingly similar uses of fate and character as explanations of one's own and others' successes and failures, discussed in Chapter Five.) If Lloyd's analysis does indeed apply to Classical Greece as the cultural source of "Western" rationality, we should hardly be surprised, by extension, to find symbolism and metaphor undergirding the most aggressively rationalistic discourses of modernity.

have reified ("essentialized") them. In particular, it misleads us
into looking for mechanical failures or "dysfunctions" rather than
for the social relationships that allow an actor to consider one
interaction a failure but another a success.

At the level of surface form, a pervasive and systematic idiom
of belonging and exclusion is used by bureaucrats and citizens
alike. It is an idiom in which the very name of "bureaucrat" carries
a considerable weight of moral commentary – most of it censorious. Officials hasten to assure the public that they are not
"bureaucrats," and that "the system" forces them to do things that
good people would rather avoid – disingenuous but extremely
common ways of reifying and demonizing the unseen sources of
authority as a common enemy. Why do these devices persist? Are
people so credulous as to take them at face value? Or are they
more or less stereotypical representations, expressions of something other than rational cause? What is their relationship to the
secular theodicy of bureaucratic life? To attempt to answer these
questions, however provisionally, we must now turn back to stereotypes, not as fixed social categories, but as rhetorical images
forever in use as the representations of restlessly changing political
relations.

CHAPTER THREE

The Creativity of Stereotypes

Stereotypes and Bureaucratic Types

Up to this point, we have been concerned mainly with the symbolic construction of bureaucratic rationality. This gave us a glimpse of some of the processes involved in the conversion of stereotypes into a supposedly objective description of reality. The present chapter deals more specifically with those processes and with the ways in which the immediacies of social interaction reproduce and reshape the stereotypes produced at the top. For not only is there a close relationship between popular stereotypes and bureaucratic classification, but the actual working of bureaucracies often, and not surprisingly, flows through channels defined in terms of this convergence.

Bureaucrats themselves are frequently the objects of such stereotyping. In addition to the common (and usually unflattering) portrait of the typical bureaucrat, certain expectations of bureaucratic behavior are channeled through national stereotypes. This is hardly less true of scholarly discussion than it is of everyday life; much of the literature on bureaucracy seeks to formulate a taxonomy of personality types. Ironically, such taxonomies proceed from precisely the sort of "innatism" – the assumption that people "naturally" fall into particular personality types – that bureaucrats use to sort out the rest of the world. As Kathy Ferguson (1984: 99–101) suggests, these typologies gloss over the personal struggles that lock individuals into one or another "personality type," and create the patterns of domination that she calls "feminization" – an apt metaphor in the context of the adrocentric imagery

71

of state. In the same way, attempts to classify bureaucratic systems according to national-character criteria, such as Crozier's (1964: 208–314; 1965: 201–206) and Peters's (1989: 40–69) summations of "cultural" factors affecting bureaucracy, suffer from the same kind of essentialist reasoning.

Many of the features that these writers attribute to bureaucrats of particular nations are real enough. This is not because the French, the Germans, or the British have the innate characteristics attributed to them, but because people everywhere adopt rhetorical strategies on the basis of a presumed "national character." Their efficacy lies not in their recognition of some unchanging reality, but in their appeal to the conventions of collective self-representation. A German bureaucrat might feel under some pressure to demonstrate "efficiency," a Briton to show impatience with "excessive bureaucracy," a French civil servant to argue in the idiom of "rationality."

There are good reasons for insisting on the centrality of rhetoric here. For what purposes are theses stereotypes used? Even Peters (1989: 41), who is careful to distinguish between stereotype and social reality, does not discuss the active role of stereotypes in national bureaucracies – the extent to which people feel pressure to conform to the stereotypes. As Peters implicitly recognizes, such conformity would not tell us how far people actually conformed to these presumed national characters in their private lives. Apparently, however, they often expend considerable effort in reproducing them. What is the point of doing so? It is clear that national stereotypes can become a means of enforcing conformity and obedience. Ferguson's apposite observation about the "feminization" of subordinates reminds us that bureaucrats are often as conscious of the power that their superiors wield over them as they are of their own nominal authority. Stereotypes are also, as we shall see in this chapter, a means whereby the clients or junior bureaucrats may try to reverse the power relationship, although almost always on the terms of those in charge – another mark of "feminization."

Stereotypes are one of the currencies of social life. They represent long-established prejudices and exclusions, and, like nationalist ideology itself, they use the terms of social life to exclude others on cultural grounds. They render intimate, and sometimes menacing, the abstraction of otherness. They are thus the building materials of practical nationalism. Their peculiar combination of

immediacy and generalization places them at the interface between street violence and patriotic fervor, between irritable minor
officialdom and the pious cant that serves as justification for
restrictive immigration and trading laws. They are the key to
understanding the nation-state's capacity to evince destructive
passion despite its dauntingly impersonal and grandiose order of
magnitude – an extraordinary phenomenon that easily takes on
the appearance of the merely self-evident.

What I suggest here does not contradict Kapferer's explanations of violence and intolerance. On the contrary, my argument,
like his, seeks the culturally specific models that make such things
possible. The present focus, however, may complement his mode
of analysis by showing how, through the rhetoric of stereotypes,
state functionaries manage the common places of everyday life,
and how social actors similarly use the logic of state for self-interested ends. Stereotypes are, above all, the idiom in which social
and cultural exclusion become mutually convertible – the means,
in short, through which nationalist ideology can present itself as
a familiar solidarity beset by equally familiar enemies, while local
actors can justify their petty tyrannies as defenses of cultural value.
Attributing some nasty character flaw to another family is not,
except in terms of scale, appreciably different from attributing it
to an ethnic group or a neighboring nation.

Stereotypes portray national characters as fixed, simple, and
unambiguous. They thus disguise their own enormous capacity for
multiple interpretation. In obviating the need to think about
whether a prejudice is justified, they also deflect attention away
from their own unstable semantics. Meanings do not inhere in
symbols; character does not inhere in nations; but stereotypes
generate certainty in support of prejudice by appearing to be
unambiguous and semantically stable – a modelling device with
enormous potential for harm. At some level – and this is a point
to which we shall return in the next chapter – the tendency of
all official discourse to treat meanings as absolute and unchanging
provides a discursive model for the essentialism of "national
character": as the words of the law stand for eternal truth, so the
people's essential genius remains forever unchanged. The lack of
any necessary connection between word and meaning, symbol and
value, or body and character gives free rein to processes of arbitrary
attribution. We may recall from the earlier discussion that the
symbolism of blood is capable of supporting a variety of different

forms of intolerance. In a wider sense, the various symbolic devices that bureaucrats and their clients share admit of a huge range of interpretations. The clash of these readings is the stuff of which bureaucratic encounters are made.

The Work of Stereotypes: Society as Nature

The ideal form of nationalism is often hostile to anything that smacks of personal or small-group interest. Weber argued that bureaucracy encourages a powerful individualism because it cannot tolerate any levels of social grouping that might come between the individual and the state. Individualism is the nearest thing to what Gellner argues must characterize all European nationalisms, namely, their similarity to each other, because it was a tenet of virtually all of them that the one thing that united all Europeans was their capacity for being highly differentiated and individualistic.[1] That assumption provided a legalistic basis for the view, especially popular among English-speaking liberals, that civil services were necessarily rational and therefore impervious to "corruption" (Pollis 1987: 588; Tsoucalas 1991). In a world of individuals working together in the paternal care of the state, who needs mediators and godfathers?

Clearly, many do feel that need. Although social actors can create a smokescreen of public virtue, as long as they can also recognize a class or regional accent or note details of dress and mannerism, they are simultaneously able both to create new social ties and to imagine the larger cultural entities to which they claim to subscribe. Nationalism exploits a wide range of imagination, to be sure, but it can only do so because the basic building blocks are already familiar, making the implicit conversion of social into cultural ties quite painless and "obvious." Most state rhetorics have a strongly familial tone, even though they treat the actual pursuit of familial or local interests as inimical to the nation's best interests.

---

1. I have developed this argument in detail elsewhere (Herzfeld 1987: 77–94). The quality of individualism could be denied another group, as when nineteenth-century writers contrasted Greek individualism with alleged Slavic communalism (see Herzfeld 1982a: 57), or, more recently, when Canadian officials overseas during World War II preferred the Poles to the Russians as immigrants because the former – presumably on current political grounds – were said to be more individualistic (Abella and Troper 1982–83: 226).

It is the intermediate social allegiances that provide some of the familial and other metaphors whereby citizens can make the otherwise unfamiliar and even obscure notion of the state at least partially comprehensible. As Fernandez (1986: 35) has argued, metaphor works by glossing an "inchoate" subject with some more comprehensible image or sign; and what more immediate signs are available than the body, the self, and the family? The history of European nationalisms is a tale of such collective efforts to persuade people that they were now also citizens.

A consequence of this focus on identity, however, is a concomitant creation of otherness (Bottomley and Lechte 1990). Power-grabbing actors have at their disposal an enormous vocabulary of intimacy that can be turned into the very means of generating indifference to the human other, even to the point – in the context of modern nuclear strategy – where "[t]he imagery that domesticates, that humanizes insentient weapons, may also serve, paradoxically, to make it all right to ignore sentient human bodies, human lives... [I]t is weapons, not bodies, that get 'killed.' 'Fratricide' occurs when one of your warheads 'kills' another of your own warheads" (Cohn 1987: 699).[2] Agnatic kinship clearly provides the moral context for drawing the lines between concern and indifference, in-group humanity and collective inhumanity.

The actual forms of this kin-based symbolism do vary in place and time. The role of images in this rhetorical process makes it especially likely, as Kapferer has argued on other grounds, that nationalism and bureaucracy will take culturally specific forms, however much these may undergo revision in the context of a modern world in which cultural isolates cannot subsist. Images provide the evidential basis for claims to uniqueness as well as commonality. As Mosse (1985: 16) remarks, "[t]he visual self-representation of the nation was just as important as the much cited literature of nationalism." Because they are the least obviously arbitrary signs, being apparently based on reality and nature, visual and other material images are better equipped than abstract concepts to serve the needs of nationalist ideologies. Such ideologies suppress differences created through time, conflate social identity with cultural sameness, and disguise the contingent history whereby they came about. Images predicated on similarity are

2. Note also the unconscious irony of being killed by "friendly fire," as has happened in the 1990–1991 war in the Persian Gulf.

ideal for propaganda because they seem "natural," and provide the foundation for a whole discourse about what is natural, normal, and national (Herzfeld 1986).

Iconic signs – signs based on resemblance – are as bound by the cultural constraints of perception as any other kind, yet they make a claim to reproduction of the natural order that is less easy to sustain in the case of such obviously artificial symbols as the flag and the coat of arms. Every bureaucratic form is the icon of some edict, every rubber stamp the icon of a state seal. This pervasive reproducibility gives each bureaucrat a rhetoric of common sense, backed by the authority of law, that challenges and deflects close inspection. It is also what makes local and national levels of identity seem mutually convertible – the key feature of stereotypes.

Reproducibility is also something all nationalist ideologies have in common. It is the formal basis of their frequent appeals to cultural (and racial) continuity, to a common language and shared customs, to the rhetoric of social pathology and normality. Externally, the result is a united front. Within the more intimate context of social life, however, state officials meet clients' real needs in a nexus defined by the adoption of kinship-like rhetorics and relations. The "godfathers" of mafia lore are a particular instance of the uses of spiritual (or fictive) kinship to promote patronage (see Campbell 1964; Boissevain 1969). Thus, the converse of the state's cooptation of the idiom of social solidarity to define a cultural unity is the citizens' equally selective assumption of fictive kinship for subverting that formal sense of common identity. Such devices effectively challenge the state's cooptation of kinship as culture. In the place of official harmony and homogeneity, they suggest a more fractious reading of social and cultural experience; in the place of individualism as national character, they serve self-interest and pragmatic coalitions.

The idealized model of kinship grounds the unity to which all European nation-states lay claim. Kinship is, in other words, the principal vehicle of what Anderson has conceptualized as the "imagining" of the larger, national community. It is the bridge between body and polity, the locus of that spectacular conversion which all successful nationalisms effect between "blood" and "culture." Nationalist ideologies make great play with a range of relevant metaphors – blood, lineage, family, motherland/fatherland – in order to legitimate the reification of culture.

Bureaucrats are forced to develop a practical understanding of these metaphors. Their actions are attempts to deny and reaffirm kinship at the same time. This, I suggest, is why so many attempts to bypass formal channels invoke kin-like concepts, such as godparenthood or paternalism, that are rather explicitly not "real" kinship. On Crete, I was often told that the role of co-godparent was closer, because holier, than that of a brother. Such reallocations of affect away from both the state-as-family and the family-as-foundation allow considerable flexibility in negotiating personal and household relationships with the state itself. Bureaucrats as well as some social scientists represent the political uses of kinship and its "alternative" forms as "corrupt." Familism, so obviously a moral concept from the standpoint of anyone situated within the community, appears to be "amoral" to those who judge from without. The deployment of kinship for practical ends creates a moral context in which both formal law and its so-called "corruption" can flourish.

Corruption is in any case very much a matter of where the observer is situated in relation to events, and as such is a key concept in the theodicy of political relations. Generic calls for cleaner administration – common in Greece, for example (Caretsos 1976: 105–106) – do not recognize social experience, although they may be grounded in it. Each side represents its opponents as "dirty," and its own reasoning as based on pure logic and honesty – a social aspect of rationality that, as we are just beginning to realize, can be traced back historically to the very invention of European rationalism in Classical Greece (see Lloyd 1990: 23). The crux of such rhetoric is after-the-fact rationalization of events. Thus, in an illuminating illustration, Zonabend (1989: 66–67) shows how people choose to work for a nuclear power station because they already have close kin inside, while those who fail to get jobs there complain about "nepotism"; even these disaffected locals are afraid to protest against the presence of the station in their midst for fear of jeopardizing others' jobs. Stereotypes of bureaucracy and the state do not exist in a social vacuum. They emerge from situated actors' relationships with the sources of power: theodicy is relative to circumstances.

In attempting to understand the tactical uses of stereotypes in civil life, we can now see that they depend on both the morality of kinship and the capacity, in Anderson's sense, to "imagine" kinship beyond the local community – not, however, as Anderson does it, purely as the basis of nationalism's appeal, but additionally and conversely as both the source of constant challenges to the central authority of the nation-state, and the argument for the exclusion of foreigners.[3]

If people can imagine a community of like-minded individuals all dedicated to the common culture, they can also imagine select groups capable of discovering mutual advantage in the state's inability to suppress the value of kinship without fatally endangering its own interests. Nationalism and patronage are thus not only far from mutually incompatible; they are cut from the same cloth. National "purity" would be both impracticable and unthinkable without the mediating "corruption" of patronage. Patronage is like a secret (and often rather deep) pocket sewn into the lining of the national uniform.

Because we usually think of kinship as social rather than cultural, we generally ignore the "cultural" attributions that people routinely make to kin groups. For example, nicknames originally marking some personal quirk tend to stick to the recipient's lineal descendants (see Herzfeld 1985: 234–237). In societies where there is a strong sense of unilineal organization, people may generalize these typifications to "all the members of such-and-such a lineage." It has been customary to treat these character attributions as an epiphenomenon of kinship ideology, or at most to view their application to rival communities as an extension of the kinship metaphor. A few writers (for example, Campbell 1964) have also noted something much more fundamental: the way in which such epithets define the boundaries of a moral community. These epithets become the basis for action, or at least of after-the-fact justifications. It is really not a very long way from one's patrikin's cries for vengeance against the evil members of a rival clan to the blood hunt of ethnic hatred and nationalistic wars. A similarly short distance separates the contempt of high-status village families for those of allegedly bad blood from the bureaucrat's contempt for weak clients – the local officials' reluctance to take seriously

3. In making this last point, I am especially bearing in mind the criticisms that Bottomley and Lechte (1990) address to Anderson's argument. It is not only officials who use nationalistic language to exclude unwanted others such as certain classes of immigrant; militant language separatists within a multicultural state may similarly choose to draw the lines of metaphorical kinship in such a way as to exclude other groups. This, for example, is clearly a component in the Québecois' concern with *patrimoine*.

"a man without a collar," as one of Campbell's Sarakatsan informants so evocatively described the prevailing attitude to him
(1964: 240).

The patrilineal emphasis is never far away. Greek marriage
announcements conventionally (and by law) announce the patriline of the bride and of her mother: even female identity is couched
in androcentric terms. In other words, the father is almost always
the crucial link. When filling out a request for a residence permit
some years ago, I expressed puzzlement about the categories of
"nationality" (*ethnikotis*, a separate category from "citizenship"
[*ipikootis*]) and "religion." In the rather literal-minded spirit of the
encounter, I explained that I was a British Jew: how should I incorporate that, if at all? "What is your father?" the official wanted
to know. That was really all that mattered. Thus was my ethnic,
religious, and personal identity established through paternal links.

Kinship is thus one rich source, though by no means the only
one, for the stereotyping process to which we now turn. It is a
common figure in the production of bureaucratic indifference:
outsiders do not deserve our attention, while those of ambiguous
status must either be incorporated or fought. Kinship, however,
is a symbol with many meanings. From interpersonal relations to
state ideology, it can be used equally to incorporate and to exclude;
to coopt enemies by making them spiritual kin through baptismal
or marriage sponsorship, or to deride them because they have
managed to make alternative – and therefore "corrupt" – arrangements elsewhere. What among allies is a sacred bond, sanctified
by religious ritual, becomes a perversion of sanctity when others
achieve it.

Steering the Stereotypes: Against Essentialism

Bureaucratic authority may, in the hands of obstructionists, become
instructively tautological: things are the way they are because that
is the way they are. In its extreme form, this is the logic by means
of which the Nazi bureaucracy forced Jews, homosexuals, and
other categorically "anomalous" groups to conform to the stereotypes that the Nazis' perverted eugenics had created for them.
Mosse (1985: 190) gives as an especially odious example the
Auschwitz commandant, who "accused the Jews in his camp of acting in a 'typically Jewish' way, shirking work, clawing at each other

in wild competition" for comforts that were denied to them by
the very conditions of the camp. Conversely, the Nazis reserved
the right to exclude from the category of Jews those whom it suited
their purposes to treat instead as Germans, such as the film director
Fritz Lang. Such arbitrary decisions, which Guillaumin (1981: 56)
ranks with the equally opportunistic classifications of South African
apartheid, clearly indicate how contingent and political are attributions of "typicality." It is in these extreme cases that we see the
real danger that lurks behind stereotypes; for every stereotype is
a categorical and arbitrary "truth" that claims an invincible
defense in "reason," "nature," or some combination of both.

It is not only the bureaucrats who categorize in order to justify
their actions, however; all social actors do so. Not only are bureaucrats able to force others to create self-fulfilling prophecies, but
they must deal with the expectations the public entertains of the
bureaucrats themselves. Most people assume that they know what
bureaucrats are likely to do – this is why excuses about the
insensitivity of bureaucrats tend to work as explanations of personal failure – and most also assume that their national bureaucrats have certain characteristics that exaggerate the worst traits
of "national character." One problem that has often plagued
attempts to examine the cultural basis of bureaucratic behavior
is that the authors of such analyses (Crozier 1964; Aberbach,
Putnam, and Rockman 1981) subscribe to exactly this form of
essentialism. They expect French bureaucrats to be rule-bound,
the Greeks to be crafty, and the British to be haughty and
"nonbureaucratic." Such labels take on a dangerous and illusory
appearance of transparency – the mark of true stereotypes. Analysis becomes trapped by its object.

The most commonly invoked stereotype of all is perhaps that
of bureaucracy itself, and it is often bureaucrats themselves who
invoke it. A feature of the symbolic world that bureaucrats share
with the other people is the ethical alibi of the heartless "system."
Bureaucrats often appeal to this image in order to explain, justify,
or excuse their seemingly arbitrary actions and decisions. That this
image is a crude caricature of bureaucrats is very much to the
point. The image is a collective representation, subject to some
variation from country to country, and necessary to the self-respect
of both the bureaucrats forced to carry out distasteful orders and
the clients forced to accept their dictates.

Functionaries of state as well as rebellious citizens often find it convenient to use these caricatures to further personal or even collective goals. We can best approach the topic, then, by a path that many previous writers on bureaucracy have ignored: the rhetoric of stereotypes. By focusing on how petty functionaries interpret their mandate to put grand truths into everyday action, and how others explain away the humiliation they receive at these functionaries' hands, we shall more easily see how their power – as well as the functionaries' own humiliation from above – rests on the deliberate separation of language categories from meaning. Empty language becomes the ultimate defensive wall: a structured system of categories whose authority comes to seem too coherent for disobedience to be possible.

Once again, let us pause to remember the constitutive force of rhetoric. Rhetoric is not simply an epiphenomenon of other sources of power. It is the key to the social production of indifference in nation-state bureaucracies. The ethical alibis it awards legalistic bureaucrats and disgruntled citizens alike paper over the contradictions between freedom and law, individualism and collective identity, personal interests and allegiance to the state. European nationalisms generally extol individualism but condemn self-interest. To which of these readings a particular action will be attributed is a matter of rhetoric.

National caricatures provide the model for the "type" of bureaucrat that exists "in the blood." In Britain, for example, aggressive and humorless "jingoism" is usually considered a violation of the national self-image, yet Margaret Thatcher determinedly attacked the "un-British" bureaucracy that she caught trying to "invade" from Brussels. Why should Thatcher bother to invoke some hypothetical British way of life, were it not for the fact that this stance might enable her government to impose instead its own peculiar bureaucratic forms? The same applies to the rhetoric of the client: why would an impresario who wanted to import some spectacularly huge South American frogs into the United States furiously protest that the Food and Drug Administration's withholding of an import permit threatened his constitutional rights to entertain the crowds with his choice of frog type, unless to deploy the seeming invariance of American individualism to practical advantage? "'I'll apply for a green card if I have to,' Koffman [the impressario] said Sunday night. 'This is what America is all about'" (Associated Press as cited in *Herald–Times*, 9 January 1990).

The stereotype translates, in everyday bureaucratic practice, into the signature. Bureaucrats tend to produce a seemingly endless chain of virtually identical signatures. These both mask and express the paradox of ideological individualism. Weber, as we have seen, remarked on the individualistic basis of bureaucracy: bureaucrats are recruited to do a job for which they are personally accountable. Ostensibly, the bureaucrat's signature is an earnest of that personal commitment. Yet it is also an icon in the sense I have indicated above. It reproduces a generalized form, just as many self-proclaimed individualists would agree on what individualizes them (property rights, the possession of a personal name that has been repeated through several generations of the same family, etc.). The anxiety that such institutionalized tautology induces is the source of bureaucratic authority. It is the pen, not the sword or gun, that maintains bureaucratic power, and this concern with the status quo means that bureaucratic procedures fit well with the timeless history that characterizes virtually all ideologies of romantic nationalism.

National identity provides the template for most bureaucratic practices. Some models of national identity ostensibly reject the more obvious forms of bureaucratism. Thus, while the Greeks' striving to "be European" seems to require ever greater concessions to the great pen, the British set up a model of personal freedom that acknowledges individual responsibility. It is this rather self-congratulatory view of British freedom that Thatcher used as a means of staking out her own moral territory against Brussels. Such freedom could only belong, it seems, to those who shared in it by heritage; it did little to mute the effects of immigration policies that sent "non-patrials" packing, back to the lands that the British had so recently and reluctantly ceded to "them".[4]

Thatcher's tactics were no less bureaucratic than what she criticized. It is nonetheless arguable that the existence of a national model of resistance to bureaucracy, which in Greece takes the form of resistance to government in general, in Britain operates at the level of interpersonal relationships (see Douglas 1988: 1144). It acknowledges that bureaucrat and client alike are social actors rather than ciphers in a machine. By the same token, however, equality has its limits, and the rhetoric of antibureaucratism may conceal some of the worst abuses. It may be even harder, in such a system, not to collude. Recently, a British cabinet minister

4. Note yet again the agnatic terminology of the new immigration laws.

"... was on his way to lunch ... when his car was stopped by a police officer. 'You can't go through here, sir. The procession for the President of Nigeria·is about to pass by.'
"'Don't you realize who I am?' spluttered [the minister].
"The officer replied: 'You're not coming through here no matter who you are. By the way, who are you?"

(*The Observer*, London, 14 May 1989, p. 11)

Note the way in which the bureaucrat-policeman produces his own miniaturized version of national identity. In a "British" and "democratic" society, rank cuts no ice with supposedly incorruptible civil servants. Policeman and newspaper in turn reproduced the national stereotype. It simply isn't cricket to be too formal, even with a government minister. We all do it nonetheless; but then we can let ourselves off the patriotic hook by making fun of our inability to live up to the ideal: "By the way, who are you?" Self-mockery and humorous understatement are the characteristic forms of British self-stereotyping: once again, language reproduces and reinforces the stereotype itself.

Compare now for contrast a Greek complaint about a priest who used his holy calling to push to the front of a post office line. The offended citizen believes that priest and employee are equally responsible, collusive in fact, and concludes:

"The easiest thing in our country is the undermining [*katastratiyisi*, literally "counter-strategizing"] of the laws. And we regard this, unfortunately, as an 'achievement,' as 'cleverness'!"

(*Kiriakatiki Eleftherotipia*, 31 July 1988, p. 20)

If the bureaucrat's "respect" for the priest bespoke a "national" attitude, it was reinterpreted as a different kind of national identity – a far less complimentary one – by the complaining correspondent. Once again, national stereotypes are invoked, images of "individualism" that would perhaps here be better glossed as "self-interest." The "strategizing" that would be an asset in a fellow citizen trying to get around some particularly silly regulation becomes a negative attribute in the context of public life. Like blood, "individualism" can have a considerable range of forms and meanings.

In the end, it perhaps does not matter greatly whether one "strategizes" from behind a mask of obedience to higher authority or from a display of one's own independence. In both cases, the national stereotype is part of the strategy, which suggests again that the nationalist combination of timeless history and referential language furnishes the legitimizing model for action that often actually contradicts the model. Just as rhetoric often denies its own rhetoricity, bureaucratic wheeling and dealing usually denies that there is anything to wheel and deal about. This kind of rhetoric translates specific interests into the terms of a legitimizing generality, drawing on the sometimes mutually contradictory attributes of national self and ethnic other in the battle for a transient legitimacy.

When Cultures Meet: An Example

It may be that overarching differences in cultural values and political structures will create some differences in the style of client-bureaucrat confrontation, but these differences are not necessarily radical. Barbara Johnstone (1989: 144) tells the story of a young American woman who tried to get a package, sent to her in care of a Greek friend at whose home she was staying, from an unhelpful Greek post office clerk. In the first instance, the American tried the kind of presentational strategy that Johnstone calls "quasi-logic" – a display of reasonableness and the use of appeals to common sense. When this failed, she returned to the attack in a more aggressive mode. Instead of attempting to reason with the clerk on the grounds that the package was manifestly intended for her, and not for her friend, she simply marched in through a door marked "private," took the parcel, and announced to the clerk that it was hers and that she was taking it away with her. Over his objections, she then walked off with the package.

Johnstone is careful not to use this anecdote to claim that Americans reason more logically than Greeks, or that other strategies might not have worked equally well (or badly). She is mainly interested in demonstrating that different cultures accord weight to different rhetorical styles. She does recognize, however, that culture does not necessarily overdetermine style, so that members of different cultures may be drawn into each other's rhetorical modalities under appropriate circumstances. On the other hand, she argues, when discord supervenes, "the interaction changes from one in which persuasion per se is the goal to one in which controlling the means of persuasion is the goal" (Johnstone 1989: 154). Presumably, the Greek clerk – who could have used a "quasilogical" mode of his own had it suited it to do so, found himself defeated in terms of the tactics that he had himself elected to use.

The young woman apparently reasoned that the package was hers because it had her name on it and because she could prove her identity. As a non-Greek, however, she was in a weak position to argue with the Greek clerk, who considered the Greek addressee (that is, her friend) to be the rightful recipient. He is likely to have reasoned, we may imagine, that he would not have to deal with the foreign woman again, whereas an aggrieved Greek could mean serious trouble. For whatever reason, he chose to adhere to a highly literal sense of "addressee." The American woman eventually countered with a display of temper, and this worked, not because of some besetting Mediterranean illogic, but because now she fitted the categorical pattern of client more convincingly and presented the bureaucrat with a convincing *force majeure* that let him off the hook (i.e., what could he do with this irrational foreigner?).

Johnstone is careful not to follow the Mediterraneanist stereotype; her argument could be used as the basis for a kind of cultural determinism were it not for the care she takes in showing how easily cultural strategies mingle in the real world. I emphasize this point because it illustrates one of the many ways in which stereotypes can become institutionalized. In the encounter she describes, each side finds the other more and more incomprehensible, until the visitor stumbles upon a way of exonerating the clerk from any possibility of blame – an important consideration, as we shall see in Chapter Five.

Conversely, the idea that "Westerners" understand the operation of bureaucracy better because they are more logical is as pernicious as it is widespread. In Brøgger's ethnography of Nazaré, a work that displays obvious discomfort every time a detail departs from the Mediterraneanist stereotype, we hear an implicit claim to that effect (Brøgger n.d.: 32): "Strength of personality often seems more important than strength of argument. This style of interaction clearly reflects the lack of recognized formal leadership in the community of fishermen." Is this the kind of "pre-bureaucratic" society that is to be contrasted with the so-called "individualism" of modern bureaucratic states? If so, there is a major shift in the meaning of "individualism." Such semantic slip-page has major consequences for the play of ideas about person-hood in modern bureaucratic practices.

The art of bureaucratic game-playing, whether from client to bureaucrat or the other way about, lies in essentializing one's own actions as logical on the strongly implied grounds that they rest on eternally valid rights or self-evidence. The other side's actions, by contrast, are capricious and irrational, based on personal or cultural flaws, and wrongheaded. This is a rhetoric that easily en-ters into the discourse of anthropology, for, as Handler (1986: 4) remarks with rather depressing acuity, "the concept of 'authen-ticity' is as deeply embedded in anthropological theory as it is in the self-conscious ethnic ideologies of many of the groups that we study." It does not help analysis to accept its claims in the rhetoric that is being analyzed. It is also extremely difficult to avoid doing so.

Witnesses or Millenarians?
Tolerance and Indifference

The metaphors of kinship extend to a wide variety of social enti-ties within the framework of nationalistic discourse: ethnic group, region, religion, profession, social class. Within the argument of nationalism, all become cultural rather than social entities, al-though their membership and status is articulated in terms of social exclusiveness.

Allied to the rich idiom of kinship as a basis of exclusion, we find an extensive array of other devices. An especially germane feature of the Greek language is the use of plurals to indicate the hopeless fragmentation and thus unreliability of categorical others, as in the phrase "the Turks are dishonorable races (*atimes ratses*)." Pluralization in Greek always implies the presence of evil and pollution, presumably because it indicates a lack of categori-cal closure. Thus, while the Holy Trinity is ultimately One, the Devil appears as an infinite multitude of demons (see Stewart 1985). It is also possible to deny the state's legitimacy by using a negative, as happens in the charges that "we have no state." A now fairly long-standing debate that conjoins these two devices concerns the question of whether the Jehovah's Witnesses (a conveniently plural category to begin with!) "have" a religion of their own. Whereas pluralization is perhaps more commonly used to suggest a source of moral weakness within the community, the negative – which means an absence of some good quality – usually characterizes outsiders: the Turks are "godless" (*athei*), and therefore "without the fear of God" (*atheofovi*) that marks civilized nations. While such usages rarely appear on paper, they imbue the overt categories that take their place with morally negative force. The Jehovah's Witnesses are not only plural in name, but their detractors deny that they have a "real" religion at all.

Such linguistic usages are most usefully considered as forming a small part of the symbolic resources available for the contestation of civil rights. Different people use these resources for distinct and often sharply contrasted purposes. In the discussion that follows, we shall see that cracks may appear in the bland surface of bureaucratic indifference, although the results do not necessarily benefit the clients. The following case concerns the status of Jehovah's Witnesses in Thessaloniki, the second largest city (and "co-capital") of Greece. As the newspaper-derived account unfolds, we see that the stereotypical "fear of responsibility" of Greek bureaucrats serves to protect individual functionaries from the consequences of an apparently illegal decision made by a highly political key actor, the city's mayor. The functionaries whom the distraught Witnesses approached take refuge in a combination of formal "officialese" and shoulder-shrugging invitations to a complicit condemnation of "the system."

First, however, some background. For most of the history of the Greek state, the Greek Orthodox Church has been the official religious institution of the country and vehemently opposed the introduction of civil marriage in 1983; it has also bitterly fought any form of proselytization by non-Orthodox Christians. If its stance seems harsh, it should be remembered that Ottoman interpretations of Islamic religious law made the death penalty mandatory for any attempt at converting Muslims to other faiths, but also protected Christians as "people of the Book" from some of the more onerous consequences of being non-Muslims. The autonomy of the religious authorities in controlling marriage was also a feature of Ottoman administrative practice.

In modern times, Jehovah's Witnesses have been persecuted on three counts. They were not an established religious group with clear ties to a physical territory – such as the Jews could claim with Israel, the Muslims with Turkey or with Mecca, or the Catholics with Rome. As pacifists, they refused to serve in the military, thereby placing their allegiance to the state in constant doubt. Finally, their evangelical fervor led them into frequent and public violations of the laws against proselytizing.[5]

The religious intolerance that they have commonly faced in public met with no serious resistance from the state authorities and reached its apogee under the irredentist, church-oriented, and totalitarian military governments in power from 1967 through 1974. In reaction to the intolerance of the colonels, however, the moderate-right government of Karamanlis dismantled many of the trappings of nationalist rhetoric, including the purist language, the use of which had been compulsory in education and all official business as well as in the media. In 1975, the Karamanlis government passed a new law that gave the Jehovah's Witnesses full recognition as a legitimate religious entity, and further legislative action the following year allowed their own registered clerics to perform marriage rites for them. Had bureaucratic procedure been a sure basis of security, their troubles should have been over.

In 1981, their situation appeared to improve still further. The socialist government of Andreas Papandreou that came to power at that time was determined to undermine the pervasive social power of the Orthodox Church. Legislation particularly aimed at this goal concerned the sequestration and redistribution of monastic lands, and the legalization of civil marriage. These acts moved government policy decisively away from the remnants of the Ottoman *millet* system, according to which each religious community managed its own affairs, into a more aggressively secular and nation-statist mode.

These changes, promising though they seemed at first, posed serious new difficulties for traditionally persecuted groups such as the Witnesses. These difficulties did not, of course, lie in the intentions of the government, which sought to free such groups from a situation in which they had, as it were, no categorical existence. Rather, the problems arose from the fact that the new legislation, once enacted, deprived the Witnesses and other sects of the dubious advantages of clandestinity without guaranteeing them much practical security. In the wider context in which they now had to defend their legitimacy on apparently equal terms with all other groups, they faced weak bureaucrats and, worse, ambi-

5. On these last two counts, see especially Pollis 1987: 609–611.

tious politicians who could tap a powerful vein of popular hostility against them.

What follows is an exceptionally good illustration of the extent to which the formal requirements of law may take on meanings and implications far removed from those of their original framers. It shows how easily the European-style rationalization of existing cultural (or, as here, religious) relations can founder – at least for a while – on the shoals of popular prejudice, political opportunism, and bureaucratic reluctance to accept responsibility for offending the powerful.

These factors reinforce the effects of the prevailing legal tradition, derived from German positivism and neo-Kantianism, which makes the law "the manifestation of an 'ideal' which is embodied in the state" and treats opposition to the state as hostility to the nation itself (Pollis 1987: 588, 601). Many Greeks may be quick to dissociate the "nation" from the "state" when they are aggrieved about their personal sufferings at the hands of bureaucrats or politicians, but they may with equal ease adopt the rhetoric of official authoritarianism when this coincides with their own distrust of religious and other outsiders.

In 1986, the governing socialist party suffered humiliating defeats in municipal elections in the three largest cities. A new mayor of Thessaloniki was among the victorious conservatives. The conservative party ("New Democracy"), to which the mayor belonged and which Karamanlis had founded in the aftermath of the colonels' rout, represented a more church-oriented form of nationalism, and took every opportunity to benefit from popular unease at Papandreou's anticlericalism. Among the several areas in which he began immediately to reverse the policies of his socialist predecessor was the question of what to do with the Jehovah's Witnesses.

In April 1988, the prefect of Macedonia, a government appointee, requested information about the progress made to date in the proper registration of "millenarians" (a generic term that includes the Witnesses). The mayor's office refused to proceed, arguing instead that a 1976 court decision in Iraklio (Crete) denying the Witnesses the status of a religious entity was currently under review by the Supreme Court in Athens. The logic of this reply is straightforward: the municipality can take no action until the legal status of the group concerned has been clarified by higher authority. In strictly legal terms, this was a perfectly defensible argument. It also appealed to the principle of *efthinofovia*, or "fear of responsibility," in a way that made it extremely hard for the Jehovah's Witnesses to counter it. How could the mayor oppose the majesty of the state, expressed in a court case taking place, as it happened, in a town still locally ruled by the socialists? Here, the mayor played off the abstract virtue of the state against the increasing embarrassment of the government, which had become embroiled in a series of scandals and a growing economic crisis. In point of fact, the mayor's supporters would in practice not have looked further for the justification of his delaying tactics than the – to them – straightforward fact that the Witnesses did not have a licit religion.

It is worth noting that the 1976 court case under review had taken place on Crete, where there are many Jehovah's Witnesses, and where the prejudice against them is often expressed with great vehemence. The development of the problem in Thessaloniki was reported in some detail in a a newspaper generally friendly to the national government (*Eleftherotipia* 31 July 1988, p. 21).

This account faithfully reproduces some of the putative stereotypes of bureaucratic behavior as well as attitudes toward the Witnesses, and thus provides a fine ethnographic illustration of the relevant public discourse.

The article reports the experiences of two Witnesses who wrote in to complain about their increasingly desperate situation. The reporter takes care to note that the original orthography and syntax have been retained. This is not merely an example of the severe preference for literal discourse that characterizes much Greek journalism (see Mackridge 1985: 348), although it is certainly that, too. It also, perhaps a little mischievously, plays the bureaucratic game against itself, using a scholastic rhetoric to suggest that the data used against the errant mayor had been free from editorial manipulation.

The first Witness reported that he had asked the municipal registrar to have his registration altered to show that he was now a "religious functionary of the Christian Witnesses of Jehovah." The registrar refused: "Although he assured me that he had received the document [a directive from the Prefecture to proceed immediately with the registration of all Jehovah's Witnesses], he told me that the view of the Municipal Administration was different and that they would only accept a [specific] order from the ministry and the Prefecture to carry out the legal[ly required] registration."

The Witness then demanded to know whether the official was prepared to interpret the law in accordance with the wishes of whichever mayor happened to be in power or as directed by "the Minister, which is the highest authority." The reply was terse: "That, sir [*kirie*, a term of address often used ironically by bureaucrats to clients of presumed lower status], is . . . a matter for my superiors and [I'll do] whatever they tell me to."

The registrar's tactic of avoiding personal responsibility by invoking higher authority was then reproduced when the Witness tried a new approach, this time to the deputy mayor. This official said:

"We as a Municipality view the matter differently." When I said to him, "But how can this be the case, so that the law and its execution are different from Municipality to Municipality? Whey doesn't this happen in the other Municipalities of our city and country? And why was this matter of registration transfer working normally two months earlier?" "That," he said, "is a matter for the Mayor's legal advisor." When I asked him, "Why didn't you respond to the requests that we filed in the Town Hall in connection with this matter?" he laughed and said, "Well – so *then* what would have happened?"

Finally, the deputy mayor told the aggrieved Witness that the matter would have to await the mayor's return from a trip; but this, as things turned out, made no difference at all.

The second Witness's experience made this lack of change all too clear. Returning with her family from a protracted period of residence abroad, she went to the Town Hall to arrange the registration of their new place of residence. Once there, she discovered that one of her papers was missing. The not unsympathetic clerk, however, told her not to bother: "'Don't waste your time bringing us the supporting documents, we can't do anything [for you] because you're Jehovah's Witnesses and the Mayor of Thessaloniki won't sign them and he doesn't want Jehovah's Witnesses in their [*sic*] Municipality.'" To the client's protests – that she would now be unable to get a voter's registration book, a passport, and a (legally compulsory) identity card – "the same clerk told me that she couldn't do anything, and indeed she suggested to me that I go to a different Municipality of our city or to some nearby village where they might want Witnesses, because, quite simply, 'My good lady, the Mayor does not want you people!'"

There are several features of this sorry tale that deserve attention. Throughout, the buck-passing is consistent: clerk to superiors, registrar to superiors, deputy mayor to mayor, mayor to prefect and minister. But this does not mean that the actors on the bureaucratic side are simply helpless pawns in a power game in which they do not participate. The clerk may well have been in such a situation, as the Witness indicated that she had shown some signs of sympathy. The suggestion to go somewhere else where "they might want Witnesses" indicates at least a degree of willingness to try for a solution – not, let us note, that the registration of citizens in places where they do not in fact reside has much to recommend it in terms of some putative bureaucratic rationality. The other actors do not appear to have been interested in helping at all. And even the relatively kindly clerk's lumping together of "you people" smacks of the characteristic indifference to individual needs that the Witnesses, as citizens "rationally" entitled to their passports and other accoutrements of insiderhood, had come to experience.

The incident also illustrates how the bureaucratic rejection of individuals as collectively "different" deprives them of their individuality. The three documents that the female Witness needed are all indexes of officially recognized personhood. The passport represents a Greek's national identity to the outside world; possession of this document is not required, and indeed has sometimes been hard to achieve in the past (under the colonels, for example). The identity card and voter's registration book, however, are compulsory possessions. Ordinary speech turns the official *dheltio taftotitas* ("identity card") into *taftotita* ("identity"), thereby equating the paper with the person. The implicit reification of words recalls the American usage, "two pieces of I.D."

By depriving the Witnesses of these documents, the local authorities were denying their identity both as Greeks and as individuals – a double exclusion, and one that takes on particular force when we recall the individualistic ideology that underlies European nationalism. This is tautology in action: if you are not a true Greek, you are not really a person; therefore, you are not really a true Greek; therefore. . ." In the present case, the Witnesses found themselves placed in an impossible situation, since they were now being forced by the law at one level to break the law at another – a further "proof," always within the same circular argument, of their incomplete humanity. The bureaucrats produced a tautologous and self-justifying indifference to these symbolically excluded Greeks: tautologous because the argument for mistreating them was based on the mistreatment they had already suffered, which was itself based on their questionable Greekness; self-justifying because the semantic unity of "the law" – an infrangible authority – masked a host of legalistic interpretations at various levels of administrative differentiation.

The larger background to these events confirms their obvious implications. The bureaucratic structures through which the Jehovah's Witnesses must work to achieve any degree of autonomous identity are loaded in favor of the equation of Orthodox believer with Greek citizen: "Included in the morass of bureaucratic regulations is a procedure whereby the Ministry of Education and Religion consults the local Orthodox Church official prior to the granting of a permit for the establishment of a house of worship by those of another faith" (Pollis 1987: 609–610).[6]

The entire incident exemplifies the social production of indifference – the embedding of categorical exclusion in self-justifying tautology. The Witnesses, to paraphrase again a phrase from earlier in this discussion, are what they are because they are not what they are not – true Greeks. Their experience shows, moreover, that attention to actors is at least as important as detailing the rhetoric, since neither makes sense in isolation from the other. The bureaucrats' seeming indifference to the Witnesses' plight is not simply the product of "the system," however convenient it may have been for them to present it as such. Rather, in a country where ideologically to be Greek means to be a member of the Orthodox Church, bureaucrats have a ready-made rhetoric for going along with what they perceive as the current balance of power. Had a more liberal mayor been in office, the clerks presumably would have made haste to put the paperwork through as the law required, and would not have used the moral alibi of superior orders to exclude these people from their rights as Greek citizens – on which, we may assume, everyone would have claimed to agree. Even in the antibureaucratic rhetoric of the newspaper

6. Note also that this comment appeared in print six years after the socialists, no friends of the Orthodox hierarchy, had come to power.

reportage,[7] it is clear that at least one of the officials felt a measure of sympathy for the Witnesses.

Bureaucratic power, which relies heavily on a rhetoric of exactitude and semantic stability (Tsoucalas 1991), becomes quite diffuse when refracted through local social conditions. Thus, officials often give idiosyncratic interpretations of the overt text, representing "the system" – or even some specified higher authority – in terms congenial to their own interests. The author of the article, himself also unequivocally an actor on the political scene, clearly recognized what was going on. Above all, we see clearly in this incident the contingent nature of segmentation: if a conservative mayor chooses, in opposition to the socialist government (rather than in compliance with its conservative predecessors!), to treat Witnesses as non-Christian, and hence as non-Greek, bureaucrats under him will also treat them as just such undifferentiated outsiders – in short, as deserving only indifference. In the logic of competition over resources, being "Christian" can become a highly relative and contestable quality (see Maynard 1988). While one relatively sympathetic clerk did permit a small chink to appear in this wall of indifference, even her stance was qualified by appeals to higher authority. Indeed, one could argue that her suggestions were designed both to placate the client and to remove the problem to another location (another municipality or village) – which is exactly what the mayor was doing, at a higher level of authority, by making the decision depend on the outcome of a Supreme Court trial in faraway Athens.

The administrative relationship between the prefect and the mayor reveals some of the strains inherent in the Greek system of municipal governance. The prefect has regional authority to ensure that all elected officials perform their duties correctly. Since prefects are appointed by the government in power, there are numerous possibilities for disagreement – but also for the careful manipulation of responsibility. In the case of the Jehovah's Witnesses, the mayor was able to thwart the prefect's instructions only by invoking the *sub judice* status of their appeal for formal recognition. With the might of Athens behind them, prefects usually get the last word.

7. The political opposition of the largely progovernment Athens newspaper to the mayor's party provides a national-level context within which to read these local events.

Order and Stereotypes

The examples discussed in this chapter all exhibit a common property: the role of stereotypes in "justifying" indifference. Whether a clerk in the post office trying to deflect an insistent foreigner or a harassed town hall official only too glad to blame the mayor for refusing recognition to an entire religious group, bureaucrats can call upon two resources in escaping personal responsibility for their decisions: higher authority and the classifications to which "the system" subjects people.

In the next chapter, we shall turn to the question of higher authority and the way it is conceptualized. Here, I would like to focus briefly on the classificatory aspect. Clearly, there is nothing in the law that would formally justify the exclusion of Jehovah's Witnesses on the grounds that they are undeserving of equal consideration and respect, nor does the foreign status of the post office customer give the clerk any legal right to be offensive or uncooperative. But a defense of the law on the grounds of "what it actually says" is a literalist argument. While it has had some currency in recent debates – "strict constitutionalism" in the United States, for example – it is anthropologically unsound. It relies on the essentialist argument that treats the law as ultimately irreducible, rather than on the pragmatic view that the law consists in its applications and that each of these is also an interpretation.

The sympathetic clerk's obvious discomfiture before the enraged Jehovah's Witness gives the lie to such literalist claims. It shows that she, at least, was aware of the latitude that interpretation can take, and the extent to which the prevalence of one or another interpretation will depend on the locus of power. This example also helps to forge the all-important link between the sort of racist essentialism we noted in Chapter One and the exercise of bureaucratic authority generally. Religion might seem to be a matter of association and not of "blood," but when the mayor "does not want you people," the implicit argument is that of a qualitative difference, and the metaphor of blood reappears – doubtless reinforced by the Witnesses' refusal to participate in military service. There is some support for this interpretation in recent Greek legislation, since the law now specifies that those who refuse to bear arms must do community service

of double duration – a discrimination apparently intended specifically to affect the Witnesses.[8]

Technically, national and religious identity have long been legally
separated in Greece, so that, for example, call-up notices in 1974
had to specify "Muslim subjects of the Greek state" as differentiated from the more popular usage of "Turks." In practice, however,
there is considerable slippage between formal legal usage and
practical applications. It is quite clear that the mayor did not fear
the consequences of his refusal. On the contrary, he invoked "the
law," thereby simultaneously protecting his employees from legal
sanctions (and perhaps also from the temptation to sympathize
too much with the Witnesses), and identifying his personal
prejudices with "the" official legal position. The fact that the law
in question was currently being challenged gave him a formal basis
for refusing to act.

Stereotypes fill a seemingly empty taxonomic space, and their
popularity makes it possible for indifference to flourish. The post
office clerk and the mayor's assistant might both have been willing
to behave in a helpful fashion. In the first instance, the foreigner's
sudden reversal of tactics provided at least a legitimate excuse to
cease being obstructive: the obstreperous foreign woman took
the case out of "our" hands. In the second, orders from above,
buttressed by widespread fear and dislike of the "anomalous"
Witnesses, acted as an effective deterrent to the mildest stirrings
of sympathy. Indifference is what faces those who are trying to
enter "our" group, and it takes the form of showing that they "do
not know the rules." In Greece, "counterstrategizing" works best,
because that is what everyone – from the defensive mayor to the
pushy priest – knows as "essential" to the national self-image. This,
I suggest, is also what the foreign woman discovered in the post
office: not that logic does not work in Greece, but that acting as
though one's right stemmed from nature works everywhere. One
should, however, know what constitutes "nature" in the particular
context of the interaction.

The Witnesses, having been debarred from the cultural category
of the "natural" by a system of ethnic and religious categories

---

8. Pollis (1987: 611) notes that, although refusal to bear arms is no longer a
punishable offense, refusing to wear the national uniform is. It seems clear that
at stake in either case is the rejection of a state-defined national identity in terms
that have considerable appeal among the population at large.

based on the retention and shedding of blood, asked too meekly for their legally constituted rights. Perhaps, even, their humility reminded the authorities of their noncombatant status. They were not "blooded" even to the extent that a "Turk," a Greek subject of Muslim religion, might be. Their actions fitted the stereotype; the stereotype fitted the law. Under these socially recognizable conditions, the fact that the law itself did not explicitly legitimize the stereotype was a matter of indifference. To "make a difference," the Witnesses would have had to find a way of reconverting their "cultural otherness" into "familiarity." Refusing to shed their blood for the national body probably was not a good way of doing this.[9]

In the next chapter, we turn to the assumption that makes "the law" such an unchallengeable source of authority: the conflation, in crude terms, of language and blood. We shall see that national language, of which the law is both the guarantor and the prime instantiation, becomes an object of veneration in bureaucratic practice. It is, so to speak, the essence of the essentialist project – as vital to nationalism as blood is to racism. Its preservation mirrors and reproduces the preservation of pure blood. It is the symbolic and ritual material with which bureaucratic practitioners conjure, converting the dross of human discomfort and inconvenience into the gold of personal power.

9. Stereotypes can be embedded in bureaucratic definitions of the crassest kind. An English couple, wishing to live in Greece and to use their two-seater truck for transportation, encountered endless difficulties because such vehicles were classified as "agricultural" and therefore could not conceivably belong to foreigners, who are not – one gathers – supposed to be farmers. The difficulty was resolved by placing a canvas enclosure around the back of the truck, thus converting it into something more akin to a car. This did not, however, mean that the owners could now take back-seat passengers, which is forbidden in trucks! They were restricted by their identity as foreigners from owning such a vehicle; thus, when this problem was eventually resolved in the manner I have just described, the vehicle remained an agricultural truck in the eyes of any police officers who might have been hoping to catch the owners out in violation of traffic regulations.

CHAPTER FOUR

The Language Fetish

Language as Fetish: Sticking Pins into Verbal Effigies

In this chapter, I shall examine the role of language in translating nationalistic theory into bureaucratic practice. Many writers have pointed to the role of language as the cement of nationalism. Others have pointed out that much of bureaucratic practice consists in applying linguistic categories to the conduct of daily business. These two phenomena are linked in an extremely important sense, especially given the parallels between the ways in which both language and law, as formal systems, lend themselves to rhetorics of normativeness that can be deployed for highly practical ends (see especially Bourdieu 1977).

Anderson's (1983) reading of the nation as an "imagined community" gives us an excellent starting point. Despite its tinge of psychological reductionism – we are never really told how we know how and what people imagine[1] – Anderson's thesis is a powerful one because it suggests the mechanism whereby local allegiances can be converted into the absolute loyalty demanded by the state. It also shows how people move from a social to a cultural understanding of loyalty; for, while the social differences among the members of a small tribal segment may be minute, they carry the same kinds of moral imperative as the larger cultural loyalties that rely, as Anderson has suggested, on cultivated

[1]. His argument can also be criticized for its dependence on the concept of an imaginary "love" from a psychoanalytic standpoint; see Bottomley and Lechte 1990: 55.

imagination rather than on social immediacy.

The shift from the social to the cultural occurs through the generalization of what, at the local level, are relatively intimate distinctions between outsiders and "our own." At the local level, the moral distinction is between those whom one (literally) knows and those whom one (literally) does not. As the level widens, however, one's knowledge becomes concerned progressively less with people and more with cultural traits.

What then occurs is a recasting of all semiotic systems, language included, as literalized metaphors. The idea of the nation as a family, or even as a body, is perhaps the model for this; but other signs are drawn into the same process. To take a celebrated example, Petr Bogatyrev (1971) long ago demonstrated that Moravian folk costumes served to differentiate village populations. This already entailed a translation of bodily specificity into social collectivity: no two individuals dress exactly alike or with equal precision, so that personal clothing expresses a tension between individual and social group. What happens at the next stage, however, is that these same costumes become reified as "national," appearing on postage stamps and in folk festivals, along with local rituals and other village practices (see also Kligman 1981). In a similar pattern, young women in the mountain villages of central and western Crete weave special hunting bags (*vouryes*) with drawstrings and a delicate linear pattern. These are made for the wedding day, and are given in recognition of manliness to the groom and his closest agnates. The practice marks the bride's transition into the patrigroup (*yenia*) of the groom. With the arrival of tourism, however, these same designs have been enlarged and simplified, and transferred to those simple square bags (*tagharia*) that are widely recognized as "Greek bags." With the pattern, the social content of the message has also been simplified. Besides, how many Greeks or foreign tourists know that these are the trappings of an agnatic kinship ideology? I am tempted, in recognition of a similar and etymologically suggestive phenomenon in the English language, to remark that they have moved from the *genealogical* sphere to the *generic*.

The reuse of such symbols as the bag design or local costume as emblems of national identity entails a process of forgetting. It would be most inconvenient for Greek nationalists were the largely Albanian origins of the "national" kilt, the *foustanella* (still a notable part of the Presidential Guard's uniform), to be widely noticed.

Although the "national dance," the *kalamatianos,* is named for a
town that was part of the Greek national territory almost from the
day that independence was declared, it is its association with the
outbreak of war against the hated Turks that legitimizes its
supremacy – a national rather than a local significance. The role
of such a dance in articulating social relationships recedes into
the background, although it may acquire new meanings in particular communities over and above its national importance (see
Cowan 1990).

We see at work in all these cases the same process of progressive
reification that Holmes observed in the Friulian practice of gift-
giving (*onoranze*): an act that had hitherto marked a tie between
landlord and tenant became instead the expression of a categorical and impersonal inequality. At the level of state policy, such
reifications are liable to systematic and large-scale organization.

Nonverbal semiotic systems, however, lack the obvious power to
organize action that we see in language. It is above all in the
creation of a "national language" – often, as Anderson (1983: 69)
notes, a dialect that has adapted successfully to the use of the print
medium – that nationalist ideologues find the most effective tool
of unification. Whether or not all Greeks carry the same kind of
bag or wear the same costume, they all speak Greek today. The
symbol of national unity is also the instrument of its achievement.

Before going on to speak of language in more detail, I would
like to discuss the change that the shift from local to national
entails. It is, in simple terms, a shift from relations to images.
Anderson (1983: 15) has suggested one important difference that
lies precisely in this intersection of scale and kind. The community
is "imagined," he argues, "because the members of even the smallest
nation will never know most of their members, meet them, or even
hear of them, yet in the minds of each lives the image of their
communion." This, then, suggests one radical difference between
nation-states and local groups: unlike Douglas's argument, it treats
scale as a central issue. It does so, however, not on the basis of
some presumed correlation between size, efficiency, and reason,
but on that of the semiotic technology required to maintain a
sense of cohesion.

Anderson's focus on image is extremely suggestive. It helps to
explain the shift from local social relations to their larger-scale
embodiment as cultural interests. National sentiment, as we have
seen, is often expressed in the language of social relations. Family,

blood, kinship, ancestry, fatherland, motherland, even (in some languages) patriline – these are the social categories that nationalists commonly use to express cultural ties. In Ceauşescu's Romania, for example, the language of paternalism explicitly resonated with that of agnatic kinship and gave sinister force to the program of sweeping ethnic "homogenization" under the principle of "dynastic socialism," through which the dictator hoped to ensure the succession of his son while simultaneously turning socialism into an "inherited" national trait (Kligman n.d.). At the end of this book, I shall return to the example of Ceauşescu's Romania, for it all too sadly illustrates what happens when bureaucratic ritualism takes control of such formulae and regulates them from the top.

These familial images of family, so common a feature of European nationalism, are a simulacrum of sociality. As such, they provide the fundamental model for other uses of similarity: physical appearance, common costume and language, shared customs, arts, and crafts. They provide the idiom for recreating a sense of shared experience, a fictive common ground of interaction that makes nationalism workable even though, as Anderson points out, it is inconceivable that most citizens should know each other.

To understand the principles at work here, we must return to the most basic units of kinship from which the state draws its self-imagery. To move from characterizing a whole family or agnatic group by some repetitive feature to making parallel generalizations about entire nations is not complicated. It is facilitated by the evocation of nature, which is where the genetic metaphors of blood and race become particularly powerful. They suggest that certain physical properties, which easily transmute into moral ones, are immanent in a given group.

Immanence is a concept more commonly found in religious contexts, but it corresponds closely to what Geertz and Greenwood have termed "essentialism." In anthropological discourse, the idea of immanence has more commonly been associated with segmentary societies such as the Nuer, whose "refraction" of the "Supreme Deity" through the social order formed the basis of Evans-Pritchard's (1956) analysis of their religion. The multiplicity of saints' cults in parts of the Christian Mediterranean belongs to a similar conceptual framework, which thus appears to be far from incompatible with life under a nation-state regime. Goody (1986: 182) also recognizes the possibility that elements of segmentation may persist in state societies. While he rightly denies that these are evolutionary survivals from some more primitive kind of polity, however, he associates them only with forms of resistance and subversion against the centralized systems that inevitably result, in his view (1986: 12–13), from the emergence of literacy. Segmentation is integral to the emergence of state structures; Sahlins (1989: 110–113) has documented it historically for the Catalan border lands of France and Spain. Segmentation both reconciles local with larger interests and encapsulates the tensions among them. Literacy does not abolish segmentation, but; on the contrary, may actually perpetuate it by disguising its potential for disruption with the discursive veneer of uniform languages and scripts.

I would like to take this argument a stage further, and suggest that the religious character of nationalism justifies talking about immanence – or essentialism, if one prefers – in the very specific context of the equation of nation with language. I propose further that it would be helpful to treat all official, bureaucratic taxonomies as "refractions" of the state order in precisely this sense. Such, I suggest, is the moral order that allows bureaucrats to make arbitrary and often highly personal use of a supposedly transcendent authority. As Lefort (1971: 303) has suggested, the paradox of bureaucracy is that the larger it grows, the more differentiated it becomes internally, and the more easily special interests are able to hide behind a mask of disinterested and objective rationality. Even at the top, then, despite Goody's account of the state as the primary agent of centralization, it is only the outer form of the discourse that is monolithic. It should hardly be a matter for surprise that the rhetoric of common interest sometimes turns out to be very thinly spread indeed.

At the risk of repetition, let me briefly recapitulate the argument for recognizing segmentation in state structures. Segmentation is the political phenomenon in which, in the absence of centralized authority, social groups subdivide and reunite according to the social distance – usually defined in genealogical terms, actual or fictive – between the principals to a given dispute. It is best represented diagrammatically. In this diagram, in which A represents the entire group ("tribe," in the colonialist language of the 1940s), a dispute between a member of H and a member of I should not involve members of any other subgroups at level 4. If a member of H kills a member of J or K, then D should be pitted in its entirety against all of *E*. This principle extends all the way upward, so that if a member of *H* attacks a member of O, *B* and *C* go to war. That, at least, is the theory in its most sere and abstract form.

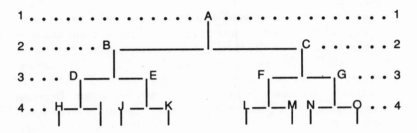

In European nation-states, the subordinate levels never cease to be important. People will even defend their local patriotisms against the state when circumstances are favorable. Bureaucratic leaders seek to control the collective imagination – or, in Anderson's terms, to fix the imagined community at the most inclusive level alone. Since, however, the language of the state depends on those far more intimate entities such as family and community, segmentation remains – at least conceptually – a paradoxically necessary component of state nationalism. Insiders – Greek *dhiki mas*, Italian *paesani* – are always those people one "knows" better. For the state, this is an ideologically unacceptable discrimination. Thus, whereas individuals may show great flexibility in using these terms, the state prefers that each individual be a "known" quantity: hence the bureaucratic habit of reducing people, quite literally, to ciphers. In other words, the state provides a highly formulaic design for imagining the other members of one's national community.

This has serious consequences for ethnic relations within relatively new nations. According to Kapferer, for example, the "European" nationalism of the Australian majority is intolerant of hyphenated ethnics. Greek-Australians, for example, emerge as a group ("all alike") that receives special treatment ("they want to be different") within the nation. This strategy offends Anglo-Australian egalitarian sensibilities because it implies that this particular group is different, and thus entitled to special treatment. The Greek's own ability to invoke a glorious "Western" and "democratic" past (Smolicz 1985: 19) and to relate it closely to notions of individualism did not endear them any further to the

Anglo-Australians, who resented it as an attempt to intrude. It is instructive here to compare the Anglo-Australians' attitude to Turks: Orientals who had the decency to remain outsiders, and who could therefore be treated as heroic foes rather than as cultural fifth columnists.

Kapferer's analysis of egalitarianism is especially useful here because, like Anderson's concept of the imagined community, it allows us to disembed the inevitable contradictions of what might best be labelled "concealed segmentation." Nationalist rhetoric conflates an idealized personhood (what Handler [1985] has identified as "possessive individualism") with the nation. Between the individual and the nation, however, lie several different levels of solidarity, each sharing a formal distinction between insiders and outsiders with the two extremes. The state, paradoxically, depends upon this segmentary logic, one result of which is that at each level units vie with one another for embodying most perfectly the immanent qualities of the whole. Such an inherently unstable system is locked into place by institutional constraints, but these cannot alter its basically segmentary constitution. This kind of segmentation produces ideologies of egalitarian individualism or of hierarchy that easily slip into harsh intolerance. When the state faces any threat from without, or when the majority of its citizens perceive such a threat, anomalous populations within become a target of the majority's search for the encompassing form of all segmentary systems – a transcendent but exclusive unity.

For the Nuer (see especially Evans-Pritchard 1956), divinity inheres in all subdivisions of the social realm. In this sense, the Nuer ought to provide a good supporting illustration of Durkheim's view that in religion a society worships itself. At each level of segmentation, there are divine spirits that Evans-Pritchard regarded as refractions of the transcendent, immanent Supreme Being (*Kwoth*) of the Nuer. Matters are not quite so straightforward, however, as the Nuer also see "divine spirit" (*kwoth*) in a range of other kinds of entities – features of the natural environment, for example. It would be truer to say that the Nuer worship a pervasive property of the world, a world of which they see themselves and their social institutions as an integral part.

I suggested in Chapter One that the Durkheimian view of religion arguably works far better when it is applied to the essentialism of modern nation-state ideologies. These have coopted nature:

landscapes become "typically English" (as in Constable's paintings, for example [Lowenthal 1985: 40]), the land takes on the rugged appearance of people even as it informs their supposed "character," the very soil is "holy." One can see the emergence of such ideas in eighteenth-century England, where landscape gardening came to suggest that all men of property and education could, by recasting "nature" as a "garden" couched nonetheless in an uncompromisingly "classical" idiom, contrast their condition with that of the oppressed French: the "informal serpentine lines of garden design" in England "opposed the rigidities of baroque gardening as it had been developed . . . at Versailles. Their absoluteness was read as representative of political absolutism. English liberty, on the other hand, threw the weight of judgment on to individual taste and sensibility" (Cosgrove 1984: 204–205). The land breathes a national spirit: nature itself is naturalized – the ultimate triumph of state ideology and bureaucracy. This selfsame sense of natural informality, of the individualistic character of the British people, reappears in Margaret Thatcher's fulminations against the "un-British" rigidity of the Brussels bureaucrats – again, an evocation of essential nature that has highly specific cultural and ideological implications.

Nation-state ideologies easily appropriate the theological principle of immanence, and, through an endlessly repetitious process of reification, make it their own. Such a view fosters intolerance because those who are outsiders in any given context lack the condition of grace or divine protection that marks their existence as social beings. For those who remain within, the maintenance of their precarious and contextual participation depends on highly redundant reaffirmations of faith. Among these reaffirmations in the modern nation-state are the daily rituals of petty bureaucracy. Informal events do the same; Lincoln (1989: 155–159), for example, proposes that All-Star Wrestling reproduces features of American identity in this way. But the less spectacular activities of bureaucracy represent an arena in which citizens affirm, willingly or otherwise, the power of those who wield the rubber-stamp and the official signature. As with public rituals, moreover, this is not always an unwilling participation: the concept of "natural right" that underlies so many appeal procedures in modern nation-state bureaucracies is a good illustration of immanence in the modern world. Where it has not become fully ensconced as part of the nation-state ideology, as in Greece, it has also been far less successful

at taking over the idioms of social identity or eradicating their
ability to function as separate from, rather than immanent in, the
state structure. Hence the coexistence of warm hospitality with
cold bureaucratic indifference, the point from which we began
this inquiry and to which we will return in the final chapter.

In nation-state ideologies, the national is immanent and ubiquitous. For the Nuer, not all refractions of the divine spirit were
through the subdivisions of the social world, but often appeared
in the natural landscape as well. Not only the subdivisions of
national entities but their conceptually denatured landscapes have
their trees and stones. If the state's tribal segments are its municipal, district, and provincial entities, its trees and stones are the
material properties that the state has taken under its control, and
are sometimes unambiguously romanticized as loci of immanence:
"In Ruskin's cosmos there were, quite literally, sermons in stones"
and the landscape taught moral lessons that "concern[ed] the
proper conduct of individual and social life" (Cosgrove 1984:
245–247). Inasmuch as real estate is taxable, it refracts the quin-
tessence of national genius. Conversely, resistance to bureaucratic
regulation of any sort, whether of people or of land, is an attack
on the immanent quality of nationhood.

In one act of disobedience, the client metonymically defies the
entire majesty of the state, whether in burning "the flag" (note
the usage of the definite article: it not merely "a" flag at that
moment) or in less visible but much more common acts of ille-
gality, such as cheating on taxes or committing bigamy or incest
– all category violations of the most obvious sort. When a hoaxer
called the harbor authorities of Piraeus to announce that a bomb
had been placed aboard a ship coming in from Rhodes and Kos,
"[t]he continuation of the investigation revealed that there had
been yet another hoax by a conscienceless 'Greek'" (*Eleftherotipia*,
12 July 1989, p. 23). The reporter's use of inverted commas suggests
a pious exclusion: the hoaxer was only "metaphorically" Greek
(see Mackridge 1985: 348, on this journalistic convention). Greeks,
by definition, must have both "(national) consciousness" in general
and "conscience" about their daily actions in particular. Both
concepts are conveyed by the same Greek term (*sinidhisi*) – a
telling conflation of individualism with conformity in the person
of each citizen-subject.

Iconic and Indexical Relations

State ideologies characteristically deny the reality of segmentation. They replace the divisive social universe with a premise of a cultural entity that is at once individualistic and homogenous – that is, a cultural entity predicated on both segmentation and its denial. The social universe is primarily a universe of shifting relativity. This means that the unifying feature of the society is above all a system of what semiotic theory calls indexical relations – that is, relationships determined by the relative positioning of actors within specific contexts. These are above all social relations.

The model of the nation-state changes all that. While such shifting relationships can and do persist in polities, and indeed sometimes are the ultimate basis for the political structure (see Davis 1987; Evans-Pritchard 1949), the state can rarely afford to acknowledge the instability that a purely segmentary arrangement of social life would imply. A consequence of the centralization of power under a nationalist ideology seems always to have been some kind of move from social relativity to cultural unity. While the idiom of blood and kinship persists, and indeed is central to the nation-state's very existence, it is "re-presented" (Handelman 1990: 57) as the genetic basis of culture rather than of sociability.

Semiotically, the indexical basis of solidarity ("I am yours because I am related to you in this way in this context") gives way to an iconic principle. Iconic relations are relations of similarity, and they form the basis of every known form of nationalist and irredentist propaganda (Herzfeld 1986). They are also the basis of what Frazer (1922: 14–49) called homeopathic or sympathetic magic, which, as I remarked in Chapter One, is also the basis of much of the conjuring that clients and bureaucrats perform with the symbols of national identity, and which has already had a distinguished history in the anthropological as well as the literary study of myth and symbol (see now also Tambiah 1990: 53, 107–110).

Everything that is similar to the national prototype, so the implicit logic goes, belongs within the nation; everything that is different, outside. Physical ("racial") types are anxiously compared to ancient statues, because the historical underpinning of national unity is historical continuity. Costumes, customs, language, music, art: all are fair game. The homogenization of folk dance and folk costume, and the refurbishing of *vouryes* as "Greek bags," illustrate the appeal of iconicity to nationalism at quite practical levels; tourists, who would perhaps prefer not to be bothered with the minutiae of local differentiation, are probably a major agent of this process. From it results a sameness that ostensibly abolishes the specificities of time and place.

Segmentation is indexical and recognizes the contingency of time; cultural homogeneity is iconic and aspires to eternity. Bureaucratic life is played somewhere in between. Bureaucrats, who hold the power to admit citizens into the national image, also serve as the godfathers and patrons who retranslate the homogeneous state back into social terms, and who control the definition of what is or is not the correct form (in both the abstract and bureaucratic senses of that word!). Where the idealizing rhetoric of the state represents each citizen in the image of an absolute cultural "type," ordinary life is much more subject to the highly relative pressures of social allegiance. Cultural identity is the material of national rhetoric, social variation that of everyday experience. The most interesting zone, however, consists of the "middle reaches" between these formal extremes, for it is here that social actors coopt the official rhetoric for their self-interested purposes, while the official rhetoric in turn tries to assimilate and expropriate the language and symbolism of social relationships in support of the homogenous "family" image of the nation. This second, unifying aspect achieves dramatic figurative force in the representations of the blood contract, already mentioned in Chapter One, whereby the Hungarian chieftains allegedly agreed to subordinate their own interests to the greater good.

Such an approach helps us to view political corruption more clearly as a symbolic construct, a complaint against categorical confusion. Such confusion is inevitable as individual interests and exigencies of state, or more generally local society and national culture, adjust to each other in the middle reaches. Here, bureaucrats and legislators offer real social bonds: godparenthood guarantees the patron electoral support, but also promises the client some kinds of material advantage as well. To those who object that such practices are unfair and corrupt, most people at the local level will respond that they are part of customary culture ("that's how we found them," as Greek villagers say with finality). In this fashion, they quickly duck back behind the cover afforded by "culture," now sanctified in turn by the encompassing virtue of the national state.

The language of national homogeneity thus coopts what is, "on the ground," a highly differentiated social reality. While local differences persist, this language puts them to work in the service of a transcendent unity. The trickle-down effect completes the task as citizens invoke the language of cultural unity to invest local social realities with the authority of national virtue: the local community "becomes" a miniature version of the state, reversing in people's consciousness the probable historical development of images of the nation-state out of the local experience. In fact, neither nation-state nor local community could function, one imagines, without the mutual convertibility of cultural homogeneity and social difference. Nation-state ideologies implicitly recognize this through their common dependence upon familial metaphors for the legitimation of their claims on their citizens' loyalty.

Taxonomies as Refractions of National Language

Nationalist ideologies are systems of classification. Most of them are very clear about what it takes to be an insider. That, at least, is the theory. In practice, however, divergent interpretations give the lie to such essentialist claims, as, to take one prominent and current example, in the debate currently raging in Israel about the definition of a Jew. Such taxonomic exercises, which anthropologists would get very excited about if they were about tribal moieties rather than modern issues, are central to the very existence of the nation-state. All other bureaucratic classifications are ultimately calibrated to the state's ability to distinguish between insiders and outsiders. Thus, as I shall suggest in more detail in a later chapter, one can see in bureaucratic encounters a ritualistic enactment of the fundamental principles upon which the very apparatus of state rests. Seen in these terms, arguments about the number on a lost driver's license or an applicant's entitlement to social security do not simply challenge or reinforce the power of particular functionaries of state. They rehearse the logic of the state itself. By quarreling with the functionaries' interpretations, clients implicitly endorse the presumption that such a logic can be clearly located through the exercise of reason.

Classification is not in itself unique to the modern nation-state. On the contrary, the state's success in imposing its will often derives from the familiarity of the categories through which its authority

is articulated, while creating and maintaining a system of classification has always, so far as we know, characterized the exercise
of power in human societies. What distinguishes the state is its
ability to infuse the common terms of sociality with absolute
meaning.

The model for this is the idea of a national language. The
national language itself becomes a sort of conventionalized image
of the total national society. All the more specialized forms of
classification are subfields of that image. Since in theory any attack
on particular segments can be treated as an attack on the whole,
each party to a bureaucratic dispute usually tries to represent its
own position as "pure," rather than as a mediated interpretation
of the fundamental text. The flag-burning debate in the United
States, in which conservative literalists and First Amendment
apologists alike claimed their respective arguments as "constitutional," offers an especially dramatic illustration of this principle
(see also Kertzer 1988: 133). These issues have been the subject
of high drama. Far more pervasive, however, are the petty irrita-
tions of everyday bureaucratic encounters. The most trivial arguments about driver's licenses or parking privileges reproduce the
same debate – a debate, in effect, between semantic fundamentalism and authoritative interpretation – in much the same way
as a theological dispute may reproduce and reaffirm the common
grounds of doctrine and the authority of the Word. Challenges
to the ground rules of such arguments are rare because the simple
fact of participation is commitment enough.

The primacy granted to language has two major consequences
for nationalistic ideologies. First, the state is usually reluctant to
grant equal rights to more than one language, or does so because
of peculiar circumstances in the historical constitution of the state
(as in the cases of Switzerland and India). The state is especially
hostile to languages its leaders or the dominant interests they
represent see as invasive; the current "one language" furor in the
United States results directly from hostility to Hispanic immigration. Second, attacks on the national language disturb the
committed complacency with which the language is thought to
stand for the purity of the people. Not all countries react as
systematically as France, where the Academy attempts to fend off
linguistic borrowings, but many have suffered the pain of seeing
their everyday tongue being carefully "cleansed" of "foreign"
influences that are in fact the coin of everyday conversation. Greece

is perhaps the most striking example of this predicament, and also the country that most dramatically illustrates the tension between claims of eternal identity and the contingencies of the moment – almost every one of its many constitutions has sought to establish that the national language was the one in which that particular constitution was written. If the single language represents a unified people, clearly any breach in the taxonomic order must also be an attack on that solidary mass. The objectification of language as the quintessential cultural property sets an immovable capstone on the inviolability of the nation and locks all classifications into place. That, at least, is the implicit intention, and the logical basis for the predication of specific bureaucratic actions on the supposedly transcendent logic of the law.

A common, if not universal, characteristic of nationalism is the insistence that one people – "our people" – should speak one language, which brings us back to the theme with which I began the present chapter. In the terms developed in the preceding two sections, the idea of a national language seeks to represent each individual's speech as an icon of the whole, a refraction of the immanent national essence; indexical relationships between speakers (the marks of differences in class or regional origin) are discounted. In a slightly different but equally important sense, the taxonomies of the state bureaucracies are also refractions of immanent national language. This is certainly not a phenomenon peculiar to European state systems. Handelman (n.d.: 6–7), in his discussion of an early Chinese text about administration, notes that its author, the Lord Shang, called for an exact correspondence of words and things. This is the myth of pure referentiality that we have already encountered in the Enlightenment-derived emergence of Greek nationalism. Here, it is explicitly connected to the simplification and remaking of the entire people as a unity, so that taxonomic divisions come to represent the internal boundaries of the state. For Shang, such boundaries represented a semantic "traversing of borders or walls." The entire taxonomy is an icon of the unity of the state.

With the development in Europe of national vernaculars, whole languages acquired this emblematic significance. Like "the" flag, the national language came, not just to stand for, but in an experiential sense to be the nation. The substitution of the sign (the national language) for its hypothetical referent (the "itself" of Durkheim's "society worshipping itself") leads to a passionate defense of the language. In the aftermath of the French Revolution, and in reaction to the temporary respectability of local patois, a priest loyal to the new order, the *abbé* Grégoire, urged others in the same position to use the national standard "in order to communicate with the Supreme Being" (Higonnet 1980: 42), the latter being equated with Sublime Reason. It would be hard to find a better parallel to the worship of *Kwoth* – the infinitely refractible Supreme Being of the Nuer – in any European context.

Multilingual policies and foreign accents pollute the all-embracing singularity of national language. Especially at times when a nation's political unity is threatened from outside, there will usually be those who react by demanding the reaffirmation of linguistic unity. In the United States, the "one language" movement demands the bureaucratic entrenchment of English as the official tongue of the American people. The resuscitation of Hebrew was the crux of Zionist essentialism, rather than the living but distressingly several languages of particular Jewish populations of the diaspora – Yiddish, Ladino, Judeo-Arabic, Judeo-Persian. Corsicans reject the idea that their speech is a dialect of Italian as linguistic imperialism, no better than the attempts to erase it in favor of French (Jaffe 1990); Greek Cypriots, paying at least lip service to the goal of eventual union with Greece, insist that what they speak is merely a dialect of Greek, albeit a "purer" form than that of Athens – such being the remarkable capacity of romantic nationalism to eat its cake and have it, too.

In a kind of reverse demonstration, the Indian civil service for years retained the British imperialists' language rather than unleash the demonic passions of language separatism that lurk in every province, and even in some local village caste systems, of their country. What is important is less who spoke a particular linguistic form before independence than to get a language accepted by everyone. It is perhaps not too cynical to suggest that almost any language will do, provided (a) that plenty of people speak it and (b) that no powerful minority is seen by others as finding in it a vehicle for secessive disruption of the encompassing nation-state.

All this is well known. The way in which it is usually presented, however, obscures the extremely important work that language does for nationalism. By appearing as the objectively determined and immanent property of national entities, language obscures its role as a surrogate for those entities. Nationalist rhetoric fastens people's attention on language as though it were an immutably perfect simulacrum of the nation itself – an icon in the technical sense in which I have used that term here. Higonnet (1980) has documented the ways in which some leaders of the French Revolution, committed to a communitarian ideology but determined not to give up their personal material advantages, objectified language as the great levelling ground for French identity. The Revolution, he suggests, was in no danger from the speakers of patois as such; by attacking their speech, he suggests, the revolutionary leaders created an issue that drew attention away from the inconsistency of their own actions and attitudes. By reifying language, these leaders hoped to distract attention away from the immediacy of their wealth and toward the immanent property of that medium through which, as the *abbé* Grégoire had pointed out, one could commune with the Supreme Being. This illustrates one of the several processes by which leaders may find it expedient to set up language as an effigy of national unity.

In the terms I have adopted here, moreover, we can see the problem as that of reconciling the two extreme ends of the segmentary model, of eating one's cake as a communitarian and having it as an individualist at the same time. This feature of simultaneity is extremely important. In segmentary polities, one's actions are defined according to circumstances: now one sides with one's immediate group, now one is fighting as a member of a much larger entity. In the modern nation-state, such shifting among levels of solidarity is inconceivable. One's personal interests are supposedly both subordinate to, and yet coincident with, those of the state. The creation of a national language, as the example of the French Revolution shows, offers an attractive way of collapsing the ramified cultural history of the nation into a single, atemporal unity, dazzling those critical eyes that might otherwise be tempted to examine more closely the inequalities and disunity that the real actions of the leaders promote.

Linguistic nationalism renders the geographical distribution of the language coterminous with that of the nation itself, so that any attack on the national language becomes, by substitution, a violation of the national borders, an illegal incursion. It is a logic that has a great deal in common with the notion of "homeopathic magic" that Frazer discerned amongst tribal peoples: if you can suppress its impurities, you can maintain the essentialist purity of the nation itself. (It is perhaps relevant that the colonels who seized power in Greece in 1967 proposed to "operate on the sick patient" of their country, a surgical procedure that included some linguistic purification that would have been hilarious had its consequences not been so traumatic: repression of education, alienation of children from their less "fortunate" parents, resistance to new ideas that the puristic neo-Classical tongue could not easily accommodate.) Language becomes a sort of conceptual effigy – one, furthermore, into which one can stick symbolic pins or on which one can practice soothing cures, according to need and inclination. The purism of nationalistic language planners is as ritualistic, and as arbitrary, as any dietary law. This is a centrally important point to which we shall shortly return.

Nationalists, then, do not only try to unify language artificially in order to provide existential unity for the nation. They also equate language with nation, and perform parallel "operations" on both. The ritual practitioners of statecraft can perform their rituals on the language, creating purist perversions of everyday speech and demanding a legalistic referentialism of all its users.

Thus, people become categorically indistinguishable from what they speak, and words take on the virtual status of things. Moreover, the treatment of the national language becomes the model for the treatment of its segments, or categories. In consequence, language appears to become a perfect tool of representation: words become the exact positional analogues of things in the only taxonomic game in town. In pre-Revolutionary France, at least, this correspondence between the singularity of national language and the pure referentiality of words was made explicit, and treated as a necessary precondition of abstract reasoning (Higonnet 1980: 50). Once people focus only on the forms of language – an act of trust – these forms assume perfect referentiality as refractions of a national truth. This is the linguistic equivalent of bureaucratic routinization in Weber's sense, as well as of a collective representation along the lines of Evans-Pritchard's reading of Durkheim. Language is not merely an instrument; it is also an emblem.

The process of reification can go beyond the fossilization of meaning to the point where meaning becomes wholly irrelevant. In Edward Albee's *Zoo Story* (1960), pork is described as so disgusting that even dogs would not eat it. According to Salman Rushdie, "This was superb anti-pork propaganda," and as such an appropriate piece of literature for Muslim audiences. A Karachi TV censor informed Salman Rushdie that he would have to delete all references to pork in a production of the play because "the word could not be spoken on Pakistani television" (Rushdie, 1983: 2).

This is the language of a shockingly transcendent referentiality, but the more familiar kinds of referentiality immortalized, for example, in Joseph Heller's wry parable, *Catch-22* (1961), or in Kafka's (1937) nightmares of justice perverted, are every bit as corrosive of individual self-respect, and ultimately produce very similar effects. There is nothing more impassable than an intransigent bureaucrat armed with a taxonomy, because the bureaucrat can always claim that the taxonomy is the state (or, as in Rushdie's encounter with the Karachi censor, the official religion). No higher arbiter is to be found. Moreover, any challenge to national language is a reminder of death, the underlying disability of all nationalisms (as Anderson [1983: 46] notes). It is in converting that basic fatality into a predestination to ultimate good that the work of nationalistic discourse lies – the abolition of death, that ultimate otherness within (Bottomley and Lechte 1990: 61).[2]

The unanswerable properties of language, especially written language, stem from its apparent transparency. I say "apparent" with good reason: the obfuscatory properties of bureaucratic jargon are well known devices of the conventional humor about bureaucracy. Both bureaucrats and humorists speak as though bureaucratic language should genuinely be transparent. But who legislates this? Even though its outer form may be quite simple, language can be made semantically obscure in order to allow bureaucratic actors to deflect attention away from the actually quite contingent character of its use. This gives new meaning to the Saussurean notion of the "arbitrariness of the linguistic sign" (Saussure 1966: 67). Language is both the instrument and the object of the action. In this regard, moreover, language is engagingly like the camel that the camel thief uses to raid other Bedouin camels (Meeker 1979): as both instrument and symbol, it can be used to violate its own kind, to impose one set of meanings over all utterances.

Bureaucratization of language thus opposes any recognition of semantic fluidity. As a model of the polity, a labile notion of

---

2. The comparison of bureaucratic denials of change with rituals, here those of death, is irresistible; for a discussion of death as ritualized other, see especially Fabian 1973; Danforth 1982.

language can only suggest that ultimate category violation: "instability." And yet everyday experience would seem to suggest that written laws are not as fixed as they appear to be. Goody (1986: 101) appears to recognize this when he points out that the Asante leaders who conducted treaty negotiations with the British colonizers overliteralized the forms, as opposed to the content, of their agreements: "Much misunderstanding arose from this tendency to equate the paper with its contents, the medium with the message." This is not, however, a consequence of the introduction of writing alone, as Goody seems to suggest; on the contrary, Salman Rushdie's conflict with the Karachi censor over the use of "pork" shows that similar overliteralization of words is perfectly possible in oral discourse.

Conversely, I find it hard to understand Goody's contention that the introduction of writing makes non sequiturs and other inconsistencies show up more clearly than happens in oral discourse (Goody 1986: 92, 141). Ideally, perhaps, this should be so. Many scholars apparently believe that it is so. Gellner (1988), for example, has argued that widespread literacy made "high culture" available to everyone, so that the members of nation-states today speak an "elaborated code" in which ambiguity and redundancy are fast disappearing. While that is undoubtedly what many governments would like to see happen, it is invariably more of an ideal type than an achieved reality. People are much more inclined to take the outer forms of bureaucratic procedure and invest them with meanings of their own.

What marks an elaborated code, according to the sociolinguist who coined the term, Basil Bernstein (1971), is freedom from the constraints of context.[3] As Goody (1986: 185) remarks, however,

3. Here my reading of Bernstein is at variance with Bloch's (1989: 25). He sees formalized political and religious language as a variety of Bernstein's "restricted code," in that it uses a limited range of stylistic, lexical, and syntactic forms. This seems to me to miss the key issue of context-sensitivity; restricted codes are restricted precisely because, lacking the presupposition of pure semantic transcendence (or possessing what Bloch calls "illocutionary" as opposed to "prepositional" force), they are ideologically committed to a very high degree of semantic indeterminacy. In practice, of course, the semantic range of formal language can be enormous; but that is not what their users wish to project. Bloch (1989: 40; my emphasis) does recognize this: "An *effect* of words and speech acts being formalized is their increasing ambiguity." While he is thus right to see the lack of semantic specificity as characteristic of restricted codes, he does not acknowledge that formalized speech – and certainly the formalized language of bureaucrats – often lays claim to total semantic transparency. One might bring our respective positions together

"nothing is ever completely 'decontextualized' nor completely 'universalistic'." But Goody still partially replicates Gellner's error here, as he treats contextual and universal meaning as possible conditions of reality rather than as rhetorical strategies. It would be more useful to avoid reifying context, and instead to speak of the appearance of context-sensitivity and context-dependence – to recognize, in other words, rhetorical modes and their tactical deployment. Despite Gellner's argument, all that mass education has been able to guarantee the citizens of the nation-state in the realm of semantics is an ideology of transcendent logic, a consequent devaluation of local meanings, while citizens may (and sometimes do) respond by inserting those same local meanings into subversive or ironic readings of official discourse.

Goody finds that writing casts a logical spotlight on law because of the immediacy of juxtaposition that it is able to produce: inconsistencies are hard to maintain when they appear in bald, decontextualized, straightforward prose. This, Goody claims, does not happen when the laws are all oral (Goody 1986: 136–137). Goody's position thus turns on very much the same kind of argument as that traditionally used to distinguish history from myth: history presents the facts and is open to critical inspection, whereas myth – especially if we follow Lévi-Strauss's (1955) famous analysis – actually encapsulates contradictions.

In practice, however, many forms of nationalistic history juxtapose contradictions as a matter of course. Like the Durkheimian view of religion, Lévi-Strauss's vision of myth may actually work best in modern nation-states, because these have a more or less consciously constructed teleology: one does not have to assume some mysterious higher purpose setting up the "functions" of religion or myth, because it may be clear – and in theory could always be investigated – whose interests are served. The contradictions of nationalistic history, moreover, are reproduced at the level of bureaucratic taxonomy and enshrined in daily rituals of obeisance, and the authority that emanates from their written form deflects rather than encourages critical inspection. Writing

---

by saying that obstructionist or self-important bureaucrats don the lexical trappings of an elaborated code to mask the semantics of a restricted one. Through this version of semiotic illusionism, they try to marshall their power, while some disgruntled clients may attempt to subvert it by implicitly or explicitly calling their bluff (see especially Balshem 1991; de Certeau 1984: 18; Ferguson 1984: 157; Scott 1985: 318).

is no guarantee of consistency or accessibility to criticism. On the contrary, as with sacred texts in numerous religions, it may deflect critical inspection and thus intensify the fetishization of language.

Greek bureaucrats are well aware of the inconsistencies that abound in the legal system they are supposed to uphold. They frequently and ruefully complain of the "multiplicity of laws" (*polinomia*) that confounds their best intentions to conform, and acknowledge the "little windows" (*parathirakia*), or loopholes, that make it possible for citizens to play one law off against another. Total clarity is a literalist dream, impossible of realization, but bureaucrats act as though the law were clear, and accept the fetishistic quality of its language: that is the lesson of Rushdie's experience with the censor, and it has little to do with whether the rules are written or oral. Or, as Vico (1744, I: cxi) bluntly expressed it over two centuries earlier, "Certainly in the laws is an obscuring of reason maintained solely by authority, which makes them inflexible in practice."

The more successfully a bureaucrat can reify "the laws," and make them "inflexible in practice," the easier it becomes to manipulate legal meetings for the purposes of self-interest. A powerful Cretan politician, visiting a village where he had many clients in early 1978, announced that for him being a parliamentary deputy meant bringing specific, understandable laws before his fellow legislators: one could not, he pontificated, be like a priest who reads the Gospel in a language that neither he nor his hearers can understand. At about the same time, this past master at obfuscation, a notorious patron of animal-thieves who had shown great dexterity at conveying the opposite of what his words literally meant, distributed leaflets declaring that he "did not want a single animal-thief voting for him." His denial of the ritualism of political life and of the law was all of a piece with this posture of literalism. Not only were his protestations entirely transparent, but they were themselves ritualistic in the extreme. The call for perfect freedom from context has a political context of its own, and we cannot realistically understand it without recourse to that context: so much for the "elaborated codes" of academic discourse as well as the law.

The fetishizing of language, its acquisition of immanent authority, often turns on just such affectations of literalism. Reed (1990), in a highly illuminating account of Portuguese rural politics, shows how the very instruments of bureaucratization – in this case, Robert's

Rules of Order – can become a symbol of both good conduct and repression, depending on one's position in the political constellation of the moment. The Portuguese rural politicians whom Reed studied flung accusations of rhetorical incompetence and ungainliness at each other, making language the board on which an intense game was played for more obviously material stakes. The contestable value in this case appears to have been "democracy." Those who possessed a sophisticated understanding of parliamentary procedure, usually conservatives with a stake in maintaining the status quo, insisted that Robert's Rules protected the rights of all to be heard. Their populist opponents, apparently with good reason, viewed this as a ploy to exploit possession of an arcane variety of knowledge in order to impose a minority will. As the debate ranged on, however, one thing became ever clearer: language itself becomes an object in its own right, to be contested as a proxy for the actualities of power.

The same process occurs institutionally, through the chronic sacralization of legal texts whose symbolic importance has long outlived their practical relevance. Goody's argument thus works better for the dreams of legislators than for the practices of bureaucrats, although in an ironic sense he is right about bureaucrats also: they use the rhetoric of semantic transparency to bring their personal goals into step with the grand sweep of history. Goody himself provides an excellent demonstration that this is so (1986: 163): "The Domesday Book was used as a source of law for over two hundred years (mainly in the later period), yet it had been a survey of the state of the nation at a particular point in time. Consequently, its actual truth-value diminished just as its perceived truth-value increased. For the written word was seen as associated with immortality." Clearly, as Goody observes, the permanence that writing brought was an important factor here. Whatever the source of its authority, any formulaic pronouncement may possess this property of apparently immutable meaning. Its formal fixity obscures the labile quality of its semantics. It is not that some forms of language are context-free, but that the exercise of power lies, in part, in the ability to represent it as such. This is why the study of bureaucratization must attend to rhetoric.

It is also important not to assume that command of formal discourse has some mysterious ability to enforce respect. On the contrary, its uses carry certain risks. Reed's Portuguese village populists, for example, were able through mockery and parody to subvert the conservatives' claims to be the guardians of democracy. Sometimes, this kind of reversal can be almost total. During the 1984 elections for the European Parliament in Greece, while the conservative leader Constantine Mitsotakis scrupulously avoided using the discredited purist (*katharevousa*) form of the national language, his opponent, the socialist Andreas Papandreou, salted his final speech with a generous array of stilted formalisms – but, cannily, only when alluding to the conservatives. In this way, he effectively encompassed the conservatives' own identity with a superior – because playful – command of the formalism that was their clearest expressive link to the bureaucratic excesses of the colonels' regime a few years earlier.

Formal language lays rhetorical claim to transcendence. In the work of Bernstein and Douglas, there is a tendency to conflate the formal properties of language and symbolism with the semantic aspects. The ironic inversions I have just described show that Robert's Rules and purist Greek are just as susceptible to ambiguity as catcalls and slang. Subversion of formality does not consist so much in simply abandoning it as in showing precisely how precarious its hold on absolute meaning really is. Bloch (1989: 27; but cf. Tambiah 1979: 152) rightly observes that formal language is meant to discourage criticism, but we are remiss if we attend only to a literal semantics; or if, to use a current literary model, we hear only the author and block out the readers' responses. Political critique has less to do with the forms of discourse than with the ability to foreground aspects of their use. Maintenance of power relies on the reification of meaning through its conflation with form. This has some clear institutional implications: "In reality, as Marx says in effect, the general interest becomes reduced to the peculiar interest of the bureaucracy, which insists on the permanence of spheres of private interest – that of corporations and states – in order to configure an imaginary universality in relation to it" (Lefort 1971: 289). By refusing to acknowledge the power of rhetoric, social science has too often turned its back on this capacity for universalizing the particular, for substituting the timeless forms of national language for the special needs of individual actors.

Within the modern nation-state, bureaucrats and politicians can often assimilate their immediate goals to explicitly national idioms of expression. This is particularly obvious in those areas where questions of identity must be negotiated – the main focus of this book. I would suggest, at least as a tentative hypothesis, that where nationalist rhetoric is given a high degree of public acceptance, it is much easier for irresponsible or selfish bureaucrats to pursue goals unrelated to their service functions. Since the hallmark of virtually all nationalist discourse is one of unity, any act of disobedience can be seen as traitorous.

Tautologies in Action

In the preceding section, I suggested that the written and legalistic form of laws may divert attention away from rather than toward their mutual incompatibility. But one should then ask: How are the inconsistencies maintained when daily practice renders them painfully obvious?

The answer lies in the tautologous form that bureaucratic pronouncements usually take. Paperwork is needed to validate facts about who people are, and then additional paperwork is needed to validate the previous paperwork. Sometimes attempts are made to counter this proliferation. The United States Reduction of Paperwork Act (1980), which requires all government agencies to indicate on each form the amount of time that completing it should take, was designed to protect the public from unnecessary information collection (Haines 1990: 254–255). One paradoxical result, however, was to increase the degree of official surveillance over minor detail. For many citizens, this was just one more paroxysm of sterile self-reference. At least, however, its stated goal and partial effect was to discourage the official habit – as it often seems – of demanding information for information's sake. The lower the level of the bureaucracy in question and the further removed from the central authority, the more such requests for cross-checking as well as for a host of ultimately useless data tend to multiply, because the minor bureaucrats' livelihoods are at correspondingly greater risk. This also has its correlate in the ontogeny of the bureaucratic organization itself. As Lefort (1971: 303) has suggested, the proliferation of offices and personnel encourages the development of personal strategies behind a facade of common goals. There are, quite simply, more backs to be guarded.

The demand for multiple signatures illustrates this well. The signature is at once a mark of individual responsibility and of impersonal power. In Greece, it sometimes used to be necessary, when cashing a traveller's check, to obtain as many as fourteen approval signatures on the paperwork. Many of these were scribbled initials, so stylized as to resemble the sign of the Cross – which indeed was often used in older documents in place of a personal signature and as witness to the sacred oath that validated the deed.

Ideally, signatures are, as Goody (1986: 73) rightly observes, "a pledge of faith; indeed, the signature is the moral person himself, or at least the legal person, *homo legens.*" In medieval Europe, as he goes on to remark, the "IOU" was "a written promise, legitimated by the signature, and sometimes . . . by a mark, in particular a cross, which is the sign of the cross, bringing supernatural sanctions into play." The Greek bank tellers' signatures, however, were not marks of individuation. They were claims to a collective authority, and a suppression of the clerical self – a clear demonstration of the principle we briefly mentioned in the last chapter, according to which the signature reduces the bureaucrat to a cipher of some generalized national entity.

Unlike the signatory to a contract, who assumed a measure of personal responsibility (Goody 1986: 124), the bureaucrat may hide behind the signature. The signature becomes an object of pure self-reference: it does not stand for the bureaucrat, but for itself – a special case of the fetishization process discussed above, as well as a way of removing any trace of accountability from the individual bureaucrat to the bureaucratic collectivity – in direct violation, be it noted, of Weber's ideal type of legal-rational bureaucracy. Such strategies are entirely consistent with the more general logic of *efthinofovia,* or "buck-passing" (literally, "responsibility phobia"). The typical signature is anonymous – a logical contradiction that reproduces the bureaucrat's conflict between self-interest and the responsibility of a national trust.

Accountability, Weber tells us, is what bureaucracy is all about; and accountability is what many bureaucrats invest enormous amounts of effort in short-circuiting or avoiding. A cynic might define power – always an elusive concept – as the right to be unaccountable. A brief tale will illustrate how far that logic can go. After an election campaign in Greece, a communist deputy complained that the Patraic Gulf was full of little plastic socialist party flags. He went to see the general secretary of the Ministry of the Interior, to whom all prefects report, saying that this pollution was the regional prefect's fault. He would not stop talking, until finally the exasperated general secretary blew up: "Look here, mister, the Prefect can't be putting little plastic flags around because she's six months pregnant!" (*Ta Nea*, 7 June 1989, p. 5).

This incident is interesting for two reasons. First, there is the deputy's clear attempt to associate the socialists with pollution, symbolically, no doubt, as well as literally. Even more revealing, however, is the presumption that the prefect was somehow directly responsible for the outrage. This pinpoints her status as a political appointee rather than as an elected official (a factor that also played its part in the travails of the Thessaloniki Jehovah's Witnesses). It was the prefect's appointed status that made it acceptable for the deputy to hold her to blame. The exasperated ministry official's response plays right into that logic. Despite (or perhaps because of) its patent absurdity, it exposes an implicit consequence of bureaucrats' pervasive refusal to accept any responsibility: the prefect's moral accountability – which was something the socialists had tried to promote – could only mean that she had virtually done the dastardly deed in person. It is hardly a matter for wonder that officials so rarely admit to having authorized any bureaucratic action at all.

Note that this anecdote takes us right back to questions of personal identity as well as accountability. In Greek political rhetoric, as I noted in Chapter One, there is a constant play of stereotypes between the Western ideal and a sort of orientalized and internalized Other. In matters pertaining to personal action, this emerges as a conflict between selfish, familistic, or party-political deviousness on the one hand, and ingenious, individualistic entrepreneurship on the other. Which of these is invoked depends on the relationship between the speaker and the subject of the conversation. The class of actions to which they belong are virtually identical; their moral implications are diametrically opposed.

Today, even as the conservative monopoly of "Western democracy" (versus "Oriental despotism") weakens or slides into irrelevance, other oppositions – fascist versus revolutionary, for example – fill the same moral spaces and inspire the same kinds of rhetorical battle. Once again, we see that far more important than the particular forms or symbols – although these are the ostensible objects of struggle – is the contest over who gets to reify meaning and under what banners.

Reifying What Others Say: Patterns of Blame

In the next chapter, we shall be examining some consequences of the avoidance of responsibility, and locating them in their cosmological context. To conclude the present chapter, however, I would like to pursue briefly the relationship between this phenomenon of buck-passing and tautology. The link is, again, through the fetishizing of language or, as I have called it, the reification of meaning.

The lack of fit between indigenous values and referential bureaucratic semantics has generated a defensive thirst for literality among Greek public officials (see Mackridge 1985; Tsoucalas 1991). Bureaucrats and clients alike are fully aware of the possibilities for mutual deception that, as de Certeau (1984) has so ably documented, the use of a common formal language usually masks. Since meanings are so easily disputed, bureaucrats reassert, over and over, their right to define terms and usages. The opposition to such semantic control may be equally ritualistic, but in a subversive fashion that punctures officious pride: such, for example, are the burlesque stereotypes played out in the Brazilian carnival (see Da Matta 1991).

This usually takes the form of an intense concern with rhetorical exactitude. Official pedantry, called "ritualism" by Merton and Blau, is actually a mark of dependency. Bureaucrats turn to language when they fear that their superiors will refuse to "cover" them. Since the national language is often ideologically homologous with the nation, and its categories are supposedly homologous with the groups of people they define, precision is not merely a perverse bureaucratic pleasure. On the contrary, it is vital to professional survival. The bureaucrat always wants to be in a position to point to a legitimating text. Even if the interpretation is in dispute, it would have to be an unusually independent superior who could insist on rejecting the subordinate's reading out of hand. It is far easier for both to assume that the subordinate was right. To pursue the analogy of nationalism with religion to its logical conclusion here, the most radical fundamentalism is arguably to be found in the offices of petty clerks.

An example of this concern with precision will also serve to illustrate the distribution of power in such situations. A "retired dentist's widow" could not get her identity card issued unless she conformed to the required format ("widow of dentist-inretirement") (*To Vima*, 7 July 1977, p. 2). But the surest way of guaranteeing referentiality is through the self-referentiality, or, rather, the self-referencing, of bureaucratic documentation (*Akropolis*, 10 November 1977, p. 2):

> "This reading is about bureaucracy. . . . In order to extend the deferral of his conscription, a student who is studying abroad must bring to the army office a certificate of identity from the Borough [of his residence]. The Borough . . . requests that he go to the civil court or to a notary and make a sworn declaration that the person who is studying abroad is one and the same person as the one who was born in such-and-such a place and is inscribed in the Borough register of males."

As with people, so with objects. In the small midwestern town where I live, a great furor broke out when the local county clerk's use of a seal-stamp marked "Monroe Circuit Court" rather than "Clerk of the Monroe Circuit Court" was challenged. When a judge finally ruled that the original seal (used since the 1850s) was in order, the clerk had to abandon the new seals he had ordered, and intended to convert them later to the original wording as well, *Herald–Times*, 6 October 1989, pp. A [I], II.

These examples illustrate the literal identification of person with label. It is a totally self-referential claim to authenticity. The panic created among the good citizens of Monroe County, Indiana, about the validity of documentation (birth, death, and marriage certificates!) stamped with the controversial seal shows how easily cowed people become. Gellner may be right in assuming that the power structures in question arise from the use of force, Gellner's "sword" and Mao's "barrel of a gun," but such illustrations show that once the system is in place, the pen is at least as mighty.

Fetishization is reification. The labelling of items brings them under the conceptual control of the state and makes their identity superficially unproblematical. An American archeologist who specializes in experimental ceramic techniques made some "prehistoric" pots and took them to a Greek museum storeroom to be photographed. When she wanted to remove them, she was told – apparently on the grounds that antiquities are national property and subject to strict export laws (which, ironically, this particular archeologist has invested a great deal of time in defending and supporting) – that they were now part of the collection. I have also been told that one cannot simply abandon any object of antiquity once it has been declared to the proper authorities, as at that point it is given a "protocol number" which guarantees its official existence.

Here we are moving away from the domain of language proper to larger issues of taxonomy and cosmology. In the next chapter I shall examine the Greek situation in rather more detail. I propose to document the conceptual framework within which the public conceptualizes bureaucratic intransigence and buck-passing, and what cosmological assumptions enable people to live with a state mechanism that inspires such dislike as well as familiarity. Bureaucracy fits widely popular notions of person and cosmos in Greece. Its evil attributes are but one rendition of the mortal burden. The next chapter examines this practical theodicy in more detail.

CHAPTER FIVE

Retrospective Fatalities

Arbitrary Writ

In this chapter, we shall take a closer look at the idiom of grumbling against the state through which people seek to excuse their humiliation at its hands – secular theodicy. The key to secular theodicy is its conventional cast. In order to show just how conventional it is, my immediate goal is to trace what we might call, in an extended sense, an etymology of concepts (see also Herzfeld 1987a: 23). Although I shall use linguistic evidence fairly freely, I am more concerned to show that the relevant images – the cosmology of the imagined community – derive from widespread ideas about personal fate, themselves embedded in the conceptual complex about blood and person that I have already discussed. This is a persistent cosmology, secularized today, but no less powerful for that reason. It is also a symbolism so common that most people do not think of it as cosmological at all. In this regard, it is like a metaphor that has gone stale through the routinization of expressive form.

The tracing of etymology is intended here as a disclosive technique, as a way of understanding how and why people become accustomed to obedience and no longer examine the terms in which it is demanded. If we look at the more outrageously arbitrary kinds of bureaucratic performance – the kinds that sometimes prompt us to wonder how on earth clerks get away with it – we can usually discern a pattern that, when we describe it to others, is equally recognizable to them. In other words, the bureaucrats have behaved, or so we like to think, as bureaucrats "always" do. Because we reduce them to stereotypes in order to explain away our own failures to ourselves or others, we usually fail to ask why such behavior should be a necessary part of bureaucracy. We simply assume that it is – which is possibly unfair, in fact, to the great majority of bureaucrats we are likely to meet!

Most Western Europeans or North Americans would be out-raged to be told that their conventional response to bureaucratic obstructionism is "fatalistic." It is basic to their sense of self that, as democratic individualists, they would fight back against curtail-ments of their liberty. Yet fatalism is precisely what many observers from the older industrialized nations have said, as we have seen, of Mediterranean and Middle Eastern peoples; and fighting back is just as precisely what the latter do when, lacking grievance devices such as the courts, they resort to patronage in high places or to religious or moral sanctions. The difference lies in historically specific institutional structures, not innate incapacities or collec-tive cultural feebleness. As in Presthus's rather condescending account of "Inshalla" in Turkey, we find that it is the very cultures that dominate Third World countries that may then "justify" their domination by opposing the combined fatalism and self-interest of the Oriental "in the dark," in Tsoucalas's phrase, to the aggressive "individualism" of the enlightened Occidental.

The charge of fatalism, as I have pointed out, is usually a vicarious one. At the personal level, one describes one's enemies as too lazy and one's clients as too stupid to fight for their rights. That, at least, is what winners and gossips say. In practice, those who com-plain of bureaucratic caprice usually continue to fight against it, just as Weber's Calvinists demanded unceasing effort as proof of their predestined access to paradise. Most of the examples dis-cussed in this chapter, for example, would never have surfaced had the victims not chosen to fight back through the media and in other ways. Their fight consists in laying bare the use of state rationality in favor of some far more restricted interest by a well-placed patron. It challenges the implications of the rhetoric of power, using rhetoric to do so. In no sense is it a resigned ac-ceptance of authority.

Fatalism and the Fates

It must be increasingly clear that the term "fatalism" is more of a problem than an analytical tool. We should nonetheless brief-

ly address what it might mean, if only because this will help us
see more clearly what uses people actually do make of the imagery
of fate. Fatalism as ordinarily conceived is a passive resignation
to the future dictates of chance. From the standpoint of technological rationalism, therefore, it represents the worst kind of
inefficiency. As such, it also belongs to that broad spectrum of supposedly maladaptive and inflexible values that are ranged against
the benefits of technological progress (Banfield 1958; Diaz 1966).
In such a view, the symbolic universe constitutes a rigid barrier
to the practical.

Once common sense and rationality are seen to incorporate
some of the forms of symbolism, their social significance appears
in a radically changed light. No longer is the issue whether a
bureaucratic argument or a client's excuse is literally credible.
What matters is that it is socially acceptable, and this in turn
means that it embodies an appropriate use of cultural form. As
Umberto Eco (1976: 256) has rightly observed, "Even prophets
have to be socially *acceptable* in order to be right; if not, they are
wrong."

This argument is grounded in speech act theory. J.L. Austin's
How To Do Things With Words (1975[1962]), for example, shows
how the way phrasing of an utterance is crucial to its social
acceptance. It constitutes perhaps the most important of what
Austin called the "felicity conditions" of an utterance – the
conditions under which the speaker's intentions would elicit an
appropriate response. Austin's eloquent "Plea for Excuses"
(1971[1956–57]) takes ethnographic analysis still further. In this
shorter piece, he seeks cultural explanations for the acceptability
and conventionality of excuses. His argument appeals, in part, to
historical speculation about the idioms people use to make excuses. Although Austin did not make the connection explicit, his
examination of cultural form is subversive of rhetorical preten-
tiousness in general, and of ideas about absolute rationality in
particular.

Austin thus continued the intellectual and political program
initiated by Giambattista Vico in the eighteenth century. Vico saw
that etymology could be used as much to demonstrate the fluidity
and impermanence of many civil institutions as to recognize their
antiquity, and was especially caustic about the utter folly – often
reproduced by scholars servile to official interests – of trying to
pretend that national institutions had remained unchanged since
the beginning of time. Austin similarly, if on a more intimate scale,

appealed to etymology in trying to debunk excuses. He argued that excuses must fit certain conventions in order to be noticed; after all, it is no use challenging to a duel someone who does not also subscribe to the honor code that legitimates such confrontations (1975[1962]: 37).

In the same way, Austin suggested, excuses draw on a substratum of ideas about causation, and these ideas, closely inspected, may no longer seem as rational as we might expect. To claim that "an accident happened to me," for example, entails drawing on the implications of the Latin root *accidit*, with its suggestion of fate "falling" from on high as the efficient cause of disaster. Not only are such connections largely invisible to their users, but making them apparent is one way to call their implied bluff. Austin (1971[1956–57]: 99–100) nicely captures this necessary elusiveness in his phrase "trailing clouds of etymology." Or, as Wittgenstein (cited in Tambiah 1990: 63) remarked, " [i]n our language a whole mythology is laid down." Etymological connections are used to justify what might on closer scrutiny turn out to be indefensible. This line of argument is very close to Vico, and serves a similarly skeptical purpose.

My own purpose in adopting a similar line of argument here is not to criticize people of any social or cultural group for failing to face up to responsibility. The cultural forms of making excuses differ, but it seems highly unlikely that some cultures would be more prone than others to self-exoneration in some measurable sense. While the systematic debunking of excuse-making tactics may from time to time serve an obvious purpose, such as maintaining a teacher's authority over a classroom, it also, in turn, rests on a symbolic order, and nowhere more so than when it is used to label an entire nation as irresponsible or immature. The rhetoric about national reasonableness – we have it, they don't – participates in the same invidious contest as the play of personal excuses and character assassination.

The line of thought from Vico to Austin is critical of nation-statism in another sense as well. Both philosophers set their faces against the idea of literal meaning: Vico by showing that the most abstractly scientific language can never entirely shake off its metaphorical origins; Austin by rejecting the idea that language could unambiguously represent fact ("statements") in favor of a focus on the ways in which people use language to create facts ("performative utterances"). Both approaches are inimical to nation-statism because they reject the very idea of semantic purity – of the "literally literal" – and do it by showing the instability of the word-meaning connection through time, the reverse of the nationalist program of using history to justify an eternal order in the present.

By extension, they also challenge bureaucratic claims to a genuinely hermetic set of categories. Their use of etymology, far from showing that the basic taxonomy belongs to an unchanging and transcendent moral order of the kind imagined by essentialists, instead connects bureaucratic thinking to historically contingent, material images. Their argument challenges the detemporalized history that justifies state power. It says, in effect, that the roots of that power do not lie in a predictable world order but in human actors' success in representing that order as foreordained.

Arguments about chance and fate are struggles for power. When a bureaucrat takes advantage of a client's apparent resignation to authority, or when a conquering army rejoices in the "fatalism" of the vanquished, these are vicarious traits. They reproduce at the level of discourse what the stronger party has achieved by means of force or vested authority. In Austin's terms, they are very successful performative utterances – stereotypes, the validity of which appears only after the fact, when those upon whom they have been wished seem to acquiesce in them – although the appearance of resignation may actually mask a powerful resistance to official interpretations (Balshem 1991; see also following paragraphs). Attributions of fatalism represent the view of the weak held by the powerful: by bureaucrats about their clients, or by great powers about client states or vanquished nations.[1] This is probably why, in countries where the arbitrary powers of bureaucrats are subject to severe legal controls and appeal mechanisms, the language of fate seems more muted. But this only reinforces the point: that accusations of fatalism follow the exercise of overbearing power, just as self-justification by appealing to fate follows failure at resisting that power.

Although, then, we should avoid generalizations about the *fatalism* of the weak, this does not meant that people are unin-

1. Stereotypically, Europeans are supposed to be neither fatalistic nor inefficient. Thus, attributions of fatalism to the Greeks, to be discussed below, are enmeshed in debates on national identity in relation to the wider sense of a European culture.

terested in *fate*. On the contrary, it constitutes the discursive context that they share with those who exercise power over them, and who may in turn be subject to their own, intrainstitutional burdens of domination and discipline. In European cultures, notions of fate are historically connected with both the idea of individual genius and the symbolism of blood as social bond. I shall open the analysis with a brief account of my sources (especially newspapers) as representing the national level of discourse most clearly analogous with the play of gossip and reputation in the local community. In this way, we can get some sense of the integration of the local community into larger political and administrative entities. As an analytical strategy, this also challenges the state's condescending assumption that local matters are less important and less rational than the discourse of officialdom; and it shows how pervasive the language of fate has become in a supposedly secular and skeptical setting. It is, in short, an antidote to the parochialism of the top.

Greek Examples

The rest of this chapter is devoted to illustrations of these issues, drawn from the ethnography of Greece. The location of that country on the conceptual boundaries separating Europe from the Orient, and its experience of the tension between these two models of identity, makes it an ideal place in which to study the meaning of rationality in civic life.

I have especially drawn on newspaper articles, many of them published during the eight years immediately following the restoration of Greek democracy in 1974. The three newspapers from which I have most frequently culled articles were largely sympathetic, at that time, to the Panhellenic Socialist Movement (PASOK) of Andreas Papandreou, in opposition until 1981. Of these, *Eleftherotipia* ("Free Press") probably had the most radical (or at least mischievous) reputation; *To Vima* ("The Platform," now a weekly) tended toward a more conventional, restrained tone; and *Ta Nea*, virtually a party newspaper, remained uncritically supportive of PASOK after the party's 1981 election victory while *Eleftherotipia* became increasingly critical of the party's record in government.

All three newspapers were consistently critical of the American military presence in Greece, British and American policies on the Cyprus issue, and "Great Power" manipulation generally; all three made a point of carrying feature articles on matters of cultural and historical interest. All three, sharply critical of the conservative New Democracy party's performance in office (1975–81), developed a lively tradition of investigative reporting to deal with it. A fourth newspaper, *Akropolis*, was largely pro-New Democracy, although it carried occasional criticisms of government mismanagement even while the conservatives were in power.

For the material on personal interaction and social life, I have drawn on published ethnographic materials and my own data from Athens, Crete, and the Dodecanese. Although I am claiming direct comparability between the journalistic and ethnographic materials, one important difference should be emphasized. Journalistic writing is not, on the whole, very friendly to the excuses of petty bureaucrats and politicians. Indeed, a significant part of investigative reporting tends to be just that kind of debunking. Denuded of such gestural support as the helpless shoulder shrug or the conspiratorial wink, excuses can be made to look damningly silly in print. Nonetheless, the newspapers give us three direct lines of access to the idiom of excuse-making. First, successful satire, by its very nature, reveals the most diagnostic formal features of what is satirized; and second, newspapers themselves often make equally "cultural" excuses for the political interests they support. In both respects, the "letters to the editor" columns offer particularly rich pickings.

A third point of access comes through media coverage of international relations. Here, where Greece is so often the injured party, there is relatively little desire to debunk the claims of maltreatment by hostile international forces – although here, too, sober commentators sometimes deride what they portray as a national penchant for passing the buck. For the opposition to accuse a sitting government of complaisance in "Great Power" machinations is a way of saying that one's ideological opponents are of poor moral fiber; to defend Greece against criticism on the grounds of "Great Power" interference is to excuse, however justifiably, one's compatriots' collective failure.

These are arguments among and about stereotypes. As such, they are ideal for our purpose of disinterring from the welter of claims and counterclaims the symbolic terms in which these are couched.

Appeals to "national character," fundamentally mythological constructions of identity, are suffused with the language of blood, kinship, and essential fate.

Blame and Self-justification

Journalistic writing in Greece reproduces on a grand and highly public scale the agonistic conventions of ordinary speech. In everyday conversation, people attribute the failure of others (or members of other social groups) to character flaws. One's own failures and those of one's kin and friends, conversely, are the result of bad luck, and it is one's successes that one attributes to qualities of character. This "character" is, quite literally, "natural" (*fisiko*) to the individual or group in question, so squabbles about contingent social slurs always take on an air of grand de-bates about matters of essential truth. All social actors try to assimilate the "natural character" of themselves and others to the grand order of nature itself, the ultimate underpinning of the official order and the national spirit. It is extraordinary how far this style of thinking – which to an anthropologist looks suspiciously like the "racial" characterology of the nineteenth and very early twentieth centuries, and which certainly reproduces the humoral-ists' practice of dividing up the world into unchanging types of people – resurfaces in current political science attempts to de-scribe the "character" of the typical bureaucrat, as we have seen. It is at once startling and instructive to encounter the same rhe-toric in a Greek village.

Much of the rural Greek assessment of character centers on how hard a person works. (Note, in passing, that this trait is therefore demonstrably not the exclusive preserve of Weber's ideal-type "Protestant ethic," the enabling condition for the bureaucratic personality, and that the post-Weberian use of this image does not look very different from village stereotypes.) To many Greek villagers (see du Boulay 1974: 52; Herzfeld 1981: 564), the attitude that outsiders would call fatalism is really just laziness. It is a character attribution, masquerading as an objective and categori-cal judgment. When certain individuals claim to be resigned to the whims of chance, villagers ordinarily assume that they are just making up excuses for inaction. The morally good life is above all one of unceasing struggle (Friedl 1962: 75), even when the cause seems hopeless from the outset.[2] At the very moment when a person seeks to justify some recent failure on the grounds of ill luck, measures should already be under way to set matters right. Thus, it is less a question of fatalism than of the self-justifying invocation of fate after the fact. It is damage control rather than prediction, rationalization rather than abstract rationality. It does not entail the "fatalistic" expectation that things just go wrong.

Ideas about fate and character are tightly interwoven. Before we take a closer look at how people operate this symbolic idiom, it might be useful to summarize its main components. They are: (1) the social basis of blame and self-exoneration; (2) a clear link between the *properties of character* that individuals are reputed to possess and the way in which fate determines how they inherit *material property*; and (3) the pervasive image of writing as the mode through which fate enforces its decisions. Let us turn to these three elements in greater detail.

The Social Dimension

Although people generally hold character responsible for their own successes and others' failures, while conversely attributing to fate their own failures and others' successes, there are occasions when self-accusation is appropriate. Such outbursts of candor do not necessarily express a guilty conscience, but represent an insider's view: "We shouldn't have done that." In other words, the usual determinant of whether people will admit to some level of failure is the extent to which their interlocutors belong to the same social entity. Fellow villagers might regret some collective decision, but bristle as soon as members of unrelated households accuse them of having misled the community at large. Nonetheless, it is important to recognize that, behind all the mutual recriminations and the braggadocio, Greeks do recognize their own responsibility for failure, provided the context does not threaten them with serious loss of social standing, and they may acknowledge that responsibility in a manner which redraws the boundaries to their personal advantage – sometimes even at considerable risk to themselves. One Rhodian villager told me – before the colonels' regime fell, when it was still dangerous to make such remarks –

2. On Crete, I was told (1981) that suicide was wrong even for a person in immense pain; one should struggle up to the appointed end of one's life.

that it was "our own donkeys (*ghaidhouria*)" who had provoked the Turkish invasion of Cyprus. In using on his "own" people an insult used only of "others,"[3] he was employing a device not unlike the junta's own habit of calling anyone who disagreed with it "anti-Greek." Popular and official rhetoric share a good deal of common ground.

Strategies of self-exoneration and blame are responsive to immediate social needs. They take account of what people know at a particular moment. A Glendiot unsuccessfully attempted to persuade a close friend to give a daughter in marriage to the first man's dishonored son. This ploy ended in a public rejection by the second man of the entire relationship between the two households. His response may be read as an attempt to throw the blame completely and unambiguously on his erstwhile friend. That he regarded friendship as ideally sacred and permanent, but also subject to social pressure in practice, is clear from his candid warning to me, to the effect that if I ever violated the local code in too obvious a manner, he would not be able to continue our relationship.

The relation between the attribution of bad character to others and the need to take personal initiative against it oneself is gruesomely illustrated by Pefkiot responses to allegations of Turkish atrocities in Cyprus in 1974. Their anger was vented in the form of a frequently reiterated call for the extermination of every Turkish woman and child. Not only were they able to endorse this programmatic crusade with an unorthodox interpretation of New Testament theology,[4] but they were also thereby able to ignore the official Greek policy of forebearance toward the unarmed Turkish-Cypriot civilian population. That policy, they assumed, was meant for external consumption, and its implementation would provide a stock of explanations for future humiliations at the Turks'

---

3. The point of the insult seems to be that the donkey is of unpredictable temper, and therefore lacking in social worth (*timi*) – a definitive trait of outsiders (see Herzfeld 1980a); this individual was also marginal to his own community in that, as a state official as well as by apparent personality, he was too inquisitive about his covillagers' affairs.

4. The allusion, taken entirely out of context, is to Jesus's response to the disciple who cut off the ear of the high priest's servant, one of those who came to take Jesus before Pilate: "Then said Jesus unto him put up the sword into his place; *for all they that take the sword shall perish by the sword*" (Matt. 26: 52; emphasis mine). This injunction inveighed against the very code of revenge that my informants sought to justify.

hands. Meanwhile, they could justify their more ferocious attitude on the grounds, first, of direct retaliation, and second, of the need to extirpate the very roots of the Turkish people. It is these arguments, public official pronouncements notwithstanding, that lie – as Loizos's (1988) report on Cyprus itself makes clear – at the very basis of the official ideology as it is internally enunciated. This internally directed ideology, moreover, abounds in the language of blood and the familial language of household, the two strands of metaphor united in their common exaltation of male belligerence. This is not passive fatalism, but a clarion call to violent action – to a violation that will balance out the violations already committed by the other side. That disaster has already occurred is another matter entirely, one that can be laid at the door of external agencies – NATO, the United States, or a diffuse and malevolent fate. The Greeks, no fatalists in practice, will now inscribe their control over events that others have set in train.

It is important to recall here that the idea of fate as a separate, external agency is only part of the picture. Onians (1951: 160–165) shows that the concept of a personal fate is encapsulated in the Roman *genius*, a patrilineally derived identity (from Greek *genos*, "patriline") said to be immanent in the self. Greeks today still personalize fate as "mine" or "yours." Thus, the separation of fate from character, so clear in the play of the willful "fate" (*mira*) and the immanent "nature" (*fisiko*) of the individual, is encapsulated by a larger sense of unity. It is this unity that the Cartesian split of the sensual from the sensible shatters irreversibly, changing mutually interdependent aspects of the person into the opposed forces of self and destiny, and social strategies into the categorical division of the world between fatalists and entrepreneurs. The Greek popular imagery I have discussed here is but one local variant of that widespread symbolism that nation-state ideologies take up in order, as Anderson suggests, to transform the fickleness of fate into a manifest and radically predictable destiny.

Fate, Character, and Inheritance

Personal and group character is said to be inherited, and therefore predictable. (This is another way of saying that it is inherited in the blood.) It is clear, however, that "inheritance" stands here for retrospective reconstruction. Gossip, for example, treats shameful deeds as "confirming" a reputation that may not have been at all obvious to anyone up to that point (see, for example, du Boulay 1974: 183), and can take the form of declarations of the "I always did say" variety about people one has never even mentioned hitherto. Such tactics allow speakers to "discover" inherited character traits by hindsight.

It is instructive to compare this way of talking about inherited character with the logic of property inheritance – a comparison of what happens to properties of personality with the distribution of personal property. The division of property among heirs is done by casting lots, a procedure that removes all possible blame for an unfair outcome from the immediate family and casts it upon the inscrutable agency of fate. There is no way of knowing how fate will determine the distribution before the lots are cast, and there is also no way in which family members can influence the outcome. While there is considerable variation throughout Greece in the specific rules for the casting of lots, the types of property so divided, and the protocol concerning which family member actually carries out the procedure, the fundamental idea is everywhere the same: to remove the potential for family conflict by redirecting any anger about unfair distribution at an external, impersonal force (Herzfeld 1980b; Levy 1956).

In Pefko, villagers make a categorical distinction between the lot and the gift. Property should pass automatically from parents to their children. Casting lots does not alter this basic principle. When inheritance is by "gift," this means that parents have perverted the normative flow of property, diverting it to someone other than their own children. It would not be appropriate to call parent-to-child transmission a gift, because property is ideally held in trust for all future generations. Thus, in casting lots, parents are not "giving" anything that does not already belong, in some timeless and essentialist sense, to their children. It is this assumption of property rights in perpetuity that also informs the rhetoric of national territory.

Ownership follows the blood. It is noteworthy that adopted children are proverbially considered to be ungrateful; villagers tell of an adopted son who volunteered to serve as hangman on behalf of the Turkish authorities in the execution of his own father when no Greek would volunteer for the hateful task – a cautionary tale of blood bonds and betrayal that unambiguously draws the symbolic parallel between national and familial identities. The essentialism of the blood metaphor is not an invention of the nation-state, but a familial ideology that the state exploits and expands. Adopted children would not normally share in the casting of lots, and any property they inherited from their adoptive parents must be "written" upon them as "gifts" by an act of law. The position of adopted children thus confirms, as a limiting case, the mutual – and uncompromisingly essentialist – association of blood, fate, and territory. That those who do not share in the blood are also excluded from the inheritance of character is an extremely ancient notion (Onians 1951: 121). Fate, in the same system of ideas, is external to the body. It is thus a fitting object for blame, especially as its very immunity from resistance allows the individual to lose any number of battles without losing self-respect. What better metaphor could serve the citizen caught between the demands of dignity and those of the tax office?

The Image of Writing

Writing occupies a pivotal position in this symbolic constellation. The symbol as well as the instrument of all bureaucratic power, it is above all the key to the reification of personal identity. Rather than being asked for a personal name as such, one is just as likely to be asked – especially in formal contexts – *pos ghrafese* ("how are you written?"). Writing, too, is the instrument of fate's irrevocable decrees (see Politis 1874: 218–219).

As I have just noted, "writing" property "on someone" is the expression used to indicate a legal act of transfer that conflicts with the writ of fate revealed in the customary division of property by lot. It turns over to the state, an intrusive agent in local life (see also Gavrielides 1976: 268), the responsibilities that "normal" parents properly assign to fate. It is clear not only that parents who invoke the law allow the state to invade important intimacies of social life, but that they also, in the process, transfer to the state the symbolic and moral attributes of the writ of destiny. Such a redirection of property transmission has important consequences for the state's ability to bureaucratize local social relations. Whether this also entails rationalization is altogether another question. The evidence gathered here suggests that an ideological continuum conjoins the respective operations of fate and the bureaucracy.

The image of a writing fate is pervasive. As one Glendiot remarked, there is a "huge pencil" (*moliva*) that records every false step a citizen makes and restricts the ambitions of all but the politically best connected – a sinister echo of the old "filing system" (*fakellosi*), by means of which the junta and its predecessors maintained surveillance of all potential dissidents. The imagery shows up everywhere, an excuse so conventionalized as to be almost unnoticeable. A Glendiot man losing at cards – a public if minor humiliation – anticipates his final defeat by remarking, "It wasn't written that I should win." He does not stop playing at this point, however, and if his luck should change he can always revise his reading of it. Meanwhile, his behavior is anything but fatalistic or resigned. While socially anticipating the need to explain away his defeat, he is cosmologically manipulating fate itself – fate is willful and will do exactly the opposite of what one expects.[5] In the very act of confronting fate, Glendiots are hardly fatalistic. On the contrary, they try to influence the course of events at every turn.

Fate is a rich source of imagery. In addition to writing out people's fortunes, fate lights a lamp that determines the length of each person's lifetime but provides no justification for its decisions; never reveals anything of its intentions; and may give every appearance of benevolence exactly at the moment when it has decided upon an evil end. Fate is thus arbitrary, secretive, and devious – all, especially the first, stereotypical characteristics of bureaucrats.

From the foregoing, it will be evident that the symbolism of fate pervades the perception, and perhaps also the actual practices, of the national bureaucracy in Greece. It is further developed in the idea of the paternalistic bureaucrat who "shares out" (*mirazi*, cognate with *mira*, "fate") favors, as in that of the "Great Powers'" alleged designs to "share out" (*mirazoun*) among themselves the control of the entire world – the largest projection of this essentialist and paternalistic metaphor. Both bribery (*dhorodhokia*, "gift-

---

5. See also Balshem 1991: 162. Glendiots, when asked how they are, usually reply, "Let's say 'well'" (*as ta leme(ne) kala*), an apparently apotropaic formula intended to deflect the evil eye or some other active embodiment of envy. In both Pefko and Glendi, there is a general reluctance to admit to good fortune, either present or prospective; pessimistic predictions, far from being fatalistic, are thought to improve one's chances. Rhetorically, too, Glendiots play on the delicate balance among the ironic, the strategic, and the apotropaic when they assure their cardplaying opponents that the latter will defeat them. Fatalistic rhetoric may mean the very opposite attitude in social pragmatics. The retrospective character of ritualistic attitudes, as a means of reordering the world after disaster has struck, is emphasized by Tambiah (1968: 201) in his discussion of Trobriand witchcraft.

giving") and betrayal (*prodhosia*, "giving away") are denoted by etymological cognates of *dhoro*, "gift." They thus recall the category of property transfer that draws in state power to subvert the "natural" order of parent-child relationships – the order whereby family territory is handed down from generation to generation along with inherited "natural character" (*fisiko*). In a land where the etymological imagination has been enhanced by the intense politicization of language, people recognize links of this sort, and through them acknowledge the suitability or inaptness of the ways in which others explain away that happens to them. Bribery and betrayal are both diversions of what rightly belongs to "us." Giving "gifts" – "giving it all away" might be an appropriately tart translation here – is the familial sin of favoring outsiders, or *kseni*.

How can we square this deprecation of the gift with the high value that Greeks place on hospitality, both officially and privately? This is a question of context. The lavish treatment of a visitor makes no permanent concessions, and may even enforce a kind of symbolic dependency on the visitor (see Chapter Six). It therefore offends no sensibilities about the preservation of what – to emphasize the congruence of familial metaphors with the interests of the state – I shall here call the patrimony. Hospitality is as much a defense of the insiders' collective good name as it is an act of consideration for the wayfarer. Very different indeed is the action of the "giver" (*dhotis*), the semiprofessional traitor who helps marauding shepherds from other communities locate his covillagers' unguarded sheep. A "gift" in this sense is a reverse theft, a conspiracy with outsiders to hurt those who share the perpetrator's "blood" and "fate."

What unites these meanings of "gift" is that they mark a relationship with outsiders; the moral evaluation of the act itself then depends on the effect it has on insiders. On the whole, the more powerful the source, the greater the suspicion of self-interest against some common good. Thus, the senior bureaucrat "shares favors" (*mirazi rousfetia*) in the same way that "fate distributes" (*i mira mirazi*), the latter phrase showing beyond doubt that Greeks play on the close etymological link between the respective terms for "fate" and "division" or "distribution." Any act of "gift-giving" that diverts resources away from the actor's own group, ranging from maldistribution of the parental property to the betrayal of the national patrimony, destroys the moral basis of trust. The bureaucrat who takes a bribe and the government that allows the enemy to attack the national interest are similarly guilty of betraying a collective mandate.

In the aftermath of the Turkish invasion of Cyprus in 1974, both NATO in general and the United States in particular were held by many Greeks to be guilty of *prodhosia* ("treason, giving away"). This is quite explicitly a familial metaphor, much more obviously so than is the English "betrayal." The United States is a father who makes an unequal distribution of his property between two quarrelsome sons. The right wing insists that this intra-NATO squabble is a "family affair" (*To Vima*, 4 April 1977, p. 16), while the center and right object to paternalism (for example, *To Vima*, 15 August 1976, p. 1). Yalta represents another "division" of the world by fate-like "Great Powers." Moreover, any and all setbacks to Greece's territorial growth, from nineteenth-century irredentism (Vivilakis 1866) to current desires for *enosi* (union) with Cyprus, are explained as "written into the program." Like a gigantic bureaucracy, the "Great Power" machine "writes" the fate of the small nations whose interests it has been supposed to hold in trust. The evocative force of familial metaphors is nowhere clearer than in these images of the usurpation of fate's writing hand.

The Letter and the Spirit: Civic Attitudes

In the modern state, the ubiquity of bureaucratic regulation reinforces the sense of its omnipotence. Above all, bureaucracy resembles fate in that both are seen as implacable, immovable forces. One can supplicate both for mercy and for special favors, but failure in each case seems – after the fact – to be an entirely predictable outcome. In the case of bureaucracy, this view is rooted in direct experience. Conventional wisdom holds that the only people who possess the power to alter the system are those whose vested interests are best served by perpetuating it (see *To Vima*, 7 July 1976, p. 2); this is the exact social counterpart to the cosmological model of fate. This impression is strongly reinforced by the bureaucrats' persistent refusal to take the slightest initiative or risk. It also presumably owes much to the prevalence of an idiom of political relations in which patrons constantly put on displays of haughty caprice to remind clients of their power to withhold favors (see Campbell 1964: 260–261; Argyriades 1968).

In general, patrons are more educated than their clients, and control the appurtenances, symbolic and practical, of "writing." This allows them to justify every dismissal of a case on legalistic grounds. They punctiliously insist on the letter of the law, arrogating to themselves the right to interpret its spirit. A rhetoric of precision may mask manipulative tactics. A widow remarried and reported to the local police station to have her identity card altered accordingly. She took with her a copy of her marriage certificate:

> The relevant inspector told me that instead of the marriage certificate, I should have brought a certification issued by the Borough. I brought the Borough document; the relevant official did not approve it, because my husband's profession was written down as "Pensioned Dentist" and it should have said "Dentist on pension." I took him that too. . . . Three months have gone by, [and I] have still not been given a new identity card (*To Vima*, 7 July 1976, p. 2).

Without such a card, as I noted in Chapter Three, one has no official existence as a Greek citizen.

Associated with the insistence on correct documentation is the concept, already encountered, of *efthinofovia* ("fear of responsibility"), the stereotypical unwillingness to take any initiative in even the most marginally anomalous situations. *Efthinofovia* is supposedly endemic (*Akropolis*, 16 April 1976, p. 2; *To Vima*, 4 August 1976, p. 2; Tamiolakis 1976: 90–91); Dimou 1976: 45). It is cited as the reason for many of the delays and inefficiencies of the bureaucracy. This means, moreover, that it partakes in that whereof it speaks. One can point an accusing finger at the *efthinofovia* of any unhelpful bureaucrat, while the latter can bemoan the difficulty of getting superiors to act because of their unwillingness to expose themselves.

In one incident, a twenty-minute power outage disabled all the electrical equipment of an Athens hospital. The hospital possessed a generator, bought at considerable cost in anticipation of precisely such a scenario:

> The generator, however, was left to rot, as the bureaucratic procedures for determining who was responsible for its functioning had not been resolved. Truly, if "someone had died of disgust" [i.e., during the power outage], who would have been responsible? (*To Vima*, 5 August 1976, p. 2).

Perhaps the extreme of *efthinofovia* arises in conjunction with the verification of personal identity. This is no small problem in a country where "how I do know another person['s thoughts]?" is a common question, and where, as we have just noted, the identity card is treated as literally essential. An extreme case is the legal requirement in the semiautonomous Cretan state (1898–1913) that Muslim women, who were veiled, had to provide two witnesses – usually Muslim men – to attest that they were who they said they were. This example conflates the boundaries of gender, religion and "nationality," and person. Such exercises in tautology are still relatively common.

A male Greek studying abroad faces the same logic when he makes a request for the deferral of his compulsory military service:

> He must take a Borough certificate of identity verification to the Military Board. The Borough, in order to give him the certificate, requires him to go to the Civil Court or to a notary public and get a sworn affidavit to the effect that the person studying abroad is the same as the one who was born in such-and-such a place and is registered in the roster of male inhabitants of such-and-such a Borough (*Akropolis*, 10 November 1977, p. 2).

The newspaper commented that the need for such a complex procedure was debatable at best. After all, if parents presented false papers on behalf of their son, "it would be a straightforward case of false identity, which is indeed severely punishable by law. And we do not believe that there exist families that would expose their children to such a danger."

This is the rhetoric of humanity against bureaucracy, of ordinary common sense against small-minded official legalism. It made, and makes, good political capital. It is, however, only one side of the picture. The bureaucrats' union has consistently claimed that government employees have little choice but to apply the letter of the law with unwavering strictness, since they are themselves liable to sanctions from above in an unbroken stream of buck-passing that only ends with a fatelike "unknown manager" (*To Vima*, 7 July 1976, p. 2). Such arguments show how the logic of *efthinofovia* is available to bureaucrats and clients alike. The content of strict legalism is itself highly negotiable, subject only to confirmation after the fact.

The strategy on both sides is to reify bureaucracy as "the system." It thus becomes an impersonal force on which all manner of individual and collective misfortunes may be blamed. This happened, for example, when villagers, desperate to gain control of afforested land long before the tedious bureaucratic procedure had ground to its appointed end, set fire to the forest and then held "the bureaucracy" responsible for what had happened (Resvanis 1977: 7). Residents of the neighborhoods of a Cretan town whose homes have been scheduled for historic conservation sometimes become so desperate waiting for permits to rebuild that they take matters into their own hands and illegally demolish the houses, then blame the authorities as the real culprits – an ironic reversal, since these authorities are specifically charged with preserving the houses they are now accused of destroying (Herzfeld 1991). In a pattern common throughout Greece, villagers blame local squabbles – embarrassing proof that a community is not as harmonious as it claims to be – on the arbitrary application of land-tenure laws by local courts (du Boulay 1974: 269–270). This last example is particularly helpful, because it shows how external agency – in this instance the courts – can deflect moral opprobrium from a group defined literally or metaphorically by blood: the family, the village.

The *endoli*, or written directive, is inflexible by definition. It provides a plausible excuse for most instances of bureaucratic intransigence, and for most cases where reasonable complaints have elicited no response. The owner of a country house near Athens discovered that his telephone service had been cut off. When he complained, he was told that his bill had not been paid:

> So he thought that nothing could be more *natural* to put an end to the whole adventure by showing his paid *invoice*. . . . But this – supposedly – official document, the receipt with official stamp and signature attesting payment, was of no interest to the telephone company employee, who simply declared, "This is the *endoli* I received" – that is, to charge the hapless subscriber over again.

The latter was thus obliged to pay his bill twice, as well as a fine and a reconnection fee (*To Vima*, 5 August 1976, p. 2; my emphases). Note that the aggrieved customer appeals to law embedded in "natural" logic in this contest between successive pieces of documentation. He tries to play the state at its own game. The strategic content of such observations does not go wholly unobserved: "it's well known that public service offices function with directives that they regard as above the law" (T. Paraskevopoulos, letter in *To Vima*, 21 August 1976, p. 5).

These extracts from journalistic commentary make it very clear that such incidents are commonplace and formulaic. The explanation in terms of written directives works because it follows an established convention that also corresponds to common experience. It works because socially the bureaucrat and the client share the need to excuse themselves; the bureaucrat for failing to help and the client for failing to change the bureaucrat's mind. Of course, decisions can be reversed. In that case, the bureaucrat "discovers" that a new document has superseded the old, just as each new reversal in a person's fortunes prompts a new reading of the most "recent" writ of fate.

If the tactic of appealing to prior writ works because it is conventional, as Austin's thesis would lead us to expect, it should by now be equally clear that this conventionality arises from the constant repetition of actual experience. Getting involved in anything official is a risky business. Villagers express their understanding of bureaucracy in a subversive reading of religious history in which Jesus appears as the victim of officious bureaucrats:

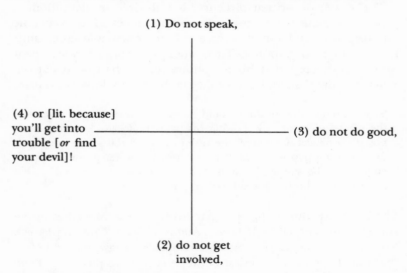

(1) Do not speak,

(4) or [lit. because] you'll get into trouble [*or* find your devil]!

(3) do not do good,

(2) do not get involved,

This figure is an encapsulated etiology. In a briefly explicated gesture, it provides current cynicism with a history – the ultimate history. Inasmuch as Greek men traditionally identified with Christ, their daily harassment by the bureaucracy appeared to be a personal and endlessly replayed Calvary.

Indeed, in this symbolism we also see how religion serves the rhetoric of nationalism (see also Dubisch 1988). The enemies of Christ are the unbelievers, whose modern descendants are the Turks and their traitorous servants. From the very beginning of Greek independence, Greek bureaucrats have had to contend with their reputed past as agents of Turkish oppression. Cretans regard the Athenian bureaucracy as the continuation of Turkish misgovernment, while, to this day, reporting certain types of offense to the authorities is regarded as "betrayal" (*prodhosia*) (Herzfeld 1985). It is certainly true that Greeks extensively staffed the Ottoman administration (Dakin 1973: 16–21), and some commentators (such as Bakoyannis 1970) have treated the present pattern of bureaucrat-client interaction as "nothing but a continuation of the landlord-serf relationship of Turkish times."

Such statements require careful evaluation. While virtually any official may behave with calculated rudeness to illiterate country folk (see, for example, Campbell 1964: 227–228, 241–242), junior bureaucrats often become cowed and unctuous in the presence of superiors. The description of the bureaucratic system as a continuation of Turkish attitudes and practices is a popular and not altogether unconvincing one in Greek political rhetoric, one that goes back to the earliest years of Greek statehood (Dakin 1973; Katsoulis 1975: 216; Kiriakidou-Nestoros 1975: 238). Employees can claim that they, too, are victims of the bureaucratic system (*To Vima*, 4 August 1976, p. 2). History, the Turks, even the hot climate (Paleologos 1976) are all blamed for the endemic evasion of bureaucratic responsibility. The grand etiology thus provides a structural model for daily practices: every excuse for inaction reproduces the arguments from religion and from history, and both are equally grounded in categorical distinctions between selves (as Christians, as Greeks, or as kin) and others (as infidels, as Turks, or as family foes).

From Antichrist to infidel Turk, and from Turk to state flunkey: these are the figures against which the modern Greek hero fights and suffers in defense of fatherland and family. Omnipotent state, petty functionaries, and harassed citizens all draw on the same cosmology, the same dualism of good and evil. The capacity to reduce time to an unchanging set of patterns is not confined to the state alone. On the contrary, it is part of the symbolic idiom that the state has taken from the timeless taxonomic order of the family and of "blood," and it appears subversively in the rhetoric of the heroic citizen defending the interests of the people (the "nation") against those of the bureaucracy (the "state").

This, then, is the logic of the "counterstrategizing" stereotype of the Greek we met in Chapter Three. While the state may punish the more obvious infractions of the law, it cannot intervene in the logic that allows the citizen to equate institutional disobedience with moral patriotism – to say, for example, that the rapacity of tax officials or merchants justifies acts of theft. To deny that logic outright would undercut its application at more encompassing levels – for example, in official criticism of "the West" for its failure to come to the country's rescue against the Turkish threat. The popular roots of official discourse allow citizens and officials to speak, in some encompassing sense, the same language.

This means, however, that the state is hostage to popular cosmology. Not only does it speak the same language, moreover, but we can now see that appeals to the ideal of rational government, in Greece no less than elsewhere, are rhetorical devices, designed to deflect attention away from so embarrassing a dependence of the "rational" upon the "symbolic."

But are not ordinary people's rationalizations an entirely different matter, some may object, from the discourse of the state itself? Such a separation, which is vital to the Cartesian logic of nation-statism, begs the question we ought to the asking. It also overlooks the fact that bureaucratic staffs, while often drawn from a relatively well educated elite, do nonetheless consist of citizens who participate in the same self-exonerating tactics as their clients.

Moreover, any argument that suggested that the state could act independently of its staff would be teleological. As such, it would reproduce the idealized logic of the state itself, the ideology of nation-statism, as well as the self-exonerating alibi of its citizens. Big Brother (a suggestively familial name!) thus gets to eat his cake and have it, too: the citizenry is obedient even when it blames the state for its ills, and resigns itself – fatalistically – to the state's control. Gellner (1988: 234) appears to accept this self-serving argument when he writes that "a liberal modern state may interfere in the lives of its citizens far more than a traditional pre-industrial despotism. The complexity and interdependence of society, and its dependence on an overall infrastructure, makes its members docile and habituated to obedience to bureaucratic instructions." Such statements are baldly teleological. "Complexity," for example, has no coercive power on its own, although it can be invested with such power by the persuasive symbolism of state pronouncements. State functionaries may be able to elicit the sort of docility that Gellner describes. Blaming the state ("the system") is the ethical alibi that enables its own functionaries to function.

The French Connection

Because the Greek bureaucratic system derives so heavily from "Western" models, and because nevertheless its apparent failures are almost always blamed on "Oriental" features in its actual operation, it would seem only fair to turn for a few moments to the heirs to that Revolution that inspired the Greeks to turn westward for emancipation. It will become apparent that the Greeks did not damage some perfect instrument, although their uncomfortable dual role as originators and passive recipients of the Western ideal might lead the careless reader to interpret my examples in that way. What follows should set the record straight.

State teleology is embedded in practices not so very different from those of nonbureaucratic social actors. Both agree on the fate-like characteristics of official power, and both derive it from the tautologous quality of all comprehensive official classifications. This symbolism is not unique to Greece. The fear of a powerful, centralized bureaucracy is also highly developed in France, perhaps the major center for the dissemination of Enlightenment theories of political life. There, too, it produces charges of fatalism. For an illustration, I turn to Françoise Zonabend's excellent ethnography of a community forced to deal with the presence of a nuclear power station. She freely uses the term "fatalism" for what would more accurately be described as self-exoneration. Her choice of term, although distracting because of its resemblance to official discourse, cannot obscure her remarkably penetrating insight into civilian reactions to an insensitive bureaucracy.

The issue centers on local resistance to the establishment of the nuclear power station in their midst. The local citizens' apparent fatalism turns out to be submission after the fact, when all available channels have apparently been exhausted, to the central

authorities' apparently foreordained decision to proceed (Zonabend 1989: 52–53). Perhaps, in point of faĉt, they could have
resisted. Some of them certainly wanted to do so. When the site
inspection nominally gave them an opportunity to object, however, they feared that voicing their opposition would only have
earned them the enmity of dangerously powerful officials without
necessarily halting construction of the power station. While it was
difficult for them to admit to such feelings of intimidation, they
could restate them as recognition of the inevitable – the so-called
"fatalism" of their response. The visiting officials' behavior does
not seem to have encouraged much hope, and is therefore a
striking example of how the functionaries of state create the very
barriers to effective communication that permit the creation of
a *fait accompli*: encountering only a guarded silence, the officials
could now say that the locals had surrendered any right to second
thoughts. At the risk of hyperbole, one might recall the horrible
racial tautologies constructed by the Auschwitz camp commandant.

Zonabend tells a fascinating story of local legends that provided the language and imagery of the inhabitants' explanation
of what had happened to them. Like tales about fate in Greece,
these folktales allow the locals some degree of self-respect in the
aftermath of their surrender to authority. As in Greece also, weather
becomes an explanation of motives. Townspeople who had once
praised the local climate now cited it as reason for leaving
(Zonabend 1989: 72–73). This is not fatalism. On the contrary,
it exhibits a good deal of care in the managing of social relations,
specifically as a means of avoiding the appearance of cowardly
desertion: "Normans don't behave like that!" This is the sort of
segmentary pride that becomes patriotism at the most inclusive
level. Here, however, it is an attitude that those who might have
an interest in doing so can use to exclude a local population, by
dismissing it as fatalistic and therefore irrational.

This appeal to a stereotype of Norman behavior is extremely
revealing. It illustrates the common invocation of essentialized
characteristics, of course, but it also shows that such arguments
are probably the only unanswerable defense – at least in Austinian
terms – against being called a coward. Such matters are also,
concurrently, questions of masculinity, and Zonabend's analysis
shows that the men who work in the town are very concerned
about the effects of prolonged exposure to nuclear emissions on

their sexual prowess. Indeed, she gives an extended discussion of the ways in which masculine symbols figure into the rhetoric of local resistance and disaffection (Zonabend 1989: 152–153). As we consider Cohn's discussion of American "defense intellectuals" and their male family of weapons, it becomes impossible to dismiss such devices as the "mere" symbolism of the unscientific and the rustic.

Gender symbolism also shows how inappropriate the label of "fatalism" is. Zonabend (1989: 150–152) argues that people actually court risk, and that their desire to do so is a reaction to the monotony of the bureaucratic regulation of life that prevails in this carefully controlled community. Security appears as an essentially female quality, the style of the kitchen and the laundry room. Deliberate risk taking is hardly the basis of fatalism. On the contrary, it entails confronting the possibility of disaster in the hope of achieving some more immediate social advantage: prestige, admiration, a reputation for virility. Given the brooding preoccupation with their sexual wholeness that Zonabend reports for the men of this community, moreover, it would appear to represent the continuing – and active – search for evidence that disaster has not struck, and that the procreation of those brave Normans who don't run away will continue forever.

For it is clear that we cannot separate the concern with masculinity from the pride in place and descent. These are two closely interwoven aspects of popular essentialism. It is the reaction of a marginalized local population to the interference of the centralized state, and its terms are an attempt to wrest the symbolic initiative from the intruders. Such brave gestures may not achieve much of an effect on events, but they do belong to an idiom that the locals share with the state. Indeed, the state, being more powerful than individuals, can mock their objections as fatalistic while using exactly the same symbolic argument to enforce its own perspective.

Sometimes this happens as a result of the secrecy with which state and citizen confront each other. The men express fear of the nuclear pollution of their sexuality. They couch this fear in terms that recognizably reproduce the older rhetoric of sexual pollution among men who worked in the local tanning industry. Because pollution is thought to be contagious, they dare not mention their fears to anyone in authority. In the same way that political patrons prey upon clients' local values to gain advantage in the larger political arena (see Campbell 1964), the authorities here capitalize on the conspiracy of silence that results from local fears of sexual contamination. They are able to proceed with their development of nuclear power as though the very source of the pollution – nuclear power – were of no local concern because local values made it very difficult for people to discuss it.

I would like to close this part of the discussion with a highly revealing anecdote. It was written down for me by a French anthropologist who had come to the United States for her graduate training. It illustrates the complicity of citizens and bureaucrats in a system in which, however, the latter hold the keys to success. The author of this account was eventually able to get what she wanted, not because she outwitted the system or went along with the formal procedures, but because she played by its unofficial rules – rules that, being French, she knew well. I give the text in full translation:

In 1970, three years after our departure from France, I was passing through Paris, when my passport was stolen along with all the luggage I had left in the car overnight. I first went to register a complaint at the neighborhood police station, thinking that it would be easy to get a new passport in view of my French citizenship (*nationalité*). There, they looked at me as if I'd come from outer space, for, despite my protestations, I didn't give off a particularly French air (I had already acquired a way of dressing and certain other external signs of the culture of young Americans, and my French was a bit slow). What was more, what French person worthy of the name would have had the stupidity to leave valuable objects in a car at night in Paris? My childhood, spent in a small village in central France, had not prepared me for this kind of thing.

I was informed that I would have to return to Touraine [*sic*], the place where the passport had been originally issued, in order to get a new one. This was of course quite annoying because my former husband and I were expected somewhere else.

When I got back to Tours, the girl clerks at the prefecture heard out my story with patience but without sympathy, and announced to me that I no longer existed. They couldn't find any trace of my identity and suggested that I should go and make inquiries at Loches because that was where my passport should have been issued in the first place. We had retraced the bureaucratic stream to its source, and by chance there was a young woman of my age waiting there, calm, intelligent, and sympathetic, for the two of us came from neighboring villages. She pondered and then said, "I'd think that they have classified your family in the aliens' bureau because you have left France." She telephoned to Tours and her theory was confirmed. I was no longer anything more than a foreigner on my beloved home ground, and more than a bit depressed [as a result].

In Tours, they told me, "Very well, then, but you will have to live in France for a minimum of three months before you can be given a new passport." I was at my wits' end, on the verge of tears, but still I tried to control myself: a Brissonnet does not make a spectacle of herself!

I was asked for an address, which I gave. "I'm visiting my aunt at Montlouis, Madame."

"The wife of the mayor who recently died, Monsieur Raoul R.?"

"That's right."

"Aha! But why didn't you tell us sooner? That changes everything!"

The next day, I had my passport. Not only was my uncle quite well known locally, but the girls who worked at the prefecture also knew my cousin well, his daughter Chantale.

Thus it was that I lost and regained within a few days the most precious thing that a French person can have: French *nationalité.*

That defiant ending – "a Brissonnet does not allow herself . . . " – is the socially minimal version of proud gestures that could be made in defense of regional pride – "Normans don't behave like that!" (Zonabend 1989: 97) – or national patriotism. Moreover, it brings the two levels of pride together, and sets the patriot against the state: the same device the Greeks use and that bureaucrats themselves sometimes employ.

A Serious Objection?

This chapter has largely dealt with the ways in which people conceptualize bureaucracy. A literalist might object that this has nothing to do with the operation of the bureaucracy itself. Are these not just the rhetorical tactics, such a critic would ask, means by which people justify their failures to deal successfully with the consequences of their own illegalities? I have already mentioned this possible objection, but now we are in a position to address it more comprehensively.

Without a doubt, self-justification is the most common motive for all the talk about a fate-like bureaucracy. We should note first of all, however, that such devices signal a very considered calculation of costs and benefits of the risks to what Bourdieu (1977) has called a person's symbolic capital. Any social actor must know that the conventionality of self-justification has two apparently irreconcilable consequences: either the story is "an old one," and so will not be believed; or, in subtle ways, it builds on the conventions of self-justification without rubbing the audience's noses in its conventionality, in which case it is socially acceptable and people can afford to respond as though they believed it.

In Greece, where Bavarian lawmakers oversaw the writing of national laws, questions of inheritance were made subject to national law only if no local, "unwritten" law could be found. This principle appeared to some to conflict with Roman law, a source of the Napoleonic Code on which the new Greek laws were partly based. The Greeks and their Bavarian advisers dealt with this in a manner that clearly shows the stamp of a shared cosmology. Claiming that "unwritten" law could often be shown to antedate codified legislation, they argued, citing the German jurist C.F. Glück, that the written-unwritten distinction was not to be taken literally, but meant instead the difference between laws promulgated – whether in writing or not – by the deliberate pronouncement of a lawmaker and those that had been passively accepted (Khrisanthopoulos 1853; see also Glück 1803).

On the basis of this argument, they could then propose that the "unwritten laws" be systematically written down, so that custom would enter the code and, converted thus into written form, would henceforward supersede any regulations with which it conflicted because the only remaining criterion was that of temporal priority. In practice, this meant that responsibility for local practice in matters relating to inheritance and property ownership – in other words, the territorial expression of social relations – lay with local custom, which appealed explicitly to fate by sanctioning the casting of lots as the most impartial instrument of distribution. Judges were to acknowledge customary law in making decisions. They could not assume that priority on the basis of personal knowledge alone, however, but were required to prove the existence (*sic*) and validity of the alleged customary law.[6] In short, the law would not

---

6. To do so meant demonstrating precedent; but since the lawmakers could reach no agreement as to how many previous decisions constituted adequate precedent, they eventually left it at "more than two" or "many times" (Khrisanthopoulos 1853).

even take responsibility for itself: wherever possible, it tried to pass that responsibility back to a generalized, antecedent body of "custom," now codified in order to prevent further erosions of a retrospectively discovered, truly national destiny, the ultimate authority and arbiter.

This resolution, if such it can be termed, left little to the judges' imagination. They could not decide independently, or on the basis of their personal experience, what constituted a "custom." The precedence of the unwritten over the written actually ceded power to another kind of writing, that of the fate that determined events through the casting of lots, while the requirement that such customs be codified allowed the state to participate in the symbolic act of writing after the fact. In case of doubt about the priority of customary law, the legislators took refuge in a nationalistic alibi: "Roman law . . . . which we took on as our legal system, is foreign to us, in that it does not spring from the very guts of the people; and since for this reason our social needs are not fulfilled, the priority of the customs among us is constituted as inevitable" (Khrisanthopoulos 1853).

The view that "Roman" – and therefore "Byzantine" – culture is a foreign importation played an important part in justifying the search for more ancient, Classical sources of folklore. Here it allows the lawgivers of the nascent nation-state the luxury of creating an idealized time before time, a declared past that could not rise up to contradict its modern interpreters, and that would let them off the hook of deciding locally difficult cases of inheritance. *Efthinofovia* is built into the very fabric of the law: there is an invisible writ that supersedes the writing of each and every judge.

Thus, importation of a "Western" legal code not only failed to displace customary law; it reinforced its validity with a further symbolic act of writing of its own. The "guts of the people" are still the best guide, although the cadre of lawmakers must give its stamp of approval. The cosmological still lurks behind the rhetoric of a humanized rationality, and it does so in systems far less obviously dependent on local symbolism than the Greek: "Today, criminal justice functions and *justifies itself* by this perpetual reference to *something other than itself*, by this unceasing reinscription in nonjudicial systems. Its *fate* is to be redefined by knowledge" (Foucault 1978: 22; my emphases). It would seem that the buck stops nowhere.

Foucault was especially concerned with the creation of knowledge as a means of removing the responsibility for inflicting violence further and further from the authorities. The shift away from direct punishment, in which the authorities visibly took upon themselves the responsibility or blame for a further act of torture or killing, has yielded, as Foucault reminds us, to an ever increasing preoccupation with the care and cure of the "soul" – a progressive disembodiment of the objects of rational government. Arguments about the appropriateness of punitive measures center on the disembodying and ultimately statistical criteria of "cruel and unusual punishment." The state itself becomes a massive machine for the evasion of responsibility, while arguing that people should "pay" for their crimes. It is not a very far cry from eugenics to judicial murder, from the eradication of bad blood to the removal – made acceptable by being supposedly painless – of bad souls. It is especially disturbing that all this should take place in the name of reason. That it is able to do so owes much to the state's built-in capacity to evade blame and to cast it upon a conveniently inchoate cosmology. In the case of Greece, the fact that legalism and referentiality were relatively late arrivals on the scene (Tsoucalas 1991) throws into sharp relief the contours of the cosmology that they claimed to supersede, and from which, in a very general way, they had themselves arisen.

We thus see that historically the bureaucratic framework of modern nation-state ideologies rests on very similar conceptual structures of self-exoneration to those used by ordinary citizens. It is obviously to the state's advantage to deny that embarrassing common derivation, just as it is to its advantage to insist on the conceptual separation of the rational and the symbolic – which amounts to exactly the same kind of defense.

To those who may now object that it is absurd to speak of "the state" in such a totalizing fashion, I would now also respond that they are absolutely right. There is no such thing as an autonomous state except in the hands of those who create and execute its ostensibly self-supporting teleology. Laws, whatever their claims to rest on eternal values, have specific histories of use and interpretation. If they seem to institutionalize the evasion of responsibility in the name of responsibility itself, this is all of a piece with the larger abolition of temporality in the name of "national history." To recover accountability, we should not simply revert to the

Weberian ideal type of the legal-rational bureaucratic state. We should instead ask who makes each decision on the basis of "the law." Restoring time and individuality to our analyses – the recognition of human agency – is the only viable defense against the reification of bureaucratic authority.

CHAPTER SIX

Declassifications

Cosmology and Classification

The euphemism "classified information" shows, perhaps more clearly than any other, the intimate links between taxonomy and bureaucratic control. It is characteristic of bureaucratic obstructionism in any society that secrecy is represented as knowledge: hence censorship as "classification." This may stand as an allegory of what can happen between the best intentions of democratic planners and the worst consequences of bureaucratic practice. Not all self-styled democracies are benign even in design, while not all the functionaries of even the most repressive state are necessarily evil; but the disjunction that occurs between ideology and practice calls for explanation – pragmatically by social actors trying to make sense ("theodicy") of their predicament, theoretically by social scientists. In this concluding chapter, I shall try to "declassify" some of the concealed processes in question.

In the preceding chapters, we have seen how the taxonomic system of a nation-state may derive, at least in part, from the same cosmology as the values of its citizens. That common set of symbols has acquired widely divergent meanings in the respective domains of official discourse and social life, and thus provides a context for the battle of systematic misunderstandings. On the one side stand the active, rational bearers of power, whose authority appears to be a self-fulfilling prophecy inasmuch as, on the other side, passive fatalists supposedly wait to be led (but perhaps think rebellious thoughts and remain unimpressed by the authorities' opinion of them).

In fact, as we have seen, this dichotomy is far too simplistic.

While bureaucrats rarely become the helpless cogs in the administrative machine that Weber foresaw in his gloomier moments, they are subject to very diffuse ramifications of power. There is a dichotomy. It does not lie in the actuality of two groups, bureaucrats serving the system and citizens oppressed by it. It lies in the play of rhetoric in which these two figures are counterposed to each other. These paired stereotypes are the key terms of a secular theodicy – the explanation of the besetting inefficiency that Marx thought was typical of bureaucracy as well as of the "iron cage" that Weber saw closing in on the modern world. Bureaucrats are often neither inefficient nor inflexible. Rather, when they do succumb to either of these characteristics, they can take absolution from personal responsibility in the conventions that treat these as marking "the system" rather than individual actors.

To the extent that citizens play along with these stereotypes in order to explain away their own failures, they are complicit in their own oppression; but enough bureaucrats can usually be found to take advantage of such expectations, and to translate them into the vindication of prophecy, that most citizens' capacity to work free of bureaucratic snares can be severely circumscribed. Weber's image of the bureaucrat has not been a universally accepted one, and its usefulness as a tool of analysis may in some respects be secondary to its faithfulness to conventional representations of bureaucracy, in the same way that his account of predestination and the will to labor seems to match the actual cosmologies of Middle Eastern villagers and the clients of patronage-peddling bureaucrats the world over. This, however, does not mean that Weber was wrong. It means that he failed to see how far, and in what respects, his models of non-Western cultural worlds resembled the condition of modernity in the "West."

In this book, I have challenged explanations of bureaucratic indifference as the more or less automatic outcome of bureaucratic structures. Such arguments, being hopelessly teleological, are far too close to the predestinations advocated by some of the more totalitarian forms of nationalism. If social boundaries emerge in social interaction, where they are constantly negotiated and redefined, blaming "the system" is implicitly to accept the argument of those who defend their territories, and who excuse their less laudable actions on the grounds that these were dictated by the system or by its supreme officials. We would do well to remember that this was the defense argument at Nuremberg.

In the crudest terms, we could say that the discussion has been about negotiating the price of admission to the polity. To be different ("my case is special") or to be confronted with indifference ("you're just like the rest of them"): that is the question. This discrimination becomes especially exigent when the question is directly one of heritage, of belonging, when admission means access to the rights and privileges of one's own identity.

At the nationalistic level, bureaucratic intransigence can simply be the means of asserting an ethnic right. The story of archeological conservation is fraught with such resistances to well-meant foreign interventions (Kardulias n.d.; Silberman 1990). The outsider is always to blame for loss and destruction because it is inconceivable that local people would contribute to the erasure of their own glories. When local people defy the state, however, they may blame "their own" bureaucrats for the same process. This is what has been happening on Crete, where official conservation of Renaissance and Turkish houses conflicts with the inhabitants' desire for "Western" amenities. Forced (as they say) to demolish the old buildings in the dead of night because of what they represent as the thoughtless delaying tactics of the bureaucracy, they hold the conservation service itself to blame for the disappearance of the historic fabric, and even blame larger entities such as the European Community and NATO for the ever-tightening bureaucratic grip on their homes (Herzfeld 1991).

Sometimes the metaphor of a price of admission takes on a literal significance. Much bureaucracy is concerned with petty financial accounting. This may come into especially revealing focus when the historic national heritage is at stake. Here, in the hands of minor officials, the forms of discrimination may assume quite explicitly "racial" terms. In Greece, a few years ago, foreigners were suddenly asked to pay admission fees to museums and archaeological sites, whereas Greeks could enter free of charge. Although the intention behind this measure was to encourage Greeks to learn more about the antiquities of their own land, it was often interpreted by site guards as a question of blood: if you spoke Greek well enough to be thought to be of Greek ancestry, admission was still free in practice. Greek critics were quick to voice their disapproval of such acts of discrimination, but there was no effective official attempt at reform – on the basis, if the usual logic was applied, that the government could not be expected to take responsibility for the misdeeds of ignorant museum and site guards.

More often, admission to the polity is based on less obvious marks of belonging and strangeness. The issue is not what people say but how they say it. A Cartesian logic, for example, is not necessarily a superior mode of arguing about licenses and post office facilities, but in some countries and in some situations it apparently works as a claim to a certain kind of identity: Western, rational, and in control. As Johnstone (1989: 145) argues with respect to the American mode that she calls "quasilogical," the goal "is to *convince*, to make it seem impossible for an audience using its powers of rationality not to accept the arguer's conclusion." Since this tactic clearly turns on the skilled use of a certain rhetorical style, it has no necessary connection with incontrovertible logic at all. The force of such devices lies not in the arguments themselves, but in the contempt implied for any alternative and the kind of identity that they implicitly project.

This argument, however, contains a trap of its own. In its extreme form, it becomes the kind of cultural determinism that Johnstone (1989: 153) herself explicitly rejects, and that is the basis of all stereotypes of "national character." Such cultural pleading, as Tambiah (1990: 128) has pointed out, can have devastating consequences; it is no less reductionist, and no less forgiving of excess, than the Nuremberg defense.

Even in more trivial situations, however, it has a certain dangerous appeal; irritated foreigners use it all the time to explain away their inability to communicate with local officials and to save their own self-respect. Moreover, such arguments are all the more pervasive because they are rarely made explicit. The American who went to receive her package from the Greek post office made the initial mistake of thinking that an interactional mode familiar to her from similar contexts at home would get results. An observer, however, might just as easily have thought that she was trying to impress the Greek clerk with her Western sophistication – in other words, that she was acting out a stereotype that she might have expected to be effective in a nominally pro-Western and politically dependent country.[1] We should not now compound the error by assuming that the only mode that works in "the West" is one that parades Cartesian forms of reasoning, or that the only argument a Greek understands is that of brute force. Of such

---

1. It is irrelevant to my point that the thought may never have crossed her mind.

misconceptions is prejudice made. It would be an extraordinarily opaque world in which we could not eventually learn the rhetorical strategies of cultural others; but it is sometimes hard to drop those strategies we stereotypically think are most appropriate to ourselves.

Equally characteristic of both modes of self-presentation is the exercise of power: power located in international relations, power located in gender, power located in immediate access to a possibly quite trivial resource. That, not logic, is what bureaucratic interaction is about. But power is a notoriously diffuse concept, as I have just remarked, and the reality of it takes many forms. It would like to suggest here that its most palpable embodiment in bureaucratic practice consists in yoking the timelessness of the state to the pace and timing of specific interactions. Let us see how that comes about.

Pace and Time

The replication of nationalistic ideology in bureaucratic daily ritual hinges on a characteristic that both share: the suppression of time. Much as national history – like myth – takes on the features of a timeless landscape, the effect of the daily interactions between bureaucrats and clients is also that of making time irrelevant.

This works in two closely cooperative ways. First, the sheer tedium of constantly having to "come back next week" deadens one's sense of the passage of time, especially in its repetitiousness. Second, the ability to demand this level of obedience expresses the bureaucrat's control over the client's time, making the latter unimportant by comparison: "Can't you see I'm very busy?"[2]

All this attrition of the client's patience and resources works to reinforce a sense of changelessness. Bureaucratic interaction truly resembles ritual, of which Buttitta and Miceli (1986: 135) write that "it has the effective capacity (and there is no religion that does not know it, no ideology that does not end up learning it) to impose the dimension of certainty, of necessity, and of absolute values on the contingent unpredictability of events" – in other words, to convert arbitrariness into necessity. In bureaucratic

2. This is an aspect of Bourdieu's concept of *tempo*. See also Goffman (1959: 67–70).

interaction, to be sure, "certainty" and "necessity" may relate to little beyond the personal power of a captious official, but they will nonetheless appear in the encounter as consequences of those "absolute values" to which bureaucrat and client supposedly both subscribe and that neither can openly abjure.

Government business allows – although it does not itself force – the bureaucrat to take over the client's time. The petty harassments and especially the often repeated advice to "come back tomorrow," the endless sets of more or less identical forms, the bureaucrat's professed inability to predict outcome and duration: all these elements, the components of indifference, conduce to the squelching of even a semblance of personal temporality. Although not necessarily invented for that purpose, they constitute, in the hands of manipulative officials, a technology for reproducing the state's monopoly of time. (The echo of Lévi-Strauss is deliberate here.)

In fact, time is a tangible presence in bureaucratic interactions. What bureaucrats do is to background their own management of this contestable commodity. The timing of their ploys – what Bourdieu (1977: 7) calls *tempo* – is a domain over which bureaucrat and client tussle for control. It is one of the dimensions in which bureaucratic interaction has much in common with hospitality, for in both the creation of a relationship of reciprocity carries implications of unequal power that can be further accentuated by skilled temporal manipulation.

Effective time management can convey, for example, the deliberately dispiriting impression that the bureaucrat is too busy with pressing and important business to engage with the humble client. In this encounter, the "Western" pose of officialdom presents a blandly indifferent face, behind which the persistent client may eventually hope to discover an "Oriental" who is willing to cut a deal. These cultural stereotypes should not fool us into accepting the notion that "Western time" is somehow radically different, more efficient, qualitatively more precise, or simply better – for this is pure self-deception, as Fabian (1983) has warned. A quarter of a century ago, Diamant (1966: 3) pointed out that it was by no means certain that the "West" still pursued the sort of goal-oriented maximization of time that one would associate with a Weberian work ethic, whereas it may be "the societies in rapid transformation who argue for speedup and for skipping stages." The stereotypes that animate bureaucrats' interpersonal poses are the key point of articulation between national ideologies and the actual conduct of business.

Bureaucrats often try not to engage with clients at all, and their method for achieving this pose of neutrality is largely to show absolutely no interest in the fact that the client's time is being wasted. Such determined refusals of temporality bring everyday administrative practice into alignment with the atemporality of nationalist historiography and the taxonomic systems that undergird it.[3] The taxa do not change, and it is up to the client – the dentist's widow, for example – to fit personal peculiarities (difference) to the indifference of this culturally constructed eternity. Whether the bureaucrat is amenable largely determines the outcome. The bureaucrat can disguise self-interest as service to the unchangeable public interest. The client has no such recourse, except by castigating the bureaucrat as "corrupt" – which is the symbolic converse of the bureaucrat's treatment of the client as "dirt." Client and bureaucrat alike use the rhetoric of purity and pollution to advance specific ends.

By appealing to the eternal truths of national character and political morality, some bureaucrats reproduce their atemporality in the little rituals of daily business. This is perhaps more likely in countries like Greece, where national identity has been forged in relatively recent times and on the often patronizing sufferance of larger or more powerful nations. Even British or American officials, however, will resort to stereotypes of "how we do things here." While each action has its specificity, rhetoric always seeks to assimilate it to a kind of generalized truth. The paraphernalia of bureaucracy provide some support for such personal tactics. Papers, rubber, stamps, stylized official signatures, insignia of state – each of these is an icon of an assumed original. They are the instruments of what Weber called "routinization," which they achieve by endlessly self-reproducing iconicity.

Forms are especially important here. Each document is a localized reenactment of an act of writing – the recording of law, which, as Goody (1986: 163–164) has pointed out, is intended to make it permanent. As every lawyer knows, reinterpretation of precedent may lead to a change in legal practice. Such appeals to

---

3. We may view this tactic as a real-life version of what Fabian (1983) calls "allochronism" – the use of narrative techniques to place the "other" in a time radically different from one's own.

precedent entail a retrospective extraction of "the" meaning, operating much like the fate-like hand of the Greek bureaucracy described in the preceding chapter. The concern with precedent, however, reveals the authorities' intense concern with creating a history that will ideally end by overwhelming itself – by, again, converting a temporal sequence into eternal fiat – and each act of bureaucratic officiousness draws on this underlying logic. The alternative is chaos. As Handelman (1978: 12) argues, "[t]his attribute of symbolic immutability ensures that bureaucracy will stand for the order of a complex division of labour, a particular system of ownership, and the rights of the state. On the other hand, again because of this symbolic immutability, the bureaucrat is highly vulnerable should sentiments of mass solidarity be turned against him" – in other words, when the bureaucrat is seen to be manipulating events and engaging with real time.

Certainly there is temporality in the interactions between bureaucrats and clients. Bureaucrats use delaying tactics to generate additional power; dissatisfied clients foreground these tactics in their complaints to gain the aura of noble victims. But these complaints are always presented as violations of the norm: they are part of the conventional grumbling about bureaucracy with which we started this exploration. Bureaucrats complain that their clients waste time with pointless fussing; clients, that the bureaucrats have no sense of responsibility to the public and cost them dearly in hours that would be better devoted to financially productive labor. Time is a crucial component in concepts of the person. By brusquely delaying action, a bureaucrat can deny the client's humanity, or, by delaying business with elaborate offers of hospitality in the form of coffee and cigarettes, can affirm, not only the client's humanity but a potential social bond – in which, however, the bureaucrat keeps the moral upper hand.

These examples show that time is a social weapon. Power can be generated by representing one's petty uses of time as aspects of the grand sweep of history. Indeed, this is a crucial point of linkage between everyday interactions and such grand visions of history as that implied by Weber's reading of the Calvinist doctrine of predestination. As I have suggested, the Protestant ethic and the supposed fatalism of Greek villagers, so utterly different when assessed by a self-congratulatory West, become remarkably similar when both are treated as social strategies. At that point, fate ceases to be an ineluctable cosmological force and instead becomes something that only the actions of the present can suggest: Greek villager and Weberian Calvinist alike must work hard to convince others that they are naturally and morally destined to succeed. This social basis of determinism surfaces even in the ever-despondent Gobineau. Arguably closer than any Mediterranean villager to the conventional image of the fatalist, he nonetheless maintained that claims to true masculine nobility could be validated by an individual's actual deeds (André 1987: 25). The logic of nation-statism pursues this logic still further by making "manifest destiny" a certainty based on collective identity and heritage (see, for example, Horsman 1981, on American Anglo-Saxonism). Exclusion from the national bounty then proceeds from the *a posteriori* assumption that certain individuals cannot have been of the national stock; inclusion in that stock proceeds, no less retrospectively, from a favorable assessment of one's deeds. This is the logic of Himmler's declaration that artistic or scholarly distinction was enough to identify a true German adult; only children had to be assessed predictively, by means of their physical characteristics (Poliakov, Delacampagne, and Girard 1976: 96–97). What seem to be the most unbreakably deterministic classifications may always be recast after the fact. Only thus, ironically, can their perfection be maintained.

The struggle over time concerns the legitimacy of claims to power and humanity. The reifying proclivities of officialdom mask interest-oriented practices; the client who wishes to challenge official claims to eternal truth must find a way of showing the inconsistency between state theory and bureaucratic practice. This, on a much larger scale, has been my goal in the present book. By following the "trailing clouds of etymology" back to their origins, I have not sought to legitimize present practices on the grounds of their antiquity, nor, conversely, have I made any claims to the effect that every bureaucrat is a self-aware tyrant whose sole desire is to reinstate ancient ideologies of fate, blood, and patriline. Any such notion would be patently absurd. On the contrary, as the phrase "trailing clouds of etymology" aptly suggests, I have pursued a far more evanescent phenomenon. Just as the person who makes an ordinary excuse may not consciously recall the historical origins of its form, and indeed usually does not, so also the clients and bureaucrats whose uneasy interactions I have discussed here are perhaps only dimly aware of couching their disputes in an idiom of enormous – if diffuse – antiquity. But the intangibility of these usages does not make them any less interesting or important. On the contrary, it would be a poor social discipline that could easily reject them as irrelevant because it did not have an easy means of measuring them, and that would consequently accept the bureaucratic imperative to stop probing and accept the dictates of the state. Whether as rebellious clients or as inquisitive anthropologists, we find that the timeless, unitary, and respectable identity common to nation-state ideologies conceals a plethora of inchoate but significant alternatives. Symbolism, we have seen, is highly labile, even when presented in the form of fixed bureaucratic categories. Thus, what has been used to conceal and repress may also, in a more disruptive temporal perspective, be used to disclose. Socially experienced time is the critical antidote to official history.

De Certeau's (1984: 36) suggestion that we may define respectability as a triumph of place over time has enormous relevance for understanding this tension between classification and temporality. Especially useful is his sense of "place" as the locus of intersection between person and value. We can get the most from it by invoking, one more time and in conjunction with de Certeau's reasoning, Douglas's perennially fertile notion of disorder as "matter out of place."

Clients occupy a certain symbolic space. When treated "like dirt," as we have noted, they are denied access to that moral topography, but – not being true fatalists – they usually go on trying to gain entrance. Claims based on common blood work best: they convert "naturally" into territorial claims. Failing that, metaphorical extensions of kinship latch onto the rhetorical strategies that European nation-state ideologies have adopted for gaining their citizens' loyalty. The national family is a spatial entity, eternal and timeless. Officials have the power to exclude individuals as outsiders: they are truly "out of place."

What then happens to them is a matter of indifference to those who have the good fortune (for such is the cosmology of luck) to find themselves already among the elect. In some of the most cynical scenarios, the supposedly liberal democracies of "the West" have repeatedly found this very argument amenable to the justification of immigration quotas in the face of genocide and political repression. Indifference to the fate of "others" becomes morally acceptable to those who would present themselves as the protectors of "our own" interests. At such times, we find hasty reclassifications, recastings of essentialist taxonomies, exposing the lability of "national identity" to a searchlight so penetrating that only the massive cohesiveness of nationalist rhetoric proves too thick for it to penetrate.

A devastating example of this is provided by Abella and Troper's (1982–83) study of Canadian reactions to Jewish refugee immigration before and during World War II. They show how the Liberal government of Mackenzie King, which did not want to admit to a callous attitude, allowed the civil servant F.C. Blair to translate his personal dislike of Jews into categorical acts of exclusion for which the government – which was more concerned with staying in power and preserving the Canadian federal structure intact than with humanitarian matters – did not have to take direct responsibility. Indeed, the government managed to sabotage the suggestion of appointing a Canadian as League of Nations High Commissioner for Refugees on the grounds that the Canadians had not yet done enough in that area to warrant getting involved at such a prominent level.

This was buck-passing of a rare order. What is more, the government's exclusionary policies reflected stereotypes that were held by particular officials and translated into official action; the rules allowed for the admission of rich farmers in preference to doctors and other professionals, for example, but rejected many applications from Jewish farmers on the grounds that the Jews did not and could not know how to farm! As Abella and Troper (1982–83: 54–55) indicate, there was a tragic irony in all this: Canada was in fact already overburdened with agriculturalists running inefficient and moribund farms. But the point at issue seems to be that since Canadians saw themselves as pioneers of the great open spaces, the most effective way of keeping it for themselves was by defining undesirable categories of others as incapable of adapting to the national environment.

Such cases can be multiplied many times over. A case in point is the U.S. distinction between political and economic refugees, the former being admissible where the latter were not (because they came from "friendly" states). It was acceptable to admit Cuban refugees even when they had a criminal record, but Haitians were another matter entirely. In Britain, the legislation defining "patrial" rights in terms of direct descent from residents has meant that many (mostly non-European) immigrants find themselves territorially excluded even when they hold British passports. In France,

right-wing ideologues actively resuscitate the arguments of Gobineau by claiming that Frenchness requires a confluence of blood,
culture, and education.

All these cases show that bureaucratic devices of exclusion only
acquire force and meaning when willing operators are in a position to seize on their possibilities. Action alone gives reality to the
potential for harm that existing cultural values bear. Without its
Blair on hand, the Canadian government might have faced its
responsibilities differently; it would have found it much harder to
deny them altogether. The converse also holds. In a rare example
of humanitarian action from within the Nazi bureaucracy, as late
as 1943, a certain Wilhelm Melchers managed to save a large
group of Turkish Jews from extinction. These Jews, with the
exception of only a handful of qualified professionals, had found
their citizenship revoked by the effectively pro-German Turkish
government, and were stranded in Vichy Paris. Melchers, a Foreign
Office official, played for time by manipulating his superiors' fears
of generating an international incident "until the Turkish government at last regained its conscience" and readmitted the entire
group (Browning 1980: 194). The interplay of high-ranking cynicism
at the Turkish government level and tactical skills from within the
virulently racist Nazi bureaucracy shows why "blaming the system"
– or indeed the Nuremberg plea of "orders from above" – cannot
provide adequate analytical models for understanding the social
production of categorical brutality and indifference.[4]

The vast majority of officials in modern nation-states do not
necessarily subscribe to the more extreme ideologies; or, if they
do, they know how to distinguish between their official mandate
and their personal feelings. Nevertheless, the available symbolism allows a good deal of play to personal agency; and this, in
turn, can lead as easily to exclusion as to acts of courage and

4. Browning (1980: 194–195) offers a further observation that is extremely
germane to my argument here: "Even before the Nazis came to power, the civil
service... [was] was strongly afflicted by both authoritarian and anti-Semitic in-
clinations, and the Nazi seizure of power intensified both of these characteristics.
Yet bureaucratic behavior cannot be understood simply by the standard alibi of
obedience to authority or the common accusation of pervasive anti-Semitism."
Thompson (1979: 50), in offering what will strike some as an outrageous link
between Nazi policies of genocide and the cultural intolerance implied by some
ways of enforcing zoning laws, nonetheless succeeds in suggesting the interdependence of taxonomy and agency in the genesis of intolerance.

compassion. Which attitudes come to prevail may reflect economic, social, political, religious, and cultural conditions, but these
should not be seen as overdetermining the outcome. Determinism
of this sort is precisely the strategy of state officials and the basis
on which they make fatalists of us all.

The discussion is clearly leading us toward the advantages of
those kinds of social theory that account for phenomena as the
products of action or agency. Before we address this central issue,
however, we should first turn to a specific area of social and symbolic play in which the manipulability of categories of belonging
and exclusion is especially clear: hospitality, the locus of moral
contests through the medium of affective exchange. Here, as we
shall see, the social actor interprets and manages the meanings
of ostensibly straightforward symbols. Inasmuch as the act of
hospitality entails treating one's guests like special kin, it is a fitting
model for our exploration of the symbolic and affective roots of
bureaucratic interaction.

Hosts and Guests

Both bureaucratic interaction and personal hospitality are deeply
concerned with defining lines of exclusion and belonging. This
revealing parallel lies at the heart of the question we asked at the
outset: how, in countries that pride themselves on the warmth they
proffer strangers, can officials turn out to be so indifferent? As
one reads account after account, it almost appears, paradoxically,
that these features are in direct rather than inverse proportion
to each other.

Imagine yourself set down, as Malinowski might have said, in
an office. The official you are visiting orders you a cup of coffee,
and plies you with compliments or questions. Or, in another
scenario, the bureaucrat keeps you standing, harangues you for
two hours and then tells you to come back the following week
with your paper in better shape. In either case, it is the bureaucrat who establishes the primacy of official space over personal
time. Your convenience is irrelevant. Your time is absorbed into
the bureaucrat's space. You may, of course, resist. If you can pace
the interview, you will thereby establish some degree of autonomy. If your ploy fails, however, the bureaucrat will announce that
time is short and you will be ushered out, with varying degrees

of ceremonious neutrality, of the space that has just rendered your calculated pacing mute and meaningless.

How strange, you will think, that such things can happen in a country where people actually do offer you coffee over a routine bank transaction or loan application; and where, even more strikingly, the most generous hospitality overflows from the poorest host. Here, however, it is important to understand what hospitality is. Certainly, it entails generosity; but that, as we know, as indeed Mauss (1967) taught us, and as every Greek villager will find occasion to remark, means that it also entails obligation – the basis of those "honorable" connections that bind patron to client and individual to kin group, and that form one of the many links between the symbolism of kinship and the practices of modern bureaucratic life.

This brings us back full circle to the point from which I began the argument of this book: symbols can carry what seem to be directly opposed sets of meanings. Just as an ideology of blood can carry messages of both egalitarianism and hierarchy (Greenwood); or, again, just as hierarchy and egalitarianism are equally capable of generating repressive effects (Kapferer); so, too, hospitality can simultaneously carry messages of incorporation and exclusion. Perhaps, after all, it is not so very strange that its incidence should show some convergence with that of indifference.

Hospitality provides the poor, the dependent, and the politically disadvantaged with unique opportunities for symbolizing the reversal of their plight. It allows them to invert their political dependence in the moral sphere (Herzfeld 1987b). While there is no reason to denigrate any individual act of hospitality or to devalue its sincerity, hospitality does, as a collectively perceived act, impose obligations of eventual reciprocity and the acknowledgment of moral indebtedness on the recipient. When I protested in Greek coffeehouses that the constant treating was placing me under too onerous a moral debt, I would be assured that this was quite all right: "One day we'll turn up in America!" Even though this did not seem very likely in many cases, the implication was clear: as the recipient of our largesse, you are now at a moral disadvantage, and we mean to keep you there – because that is probably the only way we can even temporarily reverse the political imbalance between us.

To foreign visitors, the most striking thing about the lavish hospitality they often encounter in Greek villages is the aspect of giving, a giving that makes it extremely difficult to reciprocate effectively. It is this giving that marks them off as strangers, as ambivalent friends who might well turn out to be dangerous enemies, much as the "gift" of land to a nonmember of one's own household marks that individual off as an outsider, as the bribe indicates the lack of trust on which favor-peddling is based, and as the traitor's act reinforces the identity of one's enemies. It is always the ambiguous insiders who are the real problem: hence the Australians' greater ambivalence toward Greeks ("dubious Westerners") than toward Turks ("exotic allies").

Gifts are offered to those with whom one has an ambiguous relationship. Bailey (1971: 24), following Mauss (1967), suggests that gifts are always capable of multiple interpretations: "The overgenerous gift, so big that it cannot be returned, becomes a humiliation. In short, it is not that some exchanges are competitive and others are co-operative; all exchanges have the seeds of both these opposed things within them." This is why there is always a certain amount of slippage between exchange and warfare. In social terms, those with whom one fights may also be those into whose families one marries (Leach 1965; see also Campbell 1964: 146).

Affines and spiritual kin, those whose distinguishing relationship to a given social actor does not constitute full kinship, are the unstable sources of power in the competitive world beyond the household. On Crete, one raids some shepherds' flocks in the hope of forcing them into an alliance based on spiritual kinship, while local politicians develop the same relationship with the shepherds on the basis of exchanging votes for protection from the law. Neither basis establishes absolute trust. Rather, the two kinds of situation both provide a formal framework for a use of power that contradicts that of the state, although, in the case of the politicians and their client lawyers, it works through the medium of the state system.

Now let us return to the argument about indifference. It has been my contention, throughout the preceding pages, that indifference is socially created through the selective deployment of a kin-based discrimination between selves and others. An attitude of indifference is only justifiable if directed outside the reference group – at those who are "other." But how does one determine who is "other"? The recipient of hospitality, no less than the recipient of the bureaucrat's rude rejection, remains "other" until the groaning tables can be turned, or until both chairs are moved to the same side of the desk.

This, I suggest, is the logic whereby we often find the curtest and most arbitrary-seeming bureaucrats in countries that pride themselves on their hospitality. Hospitality, after all, is a stance toward strangers – but strangers who may become useful, dangerous, or simply irritating. In Weber's ideal type of bureaucracy, such personal considerations would be irrelevant. I have tried to demonstrate, however, that this lofty image is itself a part of the negotiation of identity by stereotype that characterizes bureaucratic interaction.

Friendship, then, is an inherently unstable relationship. It is not "real" kinship; indeed, in many Balkan cultures (Simic 1982: 221), these are mutually exclusive terms. "With a leaf (*filo*, 'at the drop of a hat') you make a friend (*filo*), and with a leaf you lose the friend," runs a punning Greek proverb. It is precisely in these areas of ambiguous relationship that one finds symbolic pollution (Leach 1965). "Corruption," a suggestively bodily metaphor, is not inherent in the use of connections, any more than a plate that has served its function but not yet been washed is technically dirty – although the waiter who whisks it away will so describe it. Dirt is matter out of place, but "there is nothing that is intrinsically, inherently, and automatically anomalous" in its own right (Lincoln 1989: 165, citing Needham 1979). Accusations of corruption thus indicate the power of relations that the official ideology rejects and that social actors resent, but that neither can practically manage without. The Cypriot and Sri Lankan false attributions to prominent politicians of "polluting" affinal links connect the metaphors of affinity and nationhood in an especially revealing way.

While it might seem ungracious to compare the extraordinary hospitality of Greek villagers with the interests and motives of bureaucrats and their clients, both hinge on the association of gift-giving with ambiguous relations. In these arenas, people are engaged in a struggle to establish or deny common humanity. The consequences for those who fail are horrendous. They are kept outside the classificatory boundaries of "our people," and they can be treated with a distinct lack of humanity. This is the extreme case typified by the intracommunal killings on Cyprus about which Loizos (1988) has written so perceptively. We should also recall that Greeks sometimes express the view that Turkish visitors should receive the most generous hospitality of all. Indeed, this view often takes the form of an extended kinship metaphor: because they are more like us than some other peoples, and because we realize that commonality when we associate with them as *Gastarbeiter* among a sea of contemptuous Germans or Australians, our "blood boils" more easily with both affection and hatred than when we encounter less familial peoples. We many even invoke the biogenetic metaphor of race-as-patriline when we want to emphasize commonality: *mia fatsa, mia ratsa* ("one physiognomy, one race/patriline"). In the nationalistic propaganda of wartime, the affection disappears and only hatred remains. If, as Leach pointed out, killing is an act of classification, so, too, are marrying and gift-giving. All these areas touch on the edge of kinship, replace the common substance of blood with degrees of difference. Everyone outside that line, "beyond the pale," is undifferentiated, for which the reciprocal term and condition is indifference.

In this study, I have tried to show that the internal logic of European national bureaucracy follows from that of nationalism, in which ideology represents cultural unities as social units. It does so in two mutually complementary ways. On the one hand, its overall system of categories follows the nationalistic logic of distinguishing between insiders and outsiders, and of representing these distinctions as given in nature – as matters of essence rather than of cultural or historical contingency. On the other hand, the system of categories, founded in social experience, can be reconverted into the terms of that logic in everyday practice: since the definition of the boundary between insiders and outsiders is actually negotiable, so, too, are all the superficially fixed distinctions that official rhetoric derives from it.

Perhaps the simplest and most easily examined locus for the conversion of relationships of blood into more impersonal, generalized ties of obligation lies in acts of hospitality. These have two important consequences for the present discussion. First, they provide the most basic means of converting outsiders into insiders, albeit honorary ones. Second, hospitality is associated, throughout Europe and far beyond, with the symbols through which that conversion can be most dramatically effected: blood, bread, and wine. It easy to see how these symbols of essence can become formalized as the essentialism of both neoevolutionist racism and modern nationalism; and how, too, they can revert to pragmatic devices of social intimacy and distance in the hands of social actors.

To understand the usefulness of hospitality for finding one's way across formal social boundaries, we must recall that its very affability may be a disguise for fear, contempt, or caution (see Pitt-Rivers 1968; Herzfeld 1987b). This ambiguity provides the logical model for those many areas of contestation in which the client solicits the bureaucrat's sympathy. The bureaucrat, as "host," holds the keys to social inclusion. The "guest," by showing proper deference, hopes to gain it. The client's bad behavior, conversely, is both an insult to national integrity at the level of bureaucratic management and a violation of moral obligations to one's "host" at the level of social interaction. In both the government office and at a stranger's house, the ideals of friendly service thinly disguise mutual dependence, which may, in turn, entail a complex negotiation of relative status.

Consider, for example, the relationship between powerful political patrons and humble Sarakatsan shepherds (Campbell 1964). Relations of mutual obligation (*ipokhreosi* or *filotimo*)[5] bind host and quest. What they have to offer each other may be very different: votes on the one side, a degree of security and protection on the other. But the patron needs the shepherd's votes as much as the shepherd needs the patron's good offices, and both parties know this. The ideologies of formal social symmetry and moral obligation cloak the pragmatics of often severe inequality and mutual need, respectively. Mutual courtesy marks the clear understanding that loyalty gets protection, and protection loyalty. Patrons and clients often call each other "friends" (Loizos 1975), a clear indication that, while actual kinship is not the bond (indeed, "kinship" often forms a mutually exclusive pair with "friendship"), the moral expectations that each side has of other are predicated on kinship-like values of affect and respect.

The more distant the relationship, the less convincing such claims are likely to be. Because foreigners do not "know" the rules and strategies of insiderhood, expectations of them may be very low. While they are tourists, doing only touristy things, they are at least a source of income, and so should be treated with respect: they have something to offer. When foreigners want to outstay their visa welcome, however, and especially when they want to work in

---

5. These terms are virtually synonymous in some situations. See the discussion of "honor" in Campbell 1964; see also Herzfeld 1980a, 1987a.

the country, they immediately encounter rules of exclusion based on notions of blood and managed by potentially inimical personnel. This is why the most obvious examples of the hospitality motif are probably to be found in aliens' bureaus ("you have abused this country's hospitality" vs. "our national traditions of warmth toward all guests are at your service"). But the same principle operates at all levels of any national bureaucracy. The exacting of the client's deference is predicated on an ironic reading of the idea that the bureaucrat is a "servant," because, in fact, the client always depends upon the bureaucrat's readiness to provide "service." The client tries to insist on that service as a citizen entitled to it; the bureaucrat, if recalcitrant, responds by questioning the reality of the citizen's claims (or even questioning the citizen's claims to be a citizen at all).

I opened this book, and again this section of the final chapter, with a puzzle: how is it that some of the world's most hospitable societies seem beset by the most obstructive and callous bureaucracies? Part of the answer lies in the fact that these are often societies that have not developed a fully integrated capitalist economy, so that there is a greater need for devices of social incorporation. One may try to inveigle potential patrons into one's moral debt by overwhelming them with lavish generosity. Hospitality, viewed in these terms, becomes a basis for solidarity among equals and moral obligation on the part of the powerful toward the weak.

At the same time, hospitality is a symbolic strategy of very considerable force. The sharing of bread, meat, wine, and social space indexes the ambiguity of all host-guest relations: an equality of interest that both marks and cloaks the guest's (perhaps transitory) state of dependence. This again is the logic of moral obligation. In offering bread and wine, the host effects a model of social transubstantiation – the symbols of the Eucharist, perhaps, but also (as we have already noted) those of agnatic kinship: wine as blood, bread and meat as body. This is truly a model of reciprocal incorporation – the absorption of the familial body by newly incorporated insiders: friends, guests, clients. In the most extreme illustrations of this logic, we find hosts threatening to kill those who have threatened their guests, because the guest, having broken bread with them, is now a virtual insider – even one against whom the hosts themselves may have expectations of taking revenge at some later time (see Boehm 1984: 119). "Taking back the blood," the principal metaphor of vengeance in many societies, is explicitly predicated on the logic of reciprocity.

Sheep thieves and bureaucrats at least share this much: their circle of intimates is widened through the judicious exercise of metaphorical devices. Of course, bureaucrats are not "supposed" to act in this way. But it is clear that many do so. Moreover, such polite notions as "civil service" (and even such ironic usages as "a guest in Her Majesty's prisons") confirm that a similar mutuality of obligation is in fact implicit in the official rhetoric. The power to refuse hospitality is the basis on which indifference is built: it is a denial of common substance.

The association of hospitality with bureaucratic practice, while representing an almost stereotypical conflict of interest, is almost never absent from European daily life. A bureaucrat may offer a cup of coffee, a cigarette, or simply some friendly remarks apparently designed to put the client at ease. This is not necessarily a mark of the incompleteness of bureaucratization in certain countries, although the play of stereotypes will often represent it as such. Rather, it indicates a recognition by all parties that bureaucracy is, in practice, very much a matter of social relations.

Rationality as Symbolic System and Practice

The separation of state from local interests is but a single instance of that West-East, rational-fatalistic, intellectual-visceral Cartesianism that seems so especially blatant in Greece. It is not that petty bureaucrats depart from the values enshrined in state theory so much as that they reinterpret them socially, taking them back down from the pedestal of high culture on which Eurocentric nationalism has placed them. Dismissing their activities as survivals from the days of Turkish mismanagement is an Orientalist tactic, and, as such, a rhetorical ploy in the same struggle over symbolic resources that these bureaucrats are also conducting.

In that rhetoric, all apparent aberrations from strict adherence to the letter of the law are seen as "corruption." There is a great irony in this formulation, because corruption is itself a familial and bodily metaphor. The state system is couched in familial metaphors, validating a cultural entity. In offering protection, therefore, the godfathers and in-laws are not acting against the symbolism that the state uses, for they share in that symbolism even when they invest it with significantly different meanings. Rather, they are opposed to the state's effective monopoly of the kinship idiom. They counter that monopoly in a practical manner, by reconverting nationalist images of the family into working relationships of social life. They operate in the interstices between state absolutism and the privacies of home and body: the clerk who found me a boat ticket on the grounds that I was an "insider" used a term that could apply to the whole range of solidarities from household member to fellow citizen, but whose very applicability could be instantly revoked at the first sign of ingratitude or disloyalty on my part.

This flexibility appears at first to belie the central concept of order. That term, however, slips all too easily between two meanings: as the exercise of power and as a mode of classification – in short, as both practice and system. The existence of order is not a given, but comes about through the continuing agreement of a group of people to respect and even to create a set of regularities in the life they share. Hence Giddens' (1984) notion of the "duality of structure" – the realization that structure and agency cannot exist without one another, because the presumption that structure exists provides the necessary context within which agents can in fact make it exist.

As Brøgger (n.d.: 145) says in his own attempt to suggest the applicability of the Douglas model to the study of modern bureaucratic societies, "[t]he establishment of a number of new social categories with the rise of the modern *Gesellschaft* created an equal number of possibilities for trespassing." Yet there must always be someone to blow the police whistle. In Brøgger's model, the agents of this change are invisible, or are at least external to the local community. The local community may not seem to resist them as willfully as, say, Banfield's "amoral familists" in Montegrano, and Brøgger's description is consequently more convincing than Banfield's. Brøgger is also surely right to claim that a categorical split between mind and body characterizes the modern bureaucratic world.

I have much greater difficulty following him, however, when he makes a hard-and-fast distinction between the "pre-bureaucratic" ways of the Nazaré community and the "bureaucratic" notions of pollution and order that have succeeded it. This, in turn, suggests a past that was essentially "corporeal," in which bureaucratic rationality had not yet made its inroads, and a ratiocinative present in which logic and science (or at least organized religion) have fully displaced superstition. I would suggest that Brøgger's argument is in fact far more survivalist than my own plea for recognition of enduring cosmological symbols. Brøgger shows us a community that the world has passed by, surviving in a time capsule that the modern bureaucratic technology is about to shatter rudely; social maturity is at hand. It is the crux of survivalist arguments that older symbols represent remnants of a "childlike" past. I am suggesting, to the contrary, that the symbolism I have examined, particularly in Chapter Five, represents a conceptual technology that adapts very well to the exigencies of a life that by no stretch of the imagination conforms to a Weberian ideal type.

Brøgger's dualism illustrates the difficulty of an anthropology come "home" to Europe: our analytic categories are cut from the same cloth as the local ones of the societies we study, as is the governmental jargon with which they now have to deal. In societies where we can examine the history of civil institutions in some detail, however, we can also discern agency at work at every turn, from the founders of the state to harassed bureaucrats and equally harassed clients of everyday interaction. And while we may not be in a position to read minds and identify motives, we can at least examine what motives people conventionally attribute in the societies we study. Charges of *efthinofovia* are no sillier than structural determinism, and may be traceable to a much more identifiable culprit. This is the same argument that I made earlier in discussing Durkheim: it is easier to conceive of a reified society worshipping itself when one can identify the agents of that reification, and when one can follow its reproduction through endless petty reclassifications, than when the system of collective representations is presented as given and unchanging. When society worships itself, by contrast, it becomes the background for the social production of indifference rather than the foreground of constructive critique.

But in fact critique does occur. A theme of this book has been the local voice of skepticism about the claims of rationality. As I have emphasized, rationality – whether as science or as rational government – is itself often invoked as an after-the-fact rationalization. Discussing a dramatic convergence between science and government, Balshem (1991: 160) shows how health-care administrators attribute fatalism about cancer to Philadelphians living

in a polluted, low-income area, and shows that the latter are in
fact expressing resentment of a self-fulfilling prophecy: science
creates the pollution, now science is unable to protect us from
it. One could probably read rural Norman reactions to the establishment of a nuclear power plant, described by Zonabend as
"fatalistic," in very similar terms. This is, once again, the conceptual technology that I have identified as secular theodicy: it identifies the sources of power and recognizes that, while resistance
may not bring many actual results, it at least allows people the
collective and individual self-respect denied them by the determinisms of scientific and bureaucratic rationality.

To realize this is not necessarily to blame bureaucracy in general.
People whose dealings with bureaucrats go awry find it useful to
attack "the system," or, as in the case of Balshem's informants, to
deride professional expertise. In so doing, they explain away their
own misfortunes and at the same time give their alleged tormen-
tors – and certainly those who control their immediate environment – a handle with which to dismiss them, in turn, as fatalists.
If the common ground of cosmology is clearer in Greece than it
is in the United States, Balshem's ethnography shows that this may
have more to do with the greater influence of scientific discourse
in America than with antiquated criteria of "superstition." The
important point is a very simple one: bureaucrats (including
bureaucratic scientists) use much the same discourse as their clients
for reducing social identity to individual or collective "character."
"Character" is part of the same discourse as "fate," with which it
is dialectically engaged in arguments about people's place in the
social world. To the extent that bureaucrats can treat their clients
as fatalistic, and therefore as backward, they can justify a stance
of what the clients – rightly or wrongly – interpret and experience
as indifference.

Precisely because this rhetorical contest also involves a stereotypical characterization of bureaucrats, we must avoid treating
the latter as an analytical construct that might distance us from
what we are studying. Weber and Marx both fell into this trap,
Weber by emphasizing the inhumanity of bureaucracy, Marx by
focusing on its inefficiency and its self-perpetuating manufacture
of falsehoods. Bureaucratic structures are not essentially discrimi-
natory any more than nations are essentially constituted by the
specific properties of character, culture, or race. To attack bureaucracy in general not only mistakes the material for the method,

the conventions for analytical insight; it accedes to an essentialism of its own, lumping all bureaucrats together as a race apart. What makes so many popular accounts of bureaucracy unsatisfactory except as a palliative for irritation is their failure to escape this kind of determinism.

Bureaucrats are given various taxonomic devices with which to regulate their small sections of a civic universe. Those devices have the capacity, like the trappings of hospitality, to benefit and to demean. In the examples we have examined in the preceding chapters, most examples of indifference were tantamount to a refusal to respect difference. This is not just a play on words: successful clients are those who manage to persuade their bureaucratic interrogators to accept what makes their case "different" as belonging to the bureaucrats' "own" social world. They succeed in persuading the bureaucrats that they, the clients, are insiders: kinsfolk, fellow patriots, spiritual kin, coreligionists – in short, "one blood." Those who fail are other, outside, beyond the pale. They are not there merely because they are so classified; they are there because officials have chosen, or have been forced, to interpret their status in such a manner. In saying this, I do not deny the significance of social and semantic structure, but view that structure as taking on its specific meanings only at moments of actualization – in other words, not in an essentialist sense but through the experience of social life.[6]

The clearest sign of totalitarianism is undisguised pressure for social and culture homogenization from the top. Probably the crudest and cruellest illustration of this in recent European history is the experience of Romania under Ceauşescu, a topic to which I promised earlier to return. Ceauşescu was absolutely explicit about his desire to obliterate difference. As Kligman (n.d.) has noted, there are signs that this ideology will prove harder to eradicate in post-Ceauşescu Romania than the first flush of ecstatic liberation appeared to promise – yet another grim reminder of the semantic instability of such terms as "democracy."[7] Under

6. On "emergence," see an early statement by Tambiah (1979); on the "duality of structure" (the interplay of formal structure and human agency), see especially Giddens 1984. Haines (1990) specifically addresses the interplay of ambiguity and conformity, social indeterminacy and administrative determinism, from the perspective of a modified ethnomethodology.

7. Consider the Greek junta's use of the term, in which ideals of an inherited civic grace were combined with deliberate ambiguity: after the removal of King

Ceauşescu, moreover, it was combined with an astonishing amount of ritualization in public life at all levels. Most revealing of all, in light of the formal relationship that I have sketched between bureaucracy and hospitality, a 1974 law forbade "the lodging of anyone other than a first-degree relative without state approval. Hospitality had become dangerous" – especially after punishments for lodging foreigners were made more severe in the final phase of the regime (Kligman 1990: 399).

What does the extraordinary behavior of the odious Ceauşescu have to do with the actions of bureaucrats in a democratic state? Only this: the reification of public life from the top down, the regulation of social relationships within the paternalistic (and agnatic) horrors of "dynastic socialism," and the monopolization of hospitality by the state represent the worst transformation into state policy of what ordinarily are only the unsystematic actions of individual petty desk tyrants. It is not that liberal democracies are free of such excesses; these occur, however, at a greater remove from the centers of power, to which appeal may be made for protection – not always, to be sure, with conspicuous success, but always with a degree of hope. The barrier of indifference can be pushed back by remaining alert, not only in defense of slogans about democracy and human rights, but also in opposition to the cooptation of such concepts by the arid semantics of formal classification. An open society must resist the idea that classification is "only language." It is precisely in the absence of such warnings that bureaucratic language can acquire, by default, its sometimes seriously disquieting autonomy.

Is it possible to demand that bureaucracies recognize and accept difference as internal to the polity rather than as extraneous pollutants? Or is too utopian to suppose that a bureaucracy can transcend the limitations of good intentions and institutionalize some sort of resistance to its own conceptual inertia? For that is what we have really been talking about: the ease with which actors' reifications of arbitrary categories take hold at all political levels, the difficulty that has to be faced in resisting that process. There have certainly been calls for something of the kind, based on the same models of human diversity that actuated many earlier

---

Constantine at the end of 1967, the term was introduced to imply that the dictatorially imposed "republic" really did represent the will of the people.

revolutions now mired in curmudgeonly self-righteousness (see, for example, Bottomley and Lechte 1990).

The first step in that direction must be to realize that good intentions are actually very bad at relativizing themselves. They are prevented from doing so by the monolithic face of language. People in bureaucratic office often find it hard to see the intolerance to which their high ideals may be leading them. Others hide behind a self-righteous indignation; it is quite irrelevant (as well as pointless) to wonder whether they are sincere in so doing. As Abella and Troper (1982–83: 8–9) acknowledge, F.C. Blair deeply resented the suggestion that he was an anti-Semite; he thought of himself as simply a realistic administrator in his nation's service. We will not get very far as long as we focus on personal intentions, especially if the ritual aspect of bureaucracy is recognized. Nor, as I have tried to show, is there any point in perpetuating the stereotype of the autonomous "system," for that does nothing more than provide an ethical alibi for those who are indeed indifferent to the pleas of the different.

We can restate this barren choice in the conventional terms of arguments in social theory: methodological individualism and Durkheimian sociocentrism both ultimately fail analytically. As Haines (1990: 265) points out, bureaucratic rules, although usually filtered through social actors' ongoing interpretations of experience, are of a different kind from those of the everyday cultural order: "they constitute mandatory – if often vague, overlapping, etc. – guidelines for the actions of bureaucrats." Their claims to fixity require explanation no less than does the ambiguity that they generate in practice. Conformity, as Haines notes, must be negotiated; but the expectation remains that it is indeed conformity at which the laws are aimed. That, then, is one reading of the immediate practical problem. But the dilemma is also one of more global consequence: method is implicated in ideology. The traditional choice of methodological perspectives is mired in a contrast between the ideologies that undergird the various forms of bureaucracy itself: voluntaristic devolution or state control?

There is, however, a dialectical middle ground – no less ideological, to be sure, but perhaps more in harmony with social experience. That moral and intellectual alternative has gone by a variety of names in recent years: agency, practice, action, use, ordinary language. In the hands of such diverse thinkers as Austin (1971[1956–57]), Wittgenstein (1973), Bourdieu (1977), de

Certeau (1983), Giddens (1984), and others, it has recognized the contingent nature of structure as well as the social nature of individual action and its effects. In this middle ground, which refuses to privilege either society or the social actor, we may see more than just another theoretical fashion (though it is certainly also that). It is, at the very least, a way of resisting the temptation to reduce all social experience to a single model. Because it avoids reifying either the person or culture, but attends to the play of ideas about both in any given society, it offers a glimmer of hope for the rescue of cultural and social difference from the rigid administrative indifference of the intolerant and ungenerous.

The real danger of indifference is not that it grows out of the barrel of a gun, but that it too easily becomes habitual. It is the opium of the state drudge. Habituation, as Weber saw, is a necessary and ever-menacing precondition for discipline – a discipline, I have suggested in these pages, inculcated through the familiar (and familial) cosmology of common sense. As anthropology has increasingly had to come to terms with its origins in those racial and national ideologies that its practitioners claim to detest most, the most laudable ideals of mutual tolerance and respect similarly find that they share an embarrassing heritage stained with symbolic as well as physical blood. Hierarchy and egalitarianism, tolerance and genocide, kindly hospitality and brutal indifference: these are not mutually exclusive opposites, but the dialectics of differentiation in what we are pleased to call the modern world. Unless we can allow difference to oppose a productive discomfort to the certainties of bureaucratic classification, indifference must eventually, to cite the official cosmology that informs and maintains it, become the unblinking destiny of all.

References

Abélès, Marc. 1989. *Jours tranquilles en 89.* Paris: Odile Jacob.

Abella, Irving, and Harold Troper. 1982–83. *None is Too Many: Canada and the Jews of Europe 1933–1948.* New York: Random House.

Aberbach, Joel D., Robert D. Putnam, and Bert A. Rockman, eds. 1981. *Bureaucrats and Politicians in Western Democracies.* Cambridge: Harvard University Press.

Ahern, Emily. 1979. "The Problem of Efficacy: Strong and Weak Illocutionary Acts." *Man* (n.s.) 14:1–17.

Albee, Edward. 1960. *The Zoo Story and The Sandbox: Two Short Plays.* New York: Dramatists Play Service.

Anderson, Benedict. 1983. *Imagined Communities: Reflections on the Origin and Spread of Nationalism.* London: Verso.

André, Sylvie. 1987. *Gobineau et la féminité: Contribution à une mythologie comparée du Féminin/Masculin au XIXe siècle.* Pisa: Libreria Goliardica.

Ardener, E.W. 1971. "The Historicity of Historical Linguistics." In Edwin Ardener, ed., *Social Anthropology and Language (A.S.A. Monographs 10;* London: Tavistock), pp. 209–241.

Argyriades, D. 1968. "The Ecology of Greek Administration: Some Factors Affecting the Development of the Greek Civil Service." In J.G. Peristiany, ed., *Contributions to Mediterranean Sociology* (The Hague: Mouton), pp. 339–349.

Austin, J.L. 1971[1956–57]. "A Plea for Excuses." In Colyn Lyas, ed., *Philosophy and Linguistics* (London: Macmillan), pp. 79–101.

Austin, J.L. 1975[1962]. *How To Do Things With Words.* 2d ed., Cambridge: Harvard University Press.

Bailey, F.G. 1971. "Gifts and Poison." In F.G. Bailey, ed., *Gifts and Poison: The Politics of Reputation* (Oxford: Basil Blackwell), pp. 1–25.

Bakoyannis, P. 1977. "Opisthodhromisi s' olous tous tomis." *To Vima,* 15 March, p. 53.

Balshem, Martha. 1991. "Cancer, Control, and Causality: Talking about Cancer in a Working-Class Community." *American Ethnologist* 18: 152–172.

Banfield, E.C. 1958. *The Moral Basis of a Backward Society.* New York: Free Press.

Bauman, Richard. 1983. *Let Your Words Be Few: Symbolism of Speaking and Silence among Seventeenth-Century Quakers,* Cambridge: Cambridge University Press.

Bernstein, Basil. 1971. *Class, Codes and Control.* London: Routledge and Kegan Paul.

Béteille, André. 1990. "Race, Caste, and Gender." *Man* (n.s.) 25: 489–504.

Biddiss, Michael D. 1970. *Father of Racist Ideology: The Social and Political Thought of Count Gobineau.* New York: Weybright and Talley.

Binns, Christopher A.P. 1979–80. "The Changing Face of Power: Revolution and Development of the Soviet Ceremonial System." *Man* (n.s.) 14: 585–606 and 15: 170–187.

Blau, Peter M. 1963. *The Dynamics of Bureaucracy: A Study of Interpersonal Relationships in Two Government Agencies.* Chicago: University of Chicago Press.

Bloch, Maurice. 1989. *Ritual, History and Power: Selected Papers in Anthropology.* London: Athlone Press.

Blok, Anton. 1981. "Rams and Billy-Goats: A Key to the Mediterranean Code of Honour." *Man* (n.s.) 16: 427–440.

Boehm, Christopher. 1984. *Blood Revenge: The Enactment and Management of Conflict in Montenegro and Other Tribal Societies.* Lawrence: University Press of Kansas.

Bogatyrev, Petr. 1971. *The Functions of Folk Costume in Moravian Slovakia.* Trans. Richard G. Crum. The Hague: Mouton.

Boissevain, Jeremy. 1969. *Hal-Farrug: A Village in Malta.* New York: Holt, Rinehart and Winston.

Bolinger, Dwight. 1975. *Aspects of Language,* 2d ed. New York: Harcourt Brace Jovanovich.

Bottomley, Gill, and John Lechte. 1990. "Nation and Diversity in France." *Journal of Intercultural Studies* 11: 49–63.

Bourdieu, Pierre. 1977. *Outline of a Theory of Practice.* Trans. Richard Nice. Cambridge: Cambridge University Press.

Boyarin, Jonathan. 1991. "Jewish Ethnography and the Question of the Book." *Anthropological Quarterly* 64: 14–29.

Brandes, Stanley. 1980. *Metaphors of Masculinity: Sex and Status in Andalusian Folklore. (Publications of the American Folklore Society* [n.s.] 1.) Philadelphia: University of Pennsylvania Press.

Brettell, Caroline B. 1986. *Men Who Migrate, Women Who Wait: Population and History in a Portuguese Parish.* Princeton: Princeton University Press.

Britan, Gerald M. 1981. *Bureaucracy and Innovation: An Ethnography of Policy Change.* Beverly Hills: Sage.

Britan, G.M., and R. Cohen, eds. 1980. *Hierarchy and Society: Anthropological Perspectives on Bureaucracy.* Philadelphia: Institute for the Study of Human Issues.

Brøgger, Jan. n.d. *Pre-bureaucratic Europeans: A Study of a Portuguese Fishing Community.* Oslo: Norwegian University Press.

Browning, Christopher R. 1980. "The Government Experts." In Henry Friedlander and Sybil Milton, eds., *The Holocaust: Ideology, Bureaucracy, and Genocide* (Millwood: Kraus International), pp. 183–197.

Buttitta, Antonino, and Silvana Miceli. 1986. *Percorsi simbolici.* Palermo: S.F. Flaccovio.

Campbell, J.K. 1964. *Honour, Family, and Patronage: A Study of Institutions and Moral Values in a Greek Mountain Community.* Oxford: Clarendon Press.

Cannadine, David, and Simon Price, eds. 1987. *Rituals of Royalty: Power and Ceremonial in Traditional Society.* Cambridge: Cambridge University Press.

Caretsos, Constantine S. Caretsos. 1976. *I politiki, i ghrafiokrates, ke i politiki tis allayis: i sinepies ya tin Elladha.* Athens.

Caro Baroja, Julio. 1970. *El mito del caractér nacional: Meditaciones a contrapelo.* Madrid: Seminarios y Ediciones.

Cassirer, Ernst. 1946. *The Myth of the State.* New Haven: Yale University Press.

Chateau, Fernand. 1938. Races et groupement sanguins. *Mercure de France,* pp. 274–279.

Clark. Mari H. 1982. "Variations on Themes of Male and Female (Reflections on Gender Bias in Fieldwork in Rural Greece)." *Women's Studies* 10: 117–133.

Cohen, Abner. 1974. *Two-Dimensional Man: An Essay on the Anthropology of Power and Symbolism in Complex Society.* Berkeley: University of California Press.

Cohn, Carol. 1987. "Sex and Death in the Rational World of Defense Intellectuals." *Signs: Journal of Women in Culture and Society* 12: 687–718.

Connor, Walker. 1991. "From Tribe to Nation?" *History of European Ideas* 13: 5–18.

Cosgrove, Denis E. 1984. *Social Formation and Symbolic Landscape.* Totowa: Barnes and Noble.

Couloumbis, T.A., J.A. Petropulos, and H.J. Psomiades, eds. 1976. *Foreign Interference in Greek Politics.* New York: Pella.

Cowan, Jane K. 1990. *Dance and the Body Politic in Northern Greece.* Princeton: Princeton University Press.

Crozier, Michel. 1964. *The Bureaucratic Phenomenon.* Chicago: University of Chicago Press.

Crozier, Michel 1971. *The World of the Office Workers.* Trans. David Landau. Chicago: Chicago University Press.

Cutileiro, José. 1971. *A Portuguese Rural Society.* Oxford: Clarendon Press.

Dakin, Douglas. 1973. *The Greek Struggle for Independence, 1821–1833.* London: Batsford.

Da Matta, Roberto. 1991. *Carnivals, Rogues, and Heroes: For an Interpretation of the Brazilian Carnival.* South Bend: University of Notre Dame Press.

Danforth, Loring M. 1982: *The Death Rituals of Rural Greece.* Princeton: Princeton University Press.

Davis, John. 1973. *Land and Family in Pisticci.* London: Athlone Press.

Davis, John. 1987. *Libyan Politics: Tribe and Revolution.* Berkeley: University of California Press.

de Certeau, Michel. 1984. *The Practice of Everyday Life.* Trans. Steven Rendall. Berkeley: University of California Press.

Delaney, Carol. n.d. "Devlet Baba and Anavatan: Father State, Motherland and the Birth of the Turkish Republic." Paper presented at the annual meeting of the American Ethnological Society, New Orleans, 1991.

DeMallie, Raymond J. n.d. "Kinship and Biology in Sioux Culture." Unpublished manuscript.

Diamant, Alfred. 1962. "The Bureaucratic Model: Max Weber Rejected, Rediscovered, Reformed." In Ferrel Heady and Sybil L. Stokes, eds., *Papers in Comparative Public Administration* (Ann Arbor: Institute of Public Administration), pp. 59–96.

Diamant, Alfred. 1966. *The Temporal Dimension in Models of Administration and Organization.* Occasional Papers, Bloomington: Comparative Administration Group, American Society for Public Administration.

Diamant, Alfred. 1989. "European Bureaucratic Elites: Rising or Declining?" *History of European Ideas* 11: 545–558.

Diaz, May N. 1966. *Tonalá : Conservatism, Responsibility, and Authority in a Mexican Town,* Berkeley: University of California Press.

Di Bella, Maria Pia. 1980. "Note sul concetto di onore nelle società mediterranee." *Rassegna Italiana di Sociologia* 21: 607–615.

Di Bella, Maria Pia. 1991. "Name, Blood and Miracles: The Claims to Renown in Traditional Sicily." In J.G. Peristiany and J. Pitts-Rivers, eds., *Honour and Grace in Anthropology* (Cambridge: Cambridge University Press), pp. 151–165.

Dimou, Nikos. 1976. *I dhistikhia tou na ise Ellinas.* Athens: Ikaros.

Djilas, Milovan. 1958. *Land without Justice.* New York: Harcourt, Brace.

Douglas, Mary. 1966. *Purity and Danger: An Analysis of Concepts of Pollution and Taboo.* London: Routledge and Kegan Paul.

Douglas, Mary. 1970. *Natural Symbols: Explorations in Cosmology.* New York: Pantheon.

Douglas, Mary. 1975. *Implicit Meanings: Essays in Anthropology.* London: Routledge and Kegan Paul.

Douglas, Mary (with Baron Isherwood). 1979. *The World of Goods.* New York: Basic Books.

Douglas, Mary. 1986. *How Institutions Think.* Syracuse: Syracuse University Press.

Douglas, Mary. 1988. "Where There's Muck." *Times Literary Supplement*, 14–20 October. 1143–1144.

Dubisch, Jill. 1988. "Golden Oranges and Silver Ships: An Interpretive Approach to a Greek Holy Shrine." *Journal of Modern Greek Studies* 6: 117–134.

du Boulay, Juliet. 1974. *Portrait of a Greek Mountain Village*. Oxford: Clarendon Press.

du Boulay, Juliet. 1982. "The Greek Vampire: A Study of Cyclic Symbolism in Marriage and Death." *Man* (n.s.) 17: 219–238.

Dumont, Louis. 1966. *Homo hierarchicus: An Essay on the Caste System*. Translated by Mark Sainsbury. Chicago: University of Chicago Press.

Dumont, Louis. 1977. *From Mandeville to Marx: The Genesis and Triumph of Economic Ideology*. Chicago: University of Chicago Press.

Dumont, Louis. 1980. *Essays on Individualism: Modern Ideology in Anthropological Perspective*. Chicago: Chicago University Press.

Dupont-Bouchat, Marie-Sylvie, and Xavier Rousseaux. 1988. "Le prix du sang: sang et justice du XIVᵉ au XVIIIᵉ siècle." In Arlette Farge, ed., *Affaires de sang* (Paris: Imago), pp. 43–72.

Durkheim, Emile. 1899. De la définition des phénomènes réligieux. *Année sociologique* 2: 1–28.

Durkheim, Emile. 1915. *The Elementary Forms of the Religious Life*. Trans. Joseph Ward Swain. London: Goerge Allen and Unwin.

Eco, Umberto. 1976. *A Theory of Semiotics*. Bloomington: Indiana University Press.

Elias, Norbert. 1978. *The History of Manners*. Trans. Edmund Jephcott. Oxford: Basil Blackwell.

Evans-Pritchard, E.E. 1949. *The Sanusi of Cyrenaica*. Oxford: Clarendon Press.

Evans-Pritchard, E.E. 1956. *Nuer Religion*. Oxford: Clarendon Press.

Fabian, Johannes. 1973. "How Others Die – Reflections on the Anthropology of Death." In A. Mack, ed., *Death in American Experience* (New York: Schocken), pp. 177–201.

Fabian, Johannes. 1983. *Time and the Other: How Anthropology Makes its Object*. New York: Columbia University Press.

Fallers, Lloyd A. 1974. *The Social Anthropology of the Nation-State*. Chicago: Aldine.

Ferguson, Kathy E. 1984. *The Feminist Case Against Bureaucracy*. Philadelphia: Temple University Press.

Fernandez, James W. 1986. *Persuasions and Performances: The Play of Tropes in Culture*. Bloomington: Indiana University Press.

Foucault, Michel. 1978. *Discipline and Punish: The Birth of the Prison*. Trans. Alan Sheridan. New York: Pantheon.

Frazer, J.G. 1922. *The Golden Bough: A Study in Magic and Religion*. London: Macmillan.

Friedl, Ernestine. 1962. *Vasilika: A Village in Modern Greece.* New York: Holt, Rinehart and Winston.

Gajek, Esther. 1990. "Christmas under the Third Reich." *Anthropology Today* 6(4): 4–9.

Gavrielides, Nicolas. 1976. "The Cultural Ecology of Olive Growing in the Fourni Valley." In Muriel Dimen and Ernestine Friedl, eds., *Regional Variation in Modern Greece and Cyprus: Toward a Perspective on the Ethnography of Greece. (Annals of the New York Academy of Sciences* 268), pp. 143–157.

Geertz, Clifford. 1973. *The Interpretation of Cultures.* New York: Basic Books.

Gellner, Ernst. 1986. *Nations and Nationalism.* Ithaca: Cornell University Press.

Gellner, Ernst. 1988. *Plough, Sword, and Book.* Chicago: University of Chicago Press.

Giddens, Anthony. 1984. *The Constitution of Society: Introduction to the Theory of Structuration.* Berkeley: University of California Press.

Gilmore, David D., ed. 1987. *Honor and Shame and the Unity of the Mediterranean* (Special Publication No. 22). Washington, D.C.: American Anthropological Association.

Glück, Christian Friedrich von. 1803. *Hermeneutisch-systematische Erörterung der Lehre von der Intestaterbfolge, nach den Grundsätzen des ältern und neuern römischen Rechts, also Beytrag zur Erläuterung der Pandecten.* Erlangen: J.J. Palm.

Gobineau, Arthur de. 1984 [1856]. *The Moral and Intellectual Diversity of Races.* Reprint. New York: Garland [Philadelphia: Lippincott].

Gobineau, Comte de. 1872. *Céphalonie, Naxie, et Terre-Neuve: La mouchoir rouge, Akrivie Phrangopoulo, La chasse au caribou.* Paris: Plon.

Gobineau, Comte de. 1936. *Lettres à deux Athéniennes (1858–1881).* Athens: Castalie (Librairie Kauffmann).

Goffman, Erving, 1959. *The Presentation of Self in Everyday Life.* New York: Doubleday.

Goody, Jack. 1986. *The Logic of Writing and the Organization of Society.* Cambridge: Cambridge University Press.

Gouldner, Alvin W. 1954. *Patterns of Industrial Bureaucracy.* New York: Free Press.

Greenwood, Davydd J. 1984. *The Taming of Evolution: The Persistence of Nonevolutionary Views in the Study of Humans.* Ithaca: Cornell University Press.

Guillaumin, Colette. 1981. "Je sais bien mais quand même," ou les avatars de la notion "race," *Le Genre humain* 1: 55–65.

Guizot, François Pierre Guillaume. 1856. *Histoire de la civilisation en Europe depuis la chute de l'empire romain jusqu'à la révolution française.* 6th ed. Paris: Didier.

Haines, David W. 1990. "Conformity in the Face of Ambiguity: A Bureaucratic Dilemma." *Semiotica* 78–3/4: 249–269.

Hamayon, Roberte. 1990. *La chasse à l'âme: Esquisse d'une théorie du chamanisme sibérien.* Nanterre: Société d'ethnologie.

Hamayon, Roberte. n.d. "Shamanism in Siberia: From Partnership in Supernature to Counter-Power in Society." In Caroline Humphrey, ed., *Shamanism, History, and the State,* forthcoming.

Handelman, Don. 1976. "Bureaucratic Transactions: The Development of Official-Client Relationships in Israel." In Bruce Kapferer, ed., *Transaction and Meaning: Directions in the Anthropology of Exchange and Symbolic Behavior (ASA Essays* 1; Philadelphia: Institute for the Study of Human Issues, pp. 223–275.

Handelman, Don. 1978. "Introduction: A Recognition of Bureaucracy." In Don Handelman and Elliott Leyton, eds., *Bureaucracy and World View: Studies in the Logic of Official Interpretation* (St. John's: Institute of Social and Economic Research, Memorial University of Newfoundland, Social and Economic Studies No. 22), pp. 1–14.

Handelman, Don. 1981. "Introduction: The Idea of Bureaucratic Organization." *Social Analysis* 9: 5–23.

Handelman, Don. 1983. "Shaping Phenomenal Reality: Dialectic and Disjunction in the Bureaucratic Synthesis of Child-Abuse in Urban Newfoundland." *Social Analysis* 13: 5–40.

Handelman, Don. 1990. *Models and Mirrors: Towards an Anthropology of Public Events.* Cambridge: Cambridge University Press.

Handleman, Don, and Lea Shamgar-Handelman. 1990. "Holiday Celebrations in Israeli Kindergartens." In Don Handelman, *Models and Mirrors: Towards an Anthropology of Public Events* (Cambridge: Cambridge University Press), pp. 162–189.

Handelman, Don. n.d. "Taxonomy, Bureaucracy, and the Book of Lord Shang." Unpublished manuscript.

Handler, Richard. 1985. "On Having a Culture: Nationalism and the Preservation of Quebec's *Patrimoine.*" In George W. Stocking, Jr., ed., *Objects and Others: Essays on Museums and Material Culture (History of Anthropology* 3; Madison: University of Wisconsin Press), pp. 192–217.

Handler, Richard. 1986. "Authenticity." *Anthropology Today* 2(1): 2–4.

Handler, Richard. 1988. *Nationalism and the Politics of Culture in Quebec.* Madison: The University of Wisconsin Press.

Heller, Joseph. 1961. *Catch-22.* New York: Simon and Schuster.

Herald-Times. 1989, 1990. Bloomington, Indiana.

Herzfeld, Michael. 1980a. "Honour and Shame: Problems in the Comparative Analysis of Moral Systems." *Man* (n.s.) 15: 339–351.

Herzfeld, Michael. 1980b. "Social Tension and Inheritance by Lot in Three Greek Villages." *Anthropological Quarterly* 53: 91–100.

Herzfeld, Michael. 1981. "Meaning and Morality: A Semiotic Approach to Evil Eye Accusations in a Greek Village." *American Ethnologist* 8: 560–574.

Herzfeld, Michael. 1982a. *Ours Once More: Folklore, Ideology, and the Making of Modern Greece.* Austin: University of Texas Press.

Herzfeld, Michael. 1982b. "The Etymology of Excuses: Aspects of Rhetorical Performance in Greece." *American Ethnologist* 9: 644–663.

Herzfeld, Michael. 1985. *The Poetics of Manhood: Contest and Identity in a Cretan Mountain Village.* Princeton: Princeton University Press.

Herzfeld, Michael. 1986. "On Some Rhetorical Uses of Iconicity in Cultural Ideologies." In Paul Bouissac, Michael Herzfeld, and Roland Posner, eds., *Iconicity: Essays on the Nature of Culture* (Tübingen: Stauffenburg), pp. 401–419.

Herzfeld, Michael. 1987a. *Anthropology through the Looking-Glass: Critical Ethnography in the Margins of Europe.* Cambridge: Cambridge University Press.

Herzfeld, Michael. 1987b "'As in Your Own House': Hospitality, Ethnography, and the Stereotype of Mediterranean Society." In David D. Gilmore, ed., *Honor and Shame and the Unity of the Mediterranean* (Special Publication No. 22) (Washington, D.C.: American Anthropological Association), pp. 75–89.

Herzfeld, Michael. 1991. *A Place in History: Social and Monumental Time in a Cretan Town.* Princeton: Princeton University Press.

Higonnet, Patrice L.R. 1980. "The Politics of Linguistic Terrorism and Grammatical Hegemony during the French Revolution." *Social History* 5: 41–69.

Hirschon, Renée. 1989. *Heirs of the Greek Catastrophe: The Social Life of Asia Minor Refugees in Piraeus.* Oxford: Clarendon Press.

Hobsbwam, Eric, and Terence Ranger, eds. 1983. *The Invention of Tradition.* Cambridge: Cambridge University Press.

Holmes, Douglas R. 1989. *Cultural Disenchantments: Worker Peasantries in Northeast Italy.* Princeton; Princeton University Press.

Horsman, Reginald. 1981. *Race and Manifest Destiny: The Origins of American Racial Anglo-Saxonism.* Cambridge, Massachusetts: Harvard University Press.

Humphreys, S.C. 1978. *Anthropology and the Greeks.* London: Routledge and Kegan Paul.

Humphreys, S.C. 1990. Review of *The Cult of Pan in Ancient Greece,* by Philippe Bourgeaud. *Man* (n.s.) 25: 536–537.

Iossifides, A. Marina. 1991. "Sisters in Christ: Metaphors of Kinship among Greek Nuns." In Peter Loizos and Evthymios Papataxiarchis, eds., *Contested Identities: Gender and Kinship in Modern Greece* (Princeton: Princeton University Press), pp. 135–155.

Jacoby, Henry. 1973. *The Bureaucratization of the World.* Trans. Eveline L. Kanes. Berkeley: University of California Press.

Jaffe, Alexandra M. 1990. *Language, Identity and Resistance on Corsica.* Ph.D. diss. Indiana University, Bloomington.

Johnstone, Barbara. 1989. "Linguistic Strategies and Cultural Styles for Persuasive Discourse." In Stella Ting-Toomey and Felipe Korzenny, eds.,

Language, Communication, and Culture: Current Directions (Beverly Hills: Sage), pp. 139–156.

Just, Roger. 1989. "Triumph of the Ethnos." In Elizabeth Tonkin, Malcolm Chapman, and Maryon McDonald, eds., *History and Ethnicity* (A.S.A. Monographs 27; London: Routledge), pp. 71–88.

Kafka, Franz. 1937. *The Trial.* 1st American edition. Translated by Willa and Edwin Muir. New York: A.A. Knopf.

Kamenetsky, Christa. 1977. "Folklore and Ideology in the Third Reich." *Journal of American Folklore* 90: 168–178.

Kamenetsky, Christa. 1984. *Children's Literature in Hitler's Germany: The Cultural Policy of National Socialism.* Athens: Ohio University Press.

Kapferer, Bruce, 1988. *Legends of People, Myths of State.* Washington, D.C.: Smithsonian Institution Press.

Kaplan, Martha. 1990. "Meaning, Agency, and Colonial History: Navosavakadua and the *Tuka* Movement in Fiji." *American Ethnologist* 17: 3–22.

Kardulias, P. Nick. n.d. "Archaeology in Modern Greece: Politics, Bureaucracy, and Science." Paper presented at the annual meeting of the Archaeological Institute of America, San Francisco, 1990.

Karetsos, Kostas. *See* Caretsos, Constantine S.

Katsoulis, Yoryos D. 1975. *To Katestimeno sti Neoelliniki Istoria.* Athens: Nea Sinora.

Kertzer, David. I. 1988. *Ritual, Politics and Power.* New Haven: Yale University Press.

Kertzer, David I. 1991. "The 19th National Congress of the Italian Communist Party." In Fausto Anderlini and Robert Leonardi, eds., *Italian Politics* (London: Pinter forthcoming).

Kiriakidou-Nestoros, Alki. 1975. *Laoghrafika Meletimata.* Athens: Olkos.

Khrisanthopoulos, L. 1853. *Silloyi ton topikon tis Elladhos sinithion.* Athens: Milt. K. Garpola.

Kligman, Gail. 1981. *Căluş: Symbolic Transformation in Romanian Ritual.* Chicago: University of Chicago Press.

Kligman, Gail. 1990. "Reclaiming the Public: A Reflection on Creating Civil Society in Romania." *East European Politics and Societies* 393–438.

Kligman, Gail. n.d. "The Politics of Identity: The Return of the Repressed in Post-Ceauşescu Romania." Unpublished manuscript.

Kuper, Adam. 1988. *The Invention of Primitive Society: Transformations of an Illusion.* New York: Routledge.

Leach, Edmund. 1965. "The Nature of War." *Disarmament and Arms Control* 3: 165–183.

Lefort, Claude. 1971. *Eléments d'une critique de la bureaucratie.* Geneva: Droz.

Lévi-Strauss, Claude. 1955. "The Structural Study of Myth." *Journal of American Folklore* 68: 428–444.

Levy, Harry L. 1956. "Property Distribution by Lot in Present Day Greece." *Transactions of the American Philological Association* 87: 42–46.

Lewontin, R.C., Steven Rose, and Leon Kamin. 1984. *Not In Our Genes: Biology, Ideology, and Human Nature.* New York: Pantheon.

Lincoln, Bruce. 1989. *Discourse and the Construction of Society: Comparative Studies of Myth, Ritual, and Classification.* New York: Oxford University Press.

Linke, Uli. 1985. "Blood as Metaphor in Proto-Indo-European." *Journal of Indo-European Studies* 13: 333–376.

Linke, Uli. 1986. *Where Blood Flows a Tree Grows: A Study of Root Metaphors in German Culture.* Ph.D. diss., University of California, Berkeley.

Linke, Uli. 1990. "Folklore, Anthropology, and the Government of Social Life." *Comparative Studies in Society and History* 32: 117–148.

Lloyd, G.E.R. 1990. *Demystifying Mentalities.* Cambridge: Cambridge University Press.

Löfgren, Orvar. 1989. "The Nationalization of Culture." *Ethnologia Europaea* 19: 5–24.

Loizos, Peter. 1975. *The Greek Gift: Politics in a Cypriot Village.* Oxford: Basil Blackwell.

Loizos, Peter. 1988. "Intercommunal Killing in Cyprus." *Man* (n.s.) 23: 639–653.

Lowenthal, David. 1985. *The Past Is A Foreign Country.* Cambridge: Cambridge University Press.

Mackridge, Peter. 1985. *The Modern Greek Language.* Oxford: Clarendon Press.

Marx, Fritz Morstein. 1962. "Control and Responsibility in Administration: Comparative Aspects." In Ferrel Heady and Sybil L. Stokes, eds. *Papers in Comparative Public Administration* (Ann Arbor: Institute of Public Administration), pp. 145–171.

Mauss, Marcel. 1967. *The Gift: Forms and Functions of Exchange in Archaic Societies.* Translated by Ian Cunnison. New York: Norton.

Maynard, Kent. 1988. "On Protestants and Pastoralists: The Segmentary Nature of Socio-Cultural Organization." *Man* (n.s.) 23: 101–117.

Mayr, Ernst. 1982. *The Growth of Biological Thought.* Cambridge: Harvard University Press.

Meeker, Michael E. 1979. *Literature and Violence in North Arabia.* Cambridge: Cambridge University Press.

Merton, Robert K. 1957. *Social Theory and Social Structure.* Rev. ed. Glencoe: Free Press.

Mitchell, M. Marion. 1931. "Emile Durkheim and the Philosophy of Nationalism" *Political Science Quarterly* 46: 87–106.

Mosse, George L. 1978. *Toward the Final Solution: A History of European Racism.* New York: Howard Fertig.

Mosse, George L. 1985. *Nationalism and Sexuality: Middle-Class Morality and Sexual Norms in Modern Europe.* Madison: University of Wisconsin Press.

Mouzelis, Nicos P. 1968. *Organization and Bureaucracy: An Analysis of Modern Theories.* Chicago: Aldine.

Mouzelis, Nicos P. 1978. *Modern Greece: Facets of Underdevelopment.* London: Macmillan.

Needham, Rodney. 1972. *Belief, Language, and Experience.* Oxford: Blackwell.

Needham, Rodney. 1979. *Symbolic Classification.* Santa Monica: Goodyear.

Nisbet, Robert. 1973. *Sociology as an Art Form.* New York: Oxford University Press.

Obeyesekere, Gananath. 1968. "Theodicy, Sin and Salvation in a Sociology of Buddhism." In E.R. Leach, ed., *Dialectic in Practical Religion* (Cambridge: Cambridge University Press), pp. 7–40.

O'Neill, Brian J. 1987. *Social Inequality in a Portuguese Hamlet: Land, Late Marriage, and Bastardy, 1870–1978.* Cambridge: Cambridge University Press.

Onians, R.B. 1951. *The Origins of European Thought about the Body, the Mind, the Soul, the World, Time, and Fate.* Cambridge: Cambridge University Press.

Paleologos, Il. 1976. "To klima ghrafi istoria." *To Vima,* 14 July, p. 1.

Peristiany, J.G., ed. 1965. *Honour and Shame: The Values of Mediterranean Society.* London: Weidenfeld & Nicolson.

Peters, B. Guy. 1989. *The Politics of Bureaucracy.* 3d ed. New York: Longman.

Pina-Cabral, João de. 1991. Review of Brøgger n.d. *Man* (n.s.) 26: 174.

Pitt-Rivers, Julian. 1968. "The Stranger, the Guest, and the Hostile Host: Introduction to the Study of the Laws of Hospitality." In J.G. Peristiany, ed., *Contributions to Mediterranean Sociology* (Paris: Mouton), pp. 13–30.

Poliakov, Léon. 1968. *Histoire de l'antisémitisme de Voltaire à Wagner (Histoire de l'antisémitisme,* vol. 3.) Paris: Calmann-Lévy.

Poliakov, Léon. 1981. "Brève histoire des hiérarchies raciales." *Le Genre humain* 1: 70–82.

Poliakov, Léon. 1987[1971]. *Le mythe aryen: Essai sur les sources du racisme et des nationalismes.* Brussels: Éditions Complexe.

Poliakov, Léon, Christian Delacampagne, and Patrick Girard. 1976. *Le racisme.* Paris: Seghers.

Politis, N.G. 1874. *Neoelliniki Mitholoyia.* Part 2. Athens: N.B. Nakis and Karl Wilberg.

Pollis, Adamantia. 1987. "The State, Law, and Human Rights in Modern Greece." *Human Rights Quarterly* 9: 587–614.

Presthus, Robert V. 1973[1969]. "The Social Bases of Bureaucratic Organization." In Elihu Katz and Brenda Danet, eds., *Bureaucracy and the Public* (New York: Basic Books), pp. 50–60.

Reed, Robert R. 1990. "Are Robert's Rules of Order Counterrevolutionary?: Rhetoric and the Reconstruction of Portuguese Politics." *Anthropological Quarterly* 63: 134–144.

Resvanis, Kostas. 1977. "Ke . . . i ghrafiokratia kei ta dhasi!" *Ta Nea*, 6 April, pp. 7, 10.

Richman, Joel. 1983. *Traffic Wardens: An Ethnography of Street Administration*. Manchester: Manchester University Press.

Riggs, Fred W. 1962. "An Ecological Approach: The 'Sala' Model." In Ferrel Heady and Sybil L. Stokes, eds., *Papers in Comparative Public Administration* (Ann Arbor: Institute of Public Administration), pp. 19–36.

Rushdie, Salman. 1983. "Last Chance." *Index on Censorship* 12 (6) (December): 2.

Sahlins, Peter. 1989. *Boundaries: The Making of France and Spain in the Pyrenees*. Berkeley: University of California Press.

Saussure, Ferdinand de. 1966. *Course in General Linguistics*. Edited by Charles Bally and Albert Sechehaye in collaboration with Albert Riedlinger. Translated by Wade Baskin. New York: McGraw-Hill.

Schneider, David M. 1968. *American Kinship: A Cultural Account*. Englewood Cliffs: Prentice-Hall.

Schneider, David M. 1984. *A Critique of the Study of Kinship*. Ann Arbor: University of Michigan Press.

Schneider, William H. 1983. "Chance and Social Setting in the Application of the Discovery of Blood Groups." *Bulletin of the History of Medicine* 57: 545–562.

Schneider, William H. 1990. "The Eugenics Movement in France, 1890–1940." In Mark B. Adams, ed., *The Wellborn Science: Eugenics in Germany, France, Brazil, and Russia* (New York: Oxford University Press), pp. 69–109.

Schwartzman, Helen. 1989. *The Meeting: Gatherings in Organizations and Communities*. New York: Plenum.

Scott, James C. 1985. *Weapons of the Weak: Everyday Forms of Peasant Resistance*. New Haven: Yale University Press.

Shore, C.N. 1989. "Patronage and Bureaucracy in Complex Societies: Social Rules and Social Relations in an Italian University." *Journal of the Anthropological Society of Oxford* 20: 56–73.

Silberman, Neil. 1990. "The Politics of the Past: Archaeology and Nationalism in the Eastern Mediterranean." *Mediterranean Quarterly* 1: 99–110.

Simic, André. 1982. "Urbanization and Modernization in Yugoslavia: Adaptive and Maladaptive Aspects of Traditional Culture." In Michael Kenny and David I. Kertzer, eds., *Urban Life in Mediterranean Europe: Anthropological Perspectives* (Urbana: University of Illinois Press), pp. 203–224.

Sinkó, Katalin. 1989. "Arpád versus Saint István: Competing Heroes and Competing Interests in the Figurative Representation of Hungarian History." *Ethnologia Europaea* 19: 67–84.

Smith, Annette. 1984. *Gobineau et l'histoire naturelle*. Geneva: Droz.

Smolicz, J.J. 1985. "Greek-Australians: A Question of Survival in Multicultural Australia." *Journal of Multilingual and Multicultural Development* 6: 17–29.

Spencer, Robert F. 1958. "Culture Process and Intellectual Current." *American Anthropologist* 60: 640–657.

Stewart, Charles. 1985. "Exotika: Greek Values and their Supernatural Antitheses." *Scandinavian Yearbook of Folklore* 41: 37–64.

Stewart, Charles. 1991. *Demons and the Devil: Moral Imagination in Modern Greek Culture.* Princeton: Princeton University Press.

Strecker, Ivo. 1988. *The Social Practice of Symbolization: An Anthropological Analysis.* London: Athlone Press.

Tambiah, Stanley, J. 1968. "The Magical Power of Words." *Man* (n.s.) 3: 175–208.

Tambiah, Stanley J. 1979. "A Performative Approach to Ritual." *Proceedings of the British Academy* 65: 113–169.

Tambiah, Stanley J. 1989. "Ethnic Conflict in the World Today." *American Ethnologist* 16: 335–349.

Tambiah, Stanley J. 1990. *Magic, Science, Religion, and the Scope of Rationality.* Cambridge: Cambridge University Press.

Tamiolakis, Mikhail. 1976. *Maties sti zoi ton ghrafion.* Thessaloniki.

Taussig, Michael. 1984. "Culture of Terror – Space of Death: Roger Casement's Putumayo Report and the Explanation of Torture." *Comparative Studies in Society and History* 26: 467–497.

Tegnaeus, Harry. 1952. *Blood-Brothers: An Ethno-Sociological Study of the Institutions of Blood-Brotherhood with Special Reference to Africa.* New York: Philosophical Library.

Thompson, Michael. 1979. *Rubbish Theory: The Creation and Destruction of Value.* Oxford: Oxford University Press.

Tocqueville, Alexis de. 1989. *Œuvres complètes* (gen. ed. J.-P. Mayer), vol. 9: *Correspondance d'Alexis de Tocqueville et d'Arthur de Gobineau.* Edited by Maurice Degros. [Paris]: Gallimard.

Tönnies, Ferdinand. 1957. *Community and Society.* Translated by Charles P. Loomis. East Lansing: Michigan State University Press.

Tsoucalas, Constantine. 1991. "'Enlightened' Concepts in the 'Dark': Power and Freedom, Politics and Society." *Journal of Modern Greek Studies* 9: 1–22.

Vialles, Noélie. 1987. *Le sang et la chair: Les abattoirs des pays de d'Adour.* Paris: Maison des Sciences de l'Homme.

Vico, Giambattista. 1744. *Principij di Scienza Nuova.* 3d ed. Naples: Stamperia Muziana.

Vivilakis, E. 1866. *O proyeghrammenos Kris i o fatriasmos tis Kendrikis Epitropis.* Athens: Radhamanthios.

Weber, Max. 1946. *Max Weber: Essays in Sociology.* Ed. H.H. Gerth and C. Wright Mills. New York: Oxford University Press.

Weber, Max. 1963. *The Sociology of Religion.* Trans. Ephraim Fischoff. Boston: Beacon Press.

Weber, Max. 1968. *On Charisma and Institution Building.* Ed. S. Eisenstadt. Chicago: University of Chicago Press.

Weber, Max. 1976. *The Protestant Ethnic and the Spirit of Capitalism.* Trans. Talcott Parsons. London: George Allen and Unwin.

Wilson, Stephen. 1988. *Feuding, Conflict and Banditry in Nineteenth-Century Corsica.* Cambridge: Cambridge University Press.

Wittgenstein, Ludwig. 1973. *Philosophical Investigations.* The English text of the third edition, translated by G.E.M. Anscombe. New York: Macmillan.

Zonabend, Françoise. 1989. *La presqu' île au nucléaire.* Paris: Odile Jacob.

Index